KU-074-992

THE INSIDER'S GUIDE TO

RUSSIA

THE INSIDER'S GUIDES

AUSTRALIA • BALI • CALIFORNIA • CANADA • CHINA • EASTERN CANADA • FLORIDA • HAWAII • HONG KONG • INDIA • INDONESIA • JAPAN • KENYA • KOREA • NEPAL • NEW ENGLAND • NEW ZEALAND • MALAYSIA AND SINGAPORE • MEXICO • RUSSIA • SPAIN • THAILAND • TURKEY • WESTERN CANADA

The Insider's Guide to Russia
First Published 1993
Moorland Publishing Co Ltd
Moor Farm Road, Airfield Estate, Ashbourne, DE61HD, England
by arrangement with Novo Editions, S.A.
53 rue Beaudouin, 27700 Les Andelys, France
Telefax: (33) 32 54 54 50

© 1993 Novo Editions, S.A.

ISBN: 0 86190 394 3

Acknowledgments
The author would like to acknowledge the kind assistance given him by many people, but particularly by Mr. Vladimir Grigoriev of VAGRIUS Publishers.

Dedication
For Mrs. Diana Azhgibkova
Created, edited and produced by Novo Editions, S.A.
Editor in Chief: Allan Amsel
Original design concept: Hon Bing-wah
Picture editor and designer: Gaia Text, Munich
Text and artwork composed and information updated
using Ventura Publisher software

All rights reserved. No part of this publication may be reproduced, stored in a retrieval system, or transmitted in any form, or by any means, electronic, mechanical, photocopying, recording, or otherwise, without the written permission of the publisher.

Printed by Samhwa Printing Company Limited, Seoul, Korea

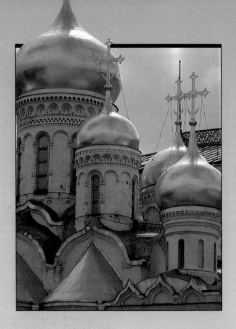

THE INSIDER'S GUIDE TO

RUSSIA

By Gleb Uspensky

Photographed by Vladimir Anokhin

MPC

Contents

MAPS

Russia	8-9
Moscow	40
Kremlin	55
St. Petersburg	92
Kiev	122
Cruising the Volga and Don Rivers	136
The European North	153
Siberia	162–163
The Far East	173

HISTORICAL CAMEOS

PRINCE VLADIMIR AND THE BAPTISM OF KIEVAN RUS	*20*
THE BOLSHEVIKS: FOOLING ALL OF THE PEOPLE, ALL OF THE TIME	*26*
THE MONGOL INVASION	*42–44*
THE EPIDEMIC OF RENAMING	*49–51*
TOWERS OF THE KREMLIN	*54*
ARISTOTLE FIORAVANTI	*56*
SIEGE OF THE "WHITE HOUSE"	*66–67*
THE LAST ATTACK	*70*
CHÂTEAU IN ABRAMTSEVO	*84*
CZAR PETER I	*94*
ANDREI VORONIKHIN	*98*
THE RUSSIAN MUSEUM	*99–100*
BALL IN THE WINTER PALACE	*102–104*
THE FLOODS	*108*
WHAT LITERATURE MEANS TO RUSSIA	*114–115*
VOLGA FISH	*137*
THE COSSACKS OF THE DON	*144–145*
RURIK AND THE RUSSES	*152*
THE RUSSIAN CONQUEST	*163*
THE GREAT EXPLORERS	*172*

WELCOME TO RUSSIA 11
Introduction 13

THE COUNTRY AND ITS PEOPLE 17
The Historical Background 19
    The Paleolithic Age • The Bronze
    Age • The Varangians • Under the
    Mongols • Ivan the Terrible •
    The Troubles • Peter the Great •
    The Palace Revolutions • Catherine
    the Great • The Napoleonic Wars •
    The Decembrists • From 1825 to
    1917 • 1917 • Proletarian
    Dictatorship • World War II •
    Cold War • Contemporary Russia •
    The Government and the Economy
Geography and Climate 32
Religion in Russia 34
Sport in Russia 35
Russian Cuisine 36

MOSCOW 39
Background 41
General Information 48
    Car Rental • Other Transportation
    Options • Passport
What to See 49
    Inside the Kremlin • Midtown
    Moscow • The Garden Ring
Art Galleries 69
    Tretiakov Gallery •
    Pushkin Museum of Fine Arts
The Monasteries 71
    Andronikov Monastery • Novodevichy
    Convent • Donskoi Monastery
Museum Estates 74
    Kolomenskoye • New Jerusalem •
    Arkhangelskoye • Izmailovo •
    Sokolniki
Where to Stay 76
    Expensive • Medium Range •
    Inexpensive (Youth Hostels)
Where to Eat 78
    Take-out

THE LAND OF WHITE STONE 81
Sergiyev Posad 83
    What to See • Where to Stay •
    Where to Eat • How to Get There
Vladimir and Suzdal 84
    Background • What to See •
    Where to Stay • Where to Eat
Other Town Museums 88
    Pereslavl-Zalessky • Rostov the Great •
    Yaroslavl • Kostroma

ST. PETERSBURG	**91**
Background	93
General Information	95
What to See	95
Peter and Paul Fortress • Nevsky • Palace Square • The Hermitage • St. Isaac's Cathedral • Vasilievsky Island • Smolny	
The Environs	109
Petrodvorets • Pavlovsk • Pushkin	
Where to Stay	114
Expensive • Medium Range	
Where to Eat	116
How to Get There	117
KIEV	**119**
Background	121
General Information	123
Specific Travel Inquiries: • Emergencies • Money • Passport	
What to See	124
Upper Town • Pechersk • Kreschatik • Podol and the Left Bank	
Where to Stay	129
Where to Eat	130
How to Get There	131

CRUISING THE VOLGA AND THE DON	**133**
Background	135
Towns en Route	138
Kazan • From Kazan to Ulianovsk • Ulianovsk (Simbirsk) • From Ulianovsk to Samara • Samara • From Samara to Volgograd (Tsaritsyn) • Volgograd (Tsaritsyn)	
From the Volga to the Don	143
The Don River	143
Rostov-on-Don	
Cruise Information	146
Lock Information	
EUROPEAN NORTH	**149**
Background	151
Novgorod	151
What to See • Where to Stay • Where to Eat	
Pskov	153
Where to Stay • Where to Eat	
Off the Beaten Track	155
Karelia • Murmansk	
SIBERIA	**159**
Background	162
Novosibirsk	163
General Information • What to See • Where to Stay • Where to Eat • How to Get There	
Irkutsk	166
General Information • What to See • Where to Stay • Where to Eat • How to Get There	

THE FAR EAST	**169**
Background	172
General Information	172
What to See	172
Where to Stay	175
Where to Eat	176
How to Get There	176
TRAVELER'S TIPS	**179**
Getting There	181
By Air • By Train • By Bus •	
By Car • By Sea	
Useful Addresses	183
Charter Flights and Tour Operators	183
In the United States • In Britain •	
Specialist Tours of Russia •	
Motoring Information	
Travel Documents	184
Customs	184
When to Go	185
What to Take	186
Getting Around	186
By Air • By Train • By Bus •	
By Taxi • By Thumb • By Car	
General Information	189
Embassies and Consulates	190
Health	190
Money	192
Accommodation	192
Etiquette	192
Public Holidays and Festivals	194
Holidays • Festivals •	
Religious Festivals	

Mail	195
Telephones	195
Emergencies	196
Other Helpful Numbers	196
Country Codes •	
Russian City Codes	
Basics	197
Time • Electricity •	
Water • Weights and Measures	
Crime	197
Radio and Television	197
Newspapers and Magazines	198
Toilets	198
Steam Baths	198
Women Alone	199
Tipping	199
Surprises	199
Staying On	200
Russian for Travelers	200
Pronunciation	
Vocabulary	201
Numbers • Calendar •	
Clock • Key Words and Phrases •	
Places and Things • On the Road •	
In the Hotel • In the Post Office •	
In Emergencies • In Restaurants •	
In Case You Get Lucky	
QUICK REFERENCE A–Z GUIDE	206
To Places and Topics of Interest	
with Listed Accommodation,	
Restaurants and	
Useful Telephone Numbers	

SYMBOLS LÉGENDE ZEICHENERKLÄRUNG

RIVER, LAKE, SEA / FLEUVE, LAC, MER / FLUSS, SEE, MEER
DIVIDED HIGHWAY / AUTOROUTE / AUTOBAHN
OTHER HIGHWAY / AUTRE ROUTE / SONSTIGE STRASSEN
RAILWAY / VOIE FERREÉ / EISENBAHN
INTERNATIONAL BOUNDARY / FRONTIÈRE D'ETAT / LANDESGRENZE
✈ AIRPORT / AEROPORT / FLUGHAFEN
✪ STATE CAPITAL / CAPITALE / HAUPTSTADT
● CITY / VILLE / STADT

375 miles
600 km

S I B E R I A

S I A

Lena River

Nikolaevsk

SAKHALIN ISLAND

SOVIET
FAR EAST

Baikal Amur Railway

Komsomolsk

Krasnoyarsk

Bratsk

Lake
Baikal

Transsiberian Railway

Belogorsk

Khabarovsk

vokuznetsk

Abakan

Angarsk

Blagoveshchensk

Birobidzan

Ulan-Ude

Irkutsk

Nakhodka

Petropavlovka

Vladivostok

SEA
OF
JAPAN

A L T A I

✈ ✪
Ulan Bator

MONGOLIA

Transsiberian Railway

✈
Beijing
(Peking)

CHINA

Welcome
to Russia

INTRODUCTION

As I bid you welcome to one of the largest countries in the world, I would like to point out that any guide that purports to cover *all* of Russia is, modestly speaking, stretching the truth to meet your expectations: you just can't have it all in one book.

There are several reasons for this, aside from the need for brevity imposed by the genre.

First, there's the vastness of the land to consider. It will be extremely difficult to squeeze all that geography into one visit. If you go for a package tour, for instance, you'll be almost certainly confined to the larger cities and there, to the universally recognized highlights. If you go alone you'll be able to enjoy greater freedom of movement; however, since most of the locations which are *not* on the group list offer inferior accommodations and tourist service generally, you may find yourself "roughing it" more than you want to.

Secondly, the condition of the various architectural monuments is such that many people have been known to exclaim, upon arrival in what most guidebooks call "a lovely thirteenth-century monastery" (yet is in reality two-and-a-half walls still standing upright through, no doubt, divine intervention): "What?! I came 100 (200, 300) miles to see *that*?"

Thirdly, internal visa restrictions will bar you from a surprising number of places that are usually dangled before the average tourist's curiosity as a lure: "Oh, Cheliabinsk is the pearl of the Urals!" the guidebooks tell you. "Oh, they have the world's most famous collection of semi-precious stones there!" Well, Cheliabinsk is nice enough, but the plain truth of the matter is that being a foreigner you cannot go there. Russia faces innumerable economic and political problems today, yet somehow international tourism has yet to be regarded among the solutions to these problems by our powers-that-be. The rules and regulations applicable to foreign travelers were written in the good old days of the Cold War, and until Russian Parliament decides to do something about it, you'll find half

of Russia totally inaccessible; for the other half, you'll need a visa for every town you want to visit. Since the state legislature has yet to pass a law permitting free international travel for Russian citizens, you may rest assured that a law permitting foreigners freedom of movement inside the country is of a second-priority nature (which means, in plain language, that we won't see it in 1993).

The final consideration is that, in my opinion at least, one does not *need* to see everything. Consequently, the Russia you will find in this book is not one huge entity stretching from the Baltic Sea to the Pacific Ocean; rather, it is a mosaic made up of cultural, ethnic, historical and psychological fragments that you as a foreigner can definitely see — and, hopefully, understand — *here and now*, not yesterday or in two years' time. These fragments were carefully chosen for a portrayal of a nation which (I hope) transcends the limitations of space, time, and state borders. For example, you won't find an essay about Krasnoyarsk, which is officially part of Russia, yet you will find a rather detailed description of Kiev, which isn't. This may annoy some people. Kiev is the capital of the Ukraine! In the context of this book, however, it matters what Kiev *was*, not what it is now. Kiev was the mother of Russian towns; Kiev was the center around which the Russians first became a nation; Kiev had precisely that quality common to all Russians which I cannot find in contemporary Russia, but which is crucial for anyone out to grasp the distinctions of Russian national character. In that sense, Kiev is as Russian as, say, Mom's apple pie is American, and without a visit to Kiev, there is no way for the reader to understand what it is that shaped the Russian nation and sustained it through a millennium of assorted calamities and catastrophes.

Needless to say, I tried to make the places and experiences the book does cover shine for you just as they did — and do — for me, so that at the end of your trip you will find that you have seen, heard and felt enough to

---

OPPOSITE: church cupolas are a familiar sight for anyone who's been in Russia for 24 hours.

have Russia planted firmly enough at the bottom of your heart for you to want to come back at least once.

At any rate, whether you go with a group or on your own, you'll find the choice of locations in this guide nearly perfect, first of all because they are easy to reach (by Russian standards) and secondly, because they are guaranteed to give you more knowledge, insight and, in the end, pure pleasure, than any other similar attraction in the shortest possible time.

I would first of all refer you to the Traveler's Tips section of this book, because the information you may find there could help you plan and prepare your trip. You will most probably be starting your acquaintance with Russia in the city of Moscow. This is why the Moscow chapter comes first. After that, you may want to take Russia just as it comes in the book, starting with the towns and cities where our ancestors built their churches, fortresses and monasteries of white stone, continuing on to enjoy the rococo splendor of St. Petersburg, and taking in the European North before moving on to Siberia and the Far East. Then again, you may want to start with a trip on the Trans-Siberian Railway and finish your journey in Moscow or St. Petersburg. Or you may be interested in the Far North only. Whatever your personal preferences, the book is structured in a way that's designed to give you quick, reliable information (and a little entertainment, as well).

For example, if you are into Ancient Russian architecture and culture, the typical guidebook will send you to a dozen locations, some of which may be many hundreds of miles apart. If you were touring Italy or the United States, it would hardly pose any problems; however, travel in Russia is never the comfortable or even luxurious experience that it is in those countries, and it is not uncommon for people to be so exhausted by the slings and arrows of getting about in Russia by the time they arrive to be past caring about whatever it is they had set out to see. To avoid this, this guide suggests Sergiyev Posad and Suzdal, two towns which are within driving distance from Moscow — and which are worth driving to, since their architectural monuments are in good condition. And once you've seen those two, you can always decide for yourself if you want more (and if you do, you'll find more in this book).

I assume, of course, that your desire to explore my country stems from the yearning to discover a culture and a people different than your own, for today's Russia is hardly a location for entertainment tourism. People don't come here to go to the beach and the nightclub, although we do have wonderful beaches and even a nightclub or two. No, people come to Russia because they want to understand that elusive entity which is usually referred to as national temperament or, poetically, "the spirit of the nation".

Let us compare this task to a jigsaw puzzle. Theoretically, you can put one together even with the pieces lying face down, but that would mean losing a lot of time on the study of minute detail with never a guarantee of success in the end. If you turn the pieces, you still face a formidable task, because up to 50 percent of a jigsaw puzzle is made up of even-colored, meaningless background, which is usually grouped around one or two vital pieces carrying parts of the picture. Put these together, and you get the adjacent background pieces where they belong in no time at all. I tried to sift through centuries and thousands of kilometers of "background" to get at the telltale "pieces" of history, culture and lifestyle which should give you a bearing in your quest to understand the "enigma inside a mystery" that is Russia. The Mongol Invasion. Christianity. The great cities. The great and the not-so-great leaders. Everyday problems. The arts and the traditions...

"National characteristics," George Orwell wrote in 1941, "are not easy to pin down, and when pinned down they often turn out to be trivialities or seem to have no connection with one another."

My jigsaw puzzle should help you find that connection. I only hope I chose the vital pieces correctly.

OPPOSITE: Russia is the architecture lover's dream. During your stay, you'll see specimens of just about every architectural school, except maybe the "Pyramids".

The Country and its People

THE HISTORICAL BACKGROUND

More than anything else, the history of Russia resembles a box-office hit from Hollywood, where the recipe for success is lots of blood, violence and destruction of private property, with a little love thrown in for good measure. It is also the perfect illustration to the famous maxim: the main lesson of history is that it teaches no lessons.

The account that follows is the briefest and most generalized that I could manage.

THE PALEOLITHIC AGE

To the best of contemporary knowledge, Homo Sapiens first came to the territory of what is now southern Russia in the early Paleolithic period (700 thousand years ago). Prehistoric dwellings half-a-million years old were discovered in the Ukraine.

By the tenth millennium BC, most of the country's contemporary territory was inhabited.

THE BRONZE AGE

It seems that we missed out on that one. All the great cultures of that distant time thrived in the warmer climates (Urartu in the territory of contemporary Armenia). Proximity of Mediterranean trade routes was another important factor. Denied both, our ancestors remained oblivious to the advantages of metal tools and weapons.

By "our ancestors" I mean the tribes who lived in the territory of present-day Russia. Yet it is a big question whether they had any relationship to the Slavs. The answer to that riddle lies in the Scythian culture, which Herodotus praised for producing "the best wheat in the world." "We are Scythians! We are Asians!" Alexander Blok, our symbolist poet, claimed in one of his better-known poems. Yet the Scythian culture vanished so abruptly that it remains unclear whether they'd had time to mingle with the tribes farther to the north.

THE VARANGIANS

Our verifiable history started approximately 1200 years ago. By the ninth century, the Slavs already had a state of their own, with a great deal of "help" from the northern Varangian tribes. Again, it is unclear whether the Varangians conquered the Slavs and their Finno-Ugrian neighbors, or, as the chronicles claim, came to rule over them "on invitation." Whatever the case, the Varangians and the Slavs clearly had the same kind of relationship that the Varangians and the Saxons had in thirteenth-century England (except that the Saxons called "their" Varangians "Normans.")

The name of our William the Conqueror was Rurik, whose lineage extends to the present day. Rurik, who came from a tribe called Russes, founded the Novgorod state. His relative Oleg later established residence in Kiev, where he attained legendary prominence: his shield "was nailed to the gates of Constantinople" (meaning that his armies besieged the mighty southern neighbor and collected tribute).

In 988, Prince Vladimir forcibly baptized his pagan realm. The baptism of Kievan Rus was probably the most important event in its history. Yet it was done, as so often happens, for all the wrong reasons.

UNDER THE MONGOLS

In the second half of the second century, the hopelessly fragmented Kievan Rus (see cameo overleaf) fell to the armies of Genghis Khan.

From the beginning, it was no contest at all. As town after town fell before the irresistible onslaught, the need for centralized rule became increasingly obvious (see more in the Moscow chapter). But it was one thing to understand this, and quite another to bring it off. In the end, the Mongols' boundless greed, Moscow's political maneuvers, bribery and, most importantly, the balancing act of the Orthodox Church (which somehow managed to please the "Tartars," as the Mongols were called in Russia, and, at the same time, retain the spiritual hold over its subjects) brought the Mongol domination to an end in 1480.

OPPOSITE: farmer getting ready for the winter. After 75 years of Communist meddling, the nation is painfully learning to feed itself.

PRINCE VLADIMIR AND THE BAPTISM OF KIEVAN RUS

Prince Vladimir of Kiev, the baptizer of Rus, lord and master of all the Russian lands, and canonized Orthodox saint, must have been, if you'll excuse the expression, quite a character. Realizing that the time for monotheism had come, he "tried on" the world's greatest religions and judged them against his personal preferences (or, more accurately, vices).

Rogned. By her he had four sons and two daughters. The Greek woman bore him Sviatopolk; by one Czech he had a son, Vysheslav; by another Sviatoslav and Mstislav; and by a Bulgarian woman, Boris and Gleb. He had 300 concubines at Vyshegorod, 300 at Belgorod, and 200 at Berestovo. He even seduced married women and violated young girls..."

Islam appealed to Vladimir the lecher (it allowed harems).

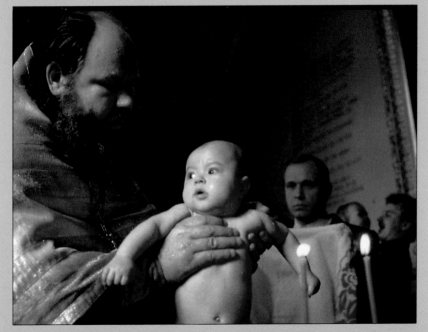

Among the first missionaries to arrive at his court were Moslems. In consequence, Vladimir had been on the brink of accepting Islam — a fact I found hard to believe until I came across the following account in the chronicles:

"Now Vladimir was overcome by lust for women. His lawful wife was

Yet it forbade drunkenness, whereas the Byzantians assured him that a good Christian could drink until he dropped. This appealed to Vladimir the drinker. In the end, the drinker prevailed over the lecher, and Russia was forever separated from the Moslem Orient.

This was preceded by the battle in Kulikovo Field near the Don (for which Prince Dmitry received the honorary title "Donskoi").

IVAN THE TERRIBLE

The translation of his title has always sounded funny to me. A more accurate

translation would be something like "awe-inspiring."

The birth of Ivan IV (the last descendant of Rurik in the Kremlin) in 1530 heralded the era of empire-building (which is drawing to a close as you read this book).

Ivan believed in ruling with an iron hand. He directed his energies at territorial expansion (conquering Kazan and Astrakhan on the Volga as well as Western Siberia), consolidation of the Russian lands around Moscow (Novgorod and Pskov acknowledged his supremacy after several bloody campaigns), and the subjugation of the great feudal overlords (known as Boyars) to the monarch's will. This may sound smooth on paper, but in reality it was blood, blood, and more blood. In fact, Ivan the Terrible had in the end proved almost too much for Russia. Ironically, it was his death that became the final straw and triggered peasant unrest, a crisis of succession, utter economic dislocation and foreign intervention known today as the Troubles.

THE TROUBLES

The period full of strictly Hollywood material: weak monarchs, powerful favorites, pretenders to the throne, amoral fathers selling their daughters for power and money, betrayal, clandestine assassinations, more betrayal, more murders, peasant revolts, villainous Cossacks, and finally, the happy end — Minin and Pozharsky ousting the Poles from Russia.

And think of the sets, too: the castles of Poland, the palaces of Sweden, the siege of Moscow... It would really make a great movie.

As a matter of fact, it has already been made into a great play, perhaps the greatest drama written in the Russian language: Boris Godunov by Alexander Pushkin.

Jokes aside, it was probably the worst period in Russian history, Mongol invasion or no Mongol invasion. When Mikhail Romanov assumed the throne in 1613, he had much fewer subjects to govern than did Ivan the Terrible in 1605. (For a detailed description of the Troubles, see page 44).

PETER THE GREAT

Peter was the first, and probably the only Romanov who was both hyperactive and successful as an empire builder. He was clearly a believer in attack as the best method of defense; striving to solve domestic problems with external conquests, he "made Russia rear up" as Pushkin phrased it, and

transformed the backward, landlocked realm that he inherited into an empire. He, by the way, was the first monarch to be called "Emperor of All Russia."

Fighting the Turks on the Black Sea, Peter constantly kept an eye on a far more dangerous enemy to the North: Sweden. The war with the Swedes lasted for more than two decades, during which Russia gained a foothold on the Baltic. A new city, St. Petersburg, was founded on the Neva River, and immediately got down to creating the vital factor of victory — the Russian navy.

I think that Peter would have made a better court favorite than a czar. He was a man of action, and all his acts were usually a reaction to some development or other. He appeared to lack the time to think, to plan ahead. It was through no fault of his own, for I'm sure that he sincerely believed in the role of the czar as the first servant of the state; yet in a way, he was like that old Genie from a popular children's tale, who

OPPOSITE: For Orthodox Christians, Baptism is the biggest — and earliest — rite.
ABOVE: Emperor Alexander I, whose victorious troops marched into Paris after defeating Napoleon and ousting the French out of Russia in 1812. Legend has it that Alexander faked his death and retired to a Siberian cave, where he led the ascetic life of a starets (holy man).

was let out of the bottle in the twentieth century. When the boy who found him asked him to make a replica of a watch, the genie promptly made one. "And this one's better, too," he boasted, "because it's solid gold." Yet the watch did not work — there was no mechanism inside. The same can be said about Peter's reforms. On the surface, everything was tip-top and European: the ships sailed the four seas, new lands were being added to the realm, schools and printing shops were being opened, young people were being sent abroad to study, palaces and even entire cities were founded, the Boyars wore close shaves to avoid the disastrous "beard tax" — and yet Russia remained as savage, oppressed and unenlightened as before his time, not in the least, perhaps, because of the savage methods he resorted to.

THE PALACE REVOLUTIONS

Five years after Peter's death, Anna of Courland, the second daughter of Ivan V, was offered the throne. The strings attached to this offer by the wily Prince Golitsyn, had all the makings of a bill of rights. Anna signed the "proposals," which took two-thirds of her power away, took the crown, and convened the Senate. There, she dramatically tore up the "conditions" and proclaimed herself empress. And that was that (Peter would have had them killed).

Anna left the boring affairs of state to her minister and lover Biron; after her death in 1740, he did not last even a month. In the first palace coup of the eighteenth century, Biron was overthrown and sent to Siberia. Soon afterward, Elizabeth, daughter of Peter the Great, lead a torchlight procession of imperial guards to the imperial palace and arrested baby emperor Ivan VI and his ministers.

Elizabeth was very beautiful and popular with the Guards, which was quite enough for her to remain in power in those days. In some ways she was quite extraordinary for her times. For instance, she released many political prisoners, abolished the death penalty and her father's charming custom of hacking off the right arm of convicts with lifelong sentences. Yet she seriously believed reading was hazardous

to health. Her chief legacies to her designated heir, Peter III, were 15 thousand dresses and enormous debts.

Peter III's greatest mistake was his marriage. Wrote his wife Catherine: "Peter III had lost the little wit he had. He wanted to change his religion, marry Elizabeth Vorontsov and shut me up." Supported by the Guards, Catherine forced Peter to abdicate. Soon afterwards, he was very probably strangled, although Catherine denied rumors of foul play.

CATHERINE THE GREAT

Born as Princess Sophie in a minor German state in 1729, she was invited to Russia by Elizabeth and paid court to her "ugly, immature and boastful" future husband (her own words). Catherine came to the throne as the best educated ruler in Russian history. She was a very passionate woman, and was very generous to her lovers after she discarded them.

She also shared Peter the Great's views of the sovereign as the first servant of the state. Yet she was "an enlightened despot." She seemed to have time for everything, ranging from domestic reform to huge construction projects to writing comedies and long letters to Voltaire and the other great philosophers of the West.

Yet she flouted the logic she so admired in the philosophes and solved problems through patience and charm. The regime of enhanced absolutism, consolidated by Catherine, was to last for more than a century.

Catherine's unloved son Paul succeeded her after her death in 1796. Suffering from a persecution mania, he built the huge Mikhailovsky Castle in Petersburg, complete with water-filled moats and cannon. Yet his policies alienated the courtiers, and in 1801 he was strangled in his own bedroom, weeks after moving into the new castle, the last victim of the age of palace revolutions.

THE NAPOLEONIC WARS

For Europe, the nineteenth century started with war. The ambitions of two of the world's most powerful rulers of the time, Napoleon and Alexander I, first clashed in the Coalition Wars. It was Britain, Austria, Sweden, Naples and Russia against Napoleon.

What the allies failed to foresee, however, was that they were going up against the greatest military genius the world had ever known. In December, 1805, Napoleon pulverized the coalition forces at Austerlitz. It was only through General Kutuzov's timely intervention that Russia managed to emerge from this battle with a part of its army.

1811, "I shall be ruler of the world; there remains only Russia, but I shall crush her."

Napoleon invaded on June 24, 1812. His armies outnumbered the Russians three to one.

Following the battle for the city of Smolensk, which the Russians had had to give up, came the famous battle at Borodino, the greatest battle of the campaign and, arguably, of Napoleon's career. Napoleon withheld his Guard after the French captured key positions. It took between 69 and 117 thousand lives (sources vary) on

Then came the Peace of Tilsit. France and Russia divided Europe into spheres of interest and secretly agreed to fight side by side in any European conflict. In Russia, these accords were highly unpopular. Russia declared war on Britain and seized the Swedish province of Finland.

But the Franco-Russian Alliance was doomed from the start, because Napoleon aimed to control all of Europe, and Alexander's ambitions extended all the way to Constantinople. In addition, things became personal: Alexander refused Napoleon the hand of his sister, after which Napoleon promptly annexed Oldenburg, a north German state ruled by a relative of Alexander. "In five years," he declared in

both sides that day. Perhaps it was a fatal mistake on his part. Whatever the case, both armies retained their positions as darkness fell. In the small hours of the dawn, General Kutuzov made a decision to withdraw. At the famous council of war in the village of Fili near Moscow, Kutuzov decided upon further retreat. "It's either lose the army and Moscow, or lose Moscow and save the army," he told his generals. Moscow was left to Napoleon.

Napoleon took it. It may well be that this, and not the decision to invade Russia, was the worst mistake of his career. From the

Hall in the Kremlin where foreign ambassadors presented their credentials to the Czars.

start, septuagenarian but by no means dim-witted Kutuzov realized that Napoleon's conquering army, like a bicycle (which had not been invented yet), had to keep moving to retain its tremendous power. When Napoleon took Kutuzov's "poisoned pawn," the bicycle stopped.

And fell: occupied with looting Moscow's not inconsiderable treasures, drinking and generally "living it up," the army quickly lost the only distinction between a band of marauders and an organized fighting force — discipline.

life. When they came back to Russia, the glaring contradictions and the injustices of which they may have remained blissfully unaware (had they not absorbed the liberal ideas of the country they occupied), were suddenly revealed to them.

They formed the Union of Salvation. The 200-member secret society comprised representatives of Russia's noblest families: Trubetskoi, Muraviev, Turgenev, Pestel, the poet Ryleev. They wanted social change: abolition of serfdom, prohibition of all social distinctions, and a constitutional monarchy.

On October 19 the French abandoned Moscow. They were not retreating, they were running. But "running for your life is the quickest way to lose it," says the Chinese proverb, and when the French counted their comrades after recrossing the Niemen River, they found that only one in twenty survived.

In 1814, Alexander I came to Paris at the head of his army.

THE DECEMBRISTS

A whiff of the West worked wonders for the educated, mostly noble, young army officers. They were struck by the enormous gulf between European and Russian social

When Alexander I suddenly died in Taganrog in 1825, they made their move. Some three thousand troops were gathered in St. Petersburg's Senate Square on December 14. It was at this moment that their greatest strength — idealism — turned into their worst liability. Indecision, poor organization, cowardice and, as Lenin said, "a terrible alienation from the people" added up to a crushing defeat from the troops which remained loyal to Nicholas I (labeled the "iron czar" after the end of his long reign).

It was probably the most romantic revolt in Russian history; as such, it inspired subsequent generations of radicals all the way to 1917.

The Country and its People

FROM 1825 TO 1917

Nicholas I never forgot December 14. His reign was marked by ultra-conservatism at home and counterrevolutionarism abroad, for which he was called "the stick-man" and the "gendarme of Europe." He increased Russia's territories after a war with the Caucasians.

He also lost the Crimean War against the French, the British and the Turks in 1853-56. The defeat, which coincided with the

Historians believe that Alexander II would have come through and maintained relative internal stability with his steam-bleeding policies if not for his assassination by terrorists from People's Will (they say that he carried a draft constitution in his pocket on the day of his death).

The last of the Romanov emperors, Nicholas II, clearly lacked the savagery which his ancestors found so useful in running the realm. During his reign, Russia suffered a humiliating defeat from Japan in 1905, went through a bloody revolution in

emperor's death, heralded the opening of a new era, the era of reforms and revolutions.

Alexander II set out to do what the Decembrists went to Siberia for. He abolished serfdom and adopted a number of decrees which made Russia a livable place for people of all classes. Local government was now independent, and the newspapers made a big thing out of court hearings where a peasant would prevail over his former landlord on some minor issue.

Alexander II also conquered most of Turkestan, the Amu Darya region, and some territory east of the Caspian. He dealt a stunning blow to Turkey, forcing Istanbul to give up Romania and most of present-day Yugoslavia.

1905-1907, the ensuing period of reaction (the only bright spot of which were Stolypin's reforms), World War I, and the February, 1917 revolution which ended with his abdication.

1917

After the czar was deposed in February, power was passed on to the so-called Provisional Government until such time as

OPPOSITE: Detail of ornament in Peter the Great's Summer Palace in Petrodvorets.
ABOVE: The battleship *Aurora*, which purportedly fired the shot signalling the beginning of the assault of the Winter Palace on October 25, 1917.

THE BOLSHEVIKS: FOOLING ALL OF THE PEOPLE, ALL OF THE TIME

In the 1991 presidential elections, one of the candidates pledged to make vodka very cheap if he were elected. He received such a substantial number of votes (6 million) that his political career was made overnight.

In the 1917 struggle for power, the Bolsheviks did not promise cheap vodka (it was cheap enough to begin with). Yet the pattern of their populism was the same. Their first "decrees" promised instant peace (because the country was sick of war), free land (because the majority of peasants could not afford it), and bread to the hungry (because the cities were starving). Is it surprising that most people believed them?

Needless to say, the immediate fulfillment of these pledges held dire consequences in store. Trotsky's famous "no peace, no war, no army" formula cost Russia half of the Ukraine and the Baltic region. Most of the land seized by the peasants during the revolution was later taken back and administered by state officials, triggering peasant revolts to which the government responded with mass deportations and deliberately-organized famines.

Yet in the heady atmosphere of October, 1917, taking power on a platform of cynical populism was easier than stealing from a blind man's pocket.

a constitutional assembly could be elected and convened.

It was a difficult time for Russia. The war dragged on, the economy was a shambles, and life was generally growing more and more difficult.

Following is an account of October 25, 1917, the way we learned it in high school.

"… On the night of October 24 Lenin wrote the historic letter in which he called for an immediate revolt and deposition of the Provisional Government.

'We must, at any price, arrest the Provisional Government tonight, disarming (and defeating if they resist) the cadets, etc.

Don't temporize! We can lose everything!

… Hesitation amounts to death!'

"The revolutionary HQ in Smolny organized the revolt with utmost energy and resolve. The Party's Military-Revolutionary Committee gave the orders to the commanders and commissars (political officers) of Red Guard units. In one of the rooms, worker delegates were lining up for order forms to receive rifles from army arsenals.

"On the evening of October 24, the revolutionary forces began their offensive. They captured the Central Telegraph. Of the ten bridges over the Neva that could be raised and, as such, were vital arteries of the city, nine were controlled by the Red Guards by

nightfall. That day, the Red Guards took Finland Railway Station. Reinforced patrols of the Military-Revolutionary Committee stood guard at all suburban stations. The units bound for Petrograd on orders from the Provisional Government were not let through.

"That night, Lenin arrived in Smolny to stand at the helm of the uprising.

"Meanwhile, the members of the Provisional Government conferred in the Winter Palace. They made speeches and aired their plans to defeat "the rebel Bolsheviks." Yet they were political corpses.

"The proletariat clearly had the upper hand. Seeking to avoid bloodshed, the Military-Revolutionary Committee asked the Provisional Government to surrender. But the ultimatum remained unanswered. At 9:45 pm the signal was given. It was the cannon shot which has remained in the consciousness of humanity as the historic 'salvo of the Aurora', which announced to the world the beginning of a new era.

"The ranks of the defenders of the Winter Palace shook. The artillery battery, some of the Cadets, the Cossacks and the women's 'battalion of death' left the palace.

"The avalanche of the storming troops reached the walls of the palace. At 2:10 am the doors of the room where the frightened members of the Provisional Government were still sitting, slammed open. The victorious proletariat spoke with power in its voice: 'Which of you are the provisionals here? This is it, your time is over' (Mayakovsky)."

PROLETARIAN DICTATORSHIP

A key ingredient of the Marxian revolutionary recipe, the dictatorship of the proletariat was a "temporary stage required to neutralize bourgeois opposition" after a proletarian revolution. It has been noted that nothing lasts longer than temporary measures, and our constitution still proclaims the now-outlawed Communist Party to be "the guiding force" of society.

households (including seeds reserved for planting the following year). People were dying by the millions on some of the richest lands on the planet. There were cases of cannibalism. In Moscow, the railway stations were fenced off, and the peasants who came to the city in hopes of finding food stayed behind the fence and died of starvation under the watchful eye of the sentries. It was all right — they were "class enemies."

Collectivization also implied deportation of the "rich" peasants. To qualify as

It was "bourgeois opposition" that led the nation into civil war. Nearly three years — and 15 million victims — later, the Red Army won, the Entente lifted the blockade of Soviet Russia, and the future of Communist rule was secure.

Then came Stalin's collectivization. Preceded by the terrible drought on the Volga, the campaign to arrange individual peasants into "collective farms" was merely a half-disguised extension of the Bolshevik war against peasants, whom they regarded as "latent counterrevolutionaries." Grain was forcibly taken away from peasant

"rich," a peasant had to have a hired hand working on his land. Or own two cows. Or merely strike the commissar as being "not quite right."

Millions of them were deported to uninhabited areas of the Urals, northern Kazakhstan, and Siberia.

In the thirties, millions more found themselves in the GULAG (an abbreviation of State Department of Camps). Fathered by Leon Trotsky and Felix Dzerzhinsky in the early twenties, the labor camps quickly

Mamayev Hill Memorial in Volgograd is a good example of what victory in World War II means to most Russians.

evolved, in the words of their chronicler Alexander Solzhenitsyn, into "an archipelago." Stalin found millions of prisoners invaluable for his program of forced industrialization.

In 1936, Stalin reported that socialism had won "totally and irreversibly."

WORLD WAR II

On June 22, 1941, Hitler invaded Russia. And although the war came to an end on September 2, 1945 (when the last Axis Country, Japan, capitulated), in some ways, we are still at war. Monuments to war dead are everywhere. Every family lost someone in those four years. War films are still popular, as are thousands of books about it. In the United States, kids play "cowboys and Indians." In Russia, it's "Fascists and us." Every May 9, veterans put on their decorations and gather in the city (town, village) square, although their crowds get thinner with each passing year.

There are two reasons for this, of course. One is that any totalitarian regime needs an enemy to keep its subjects in line. For us, it was the Germans. I used to hate the Germans when I was a kid — and surprised to learn that Napoleon wasn't German. He was a bad guy, wasn't he? Then why wasn't he German?

The other — and infinitely more important — reason is that the war, of all the calamities suffered by the Russian people in our century, was the only one with a happy end. We won. Justice triumphed. After all, they attacked us first. The 32 million victims did not die in vain. You could take pride in them, and speak about them openly (which you could not if they died in a famine or in the camps).

And another thing. The war showed that on the "hate list" of Slav peoples, the invader is always N°1. Dictatorships come second if they are our dictatorships. In part, this should answer Winston Churchill's famous "Riddle wrapped in a mystery inside an enigma" maxim. Goebbels never grew tired of repeating that Germany was at war with communism first, and Russia second. It was a bid to split the opposing side. Yet it did not work.

COLD WAR

The Soviet Union lost about a third of its national wealth in World War II. It would seem that Stalin would draw the obvious conclusions and alter his foreign policy. Nothing doing. As party members were told at "closed" party meetings, "the war on Fascism ends, the war on capitalism begins." War was inevitable while capitalism survived.

The West heeded these warnings — perhaps too well. Speaking at Fulton, Missouri, in 1946, Winston Churchill coined an expression which was to last for at least a quarter of a century: "From Settin on the Baltic to Trieste on the Adriatic an iron curtain has descended across the Continent."

After the Americans came up with the hare-brained scheme to drop nuclear bombs on more than fifty Soviet cities, there was no averting a cold war. In fact, until the country came up with a nuclear bomb of its own, the danger of a real war seemed quite real.

Then Stalin died in March 1953, and things began to move very quickly indeed. Nikita Khrushchev dominated the political scene for the next eleven years. He will be remembered for three things: his famous "secret speech" at the 22d Party Congress, in which he denounced Stalin and Stalinism, his space program, which put Yury Gagarin in orbit, and the Cuban missile crisis, which surprisingly improved Soviet-American relations after it became apparent to everyone that New York city and half of Europe would not be blown to smithereens. Then, of course, there was the famous shoe-banging episode (they still ask me in the United States who Kuzka's Mother might have been. "I'll show you Kuzka's Mother!" roughly corresponds to the English "I'll show you!" It's not a very elegant expression, but then, Khrushchev was never a man to mince words.)

In 1964, Khrushchev was ousted from office. Although his removal from power had been an illegal act, he was not eliminated or even imprisoned. This showed that his efforts to de-Stalinize his country bore fruit. The totalitarian regime became milder. The era of "stagnation" was here.

CONTEMPORARY RUSSIA

When Leonid Brezhnev died a decade ago, he left behind a country whose beleaguered economy was sliding downhill and a leadership divided by a power struggle. There were other assorted problems, such as the insane war in Afghanistan, an increasingly hostile Eastern Europe, and looming American superiority in the field of space weapons.

Yet many of my countrymen long for those years. Seen from the grass-roots

Russia and the CIS can now be counted on, within limits, of course, not to blow our planet away. At home, however, his popularity has waned steadily since 1985, the year perestroika (which means "remodelling" or "restructuring") was introduced. Gorbachev swayed from right to left in those seven years; his orthodox communist and imperialist views, critics say, make him a political has-been. It is my belief, however, that Russia owes Mikhail Gorbachev a debt of gratitude for the courage it took him to declare that the king was naked. His honesty

level, sitting at boring party meetings and lauding "our dear comrade, the greatest political figure of the century Leonid Brezhnev," had been a small price to pay for a standard of living that Russia has vainly been trying to reattain since 1985. Brezhnev's corrupt, slovenly administration followed a "live and let live" philosophy (the only people the system could not digest were the dissidents). This scratch-my-back-and-I'll-scratch-yours lifestyle went a long way in Brezhnev's Russia.

Then came perestroika, Mikhail Gorbachev's pet policy which has so far brought our nation nothing but trouble. Like Alexander I before him, Gorbachev is very well-liked abroad, which is understandable: the

ended a decade of farce so truthfully described in one of our interminable anecdotes.

Lenin, Stalin, and Brezhnev were riding in a train. Suddenly it stopped. "All right, comrades," Lenin said, "let's organize our enthusiasts. The belief in communist ideals will get us moving."

And it did. After a while, the train stopped for the second time. "What we have to do, comrades," said Stalin taking a puff on his pipe, "is to shoot half of the train

ABOVE: whether they live in Moscow's suburbia or in the steppes of Siberia, our women see themselves as keepers of the home hearth first and foremost. In a country where dishwashers are nonexistent, this means work, work, and more work.

personnel — the other half will get us moving in no time at all."

And they did. But the train soon stopped for a third time. It was Brezhnev's turn now. He said: "All right, everybody, let's put blinds on the windows and have everybody rocking the carriage from side to side — people will think we are moving."

The train had not moved for a long time, and Gorbachev acknowledged the fact.

However, some people did not like that at all. In August, 1991, they finally crawled out of the woodwork, and attempted to take power.

It may seem funny today, but our former vice-president and his "Provisional Government" had the country (and, very probably, the world) scared for a couple of days: there were tanks in the streets of Moscow, the nuclear arsenal was controlled by our rebellious defense minister, and the president was cut off from the world at large at his summer residence in the Crimea (Khrushchev immediately comes to mind — he was ousted in absentia, too).

But Yeltsin decided to hang tough and, more importantly, the people had changed in those six years. When my middle-aged aunt, who is by no means a political activist, went to the barricades surrounding Yeltsin's White House in Moscow, I realized that the neo-Stalinist coup was doomed.

Wherever Russia was going, it was not back to socialism.

THE GOVERNMENT AND THE ECONOMY

The Russia of today is incredibly (some even say perilously) politicized. When people aren't talking food prices, they talk politics. Mass rallies and manifestations are held in major cities almost every weekend. TV and radio, films and books are full of politics.

The political scene is overcrowded and fragmented. Where shall Russia go? is the question that is answered in at least six ways in this country. First of all, there are the pro-Westerners, people who exalt the United States and favor the market economy. Then there are the assorted populists, ranging from left-wingers who want a "socialism with a human face" (whatever that may be) to ultra-conservatives who advo-

cate strong rule, discipline, and law and order. Then come the authoritarianists, who still believe that Lenin will get us out of our current predicament, and nationalists who blame everything on "non-Russians." Still others worry about the imminent ecological catastrophe.

In his first five years as President of the Union of Soviet Socialist Republics, Mikhail Gorbachev reorganized the country's governing bodies so many times that it would now take an experienced politologist to explain how the responsibilities of running the former empire were distributed. I'll spare you the finer details, yet a description of what is currently going on in "the center," as Russians call the federal government, is clearly in order since it affects the present and future of Russia.

After the abortive August 1991 coup, Gorbachev dissolved his council of ministers, substituting it with a board of presidential advisers, and temporarily suspended the sessions of the Supreme Soviet (parliament). Its economic functions were delegated to an inter-republican economic consultative committee. The post of vice-president was, quite understandably in my view, abolished (it was Vice-President Yanayev who headed the coup). Meanwhile, Boris Yeltsin outlawed the other, and perhaps more powerful, governing structure — the Communist Party of the Soviet Union — in Russian territory, precipitating an avalanche of similar bans in the former republics. In November, 1991, Gorbachev announced that he would resign if a new Union Treaty were not signed before the year was out. It wasn't, and, surprisingly to some, he did.

This left Yeltsin in command. Elected Russia's first president in 1991, he enjoys tremendous popularity (well-deserved, I might add). His uncompromising stand during the August coup showed that Boris Yeltsin is certainly worthy of the office entrusted him by the nation. The president of Russia works together with a democratically elected Supreme Soviet (parliament). He is the current prime minister (head of the cabinet) and the commander-in-chief of the armed forces. Critics say it is too much; Yeltsin defends himself by saying that times are hard, and a politician of lesser stature and popularity could not last through the winter. As it were, of all the former republics of the former Soviet Union, Russia has the most logical system of government — another feather in Yeltsin's cap.

There are many political parties, but none of them is influential — or numerous — enough to make political waves. This is understandable: after the downfall of the communists, Russian voters are wary of partisan politics (Yeltsin himself was elected on a non-partisan platform). The list of active political parties includes such serious organizations as the New Russian Democratic Party, the neo-Marxists, the anarchists and the Greens; but many people prefer the less serious Party of Fools and Party of Beer Lovers, both of which have won over many voters' hearts.

What the country clearly needs is something I'd tentatively term a Party of Economic Problems, because economic programs of nearly all the existing parties are so similar that they could have been carbon copies of a common original. Given the state of our economy, it makes one wonder what the future holds in store, particularly when the government announces far and wide that the way to a bearable future lies through an economic miracle.

The Russian economy has traditionally relied on exports of mineral resources and raw materials. And with good reason, since Russia is an incredibly rich country in that respect. Unfortunately, the economic system, or, rather, the remnants of an economic system that we have today, makes it easier to supply half of Europe with, say, oil and natural gas, than to make it readily available on the domestic market (you'll see for yourself the first time you'll go to a gas station).

Another problem is that our money isn't money in the exact sense of the word. Abroad, the rouble is not convertible into any of the world's recognized currencies; at home, having money does not necessarily mean being able to acquire what you require. It is all based on a sophisticated system of privileges, coupons, seniority and the like. It is customary to see the following sign at a Russian food store: Veterans of World War II Served Without Waiting (meaning standing in line, which takes up to five hours a week for the average Homo Sovieticus nowadays). Those of us who did not fight in the war, yet still want to buy a new refrigerator, find other ways to get around the system. Cronyism thrives, and the country's overblown bureaucracy is corrupt to the core.

If there is a chance, it lies in radical economic change. Yegor Gaidar, who spearheads the "shock therapy" reforms of the Yeltsin Cabinet, pins his hopes on a three-

stage "privatization" program (whereby state-owned property would be given away or sold to private companies); he also believes that the rouble must be made convertible with help from the West. Given the current rate of hyperinflation (the dollar cost 75 roubles on the black market in November 1991, 185 roubles in August 1992, and was rising), this isn't a bad idea at all. Another huge problem addressed by the cabinet is the snail's pace of conversion in the defense industry.

I'd say there's reason to doubt such rosy predictions.

Yet hope dies last. If Yeltsin and his team can manage to come up with a working system to reorient the national economy toward good old capitalism; if our military expenditures are cut down to reasonable proportions; if the West lends a hand… We'll wait and see.

ABOVE: *Passazh* is one of Petersburg's largest department stores.

GEOGRAPHY AND CLIMATE

In a sense, both have produced as tangible an impact on Russian character as the country's history. Here is why.

The Russian Republic, usually referred to as "Russia" in this country, is the largest republic of what, at the writing at this book, still holds together and continues to be the largest country in the world. It covers some seventeen million square kilometers (seven million square miles) of eastern Europe and northern Asia.

Most of Russia is a huge plain extending east from Poland almost to the Pacific coast. This expanse is cut into European and Siberian (Asian) Russia by the old Ural Mountains with a maximum height of 1,895 m (6,214 ft). The highest mountain ranges are situated along the frontiers: the Carpathians in the southwest, the Caucasus to the south and the Altai mountains on the China border.

European Russia is for the most part flat and low. The highest elevation whence the great Russian rivers rise — the Valdai Hills — reaches a mere 300 m (1,000 ft) above sea level.

Throughout history, the country's three million rivers have played key roles as arteries of communications and commerce. The Northern Dvina and the Pechora flow northward into the Arctic basin; most of the others flow southward: the Dniester, Bug, Dnieper and Don into the Black Sea and the Sea of Azov, and the Volga, the "mother of all Russians" into the Caspian Sea. These rivers, together with their tributaries and connecting canals, are still of considerable transportation value, whereas in Siberia (the region west of the Urals and north of Central Asia), the Ob, Lena, Enisei and Kolyma rivers, moving northward into the frozen Arctic, are of limited commercial import (which does not detract from their primeval beauty in the slightest). In Siberia, only the Amur, part of the modern boundary with China, flows eastward into the Pacific.

Sorry for the lecture, but the country is so big that even a simple list of its major cities would take up a couple of pages. Now, then…

Russia is the land of huge hydroelectric power stations. The largest are located in Siberia, on the Angara, which flows out of

Lake Baikal, one of the world's largest and deepest lakes. We also have nuclear power stations, which, alas, are not the most reliable in the world. Russia leads the world in deposits of coal, iron ores, and natural gas. There are also emeralds and rubies in the Urals, and gold and diamonds in Siberia.

The climate is continental, that is, marked by extremes of heat and cold. Most of Russia lies in the latitudes of Canada and Alaska. In fact, Russia has both of the world's largest northern cities — Murmansk (beyond the Arctic circle) and St.Petersburg.

The temperature swing increases towards the east, but even in European Russia there are no internal mountainous partitions to keep icy winds from sweeping to the Black Sea. Northeast Siberia is one of the

world's coldest regions: temperatures as low as -70°C (-90°F) have been recorded near Verkhoiansk. During the summer, however, heat waves occur even there.

Precipitation is generally moderate or light, and heaviest in summer (although we do get ferocious snowstorms sometimes even in Moscow).

There are five major soil and vegetation zones. About 15 percent of the country is in the extreme north. It comes alive only in "summer" — the two weeks in July when the local inhabitants: Polar bears, white foxes etc. can eat mushrooms instead of each other (which they do for the rest of the year).

To the south lies the *taiga,* the largest belt of evergreen forest in the world, which covers over half the territory of Russia. An agricultural headache, the forests are at the same time a source of what our ancestors used for money: fur. The population of bears, wolves, foxes, lynxes, sables and, in the Far East, tigers and leopards, make the taiga a hunter's paradise.

Still further to the south, the forest shades into wooded steppe or meadow, noted as much for its fertile black soil as for the notorious inability of our lunatic farming system to grow bread there.

East of the Caspian Sea lies the desert. In the Crimea there's a relatively small subtropical region, the closest thing we have to the Riviera.

Fun in the snow in the Taimyr Peninsula beyond the Arctic Circle.

RELIGION IN RUSSIA

There are forty religions in Russia. With 76 dioceses and 11 vicariates (some on foreign soil), the Russian Orthodox Church is the greatest religious authority in the land. It is headed by the Patriarch of Moscow and All Russia (Aleksiy II at the writing of this book), and administered by the Holy Synod. There are about seven thousand churches and 28 functioning monasteries. The seat of the Patriarch is in the St. Daniel Monastery.

and what could be better than the church with its ten centuries of unbroken tradition?

Islam has the second largest number of followers. Most of our Moslems are Sunnites. Some live in Moscow, where they attend the only mosque the capital has (at N°7 Vypolzov Pereulok).

Russia has approximately two million ethnic Jews. Synagogue attendance is not high, ranging from 3 to 10 percent in different places. The Moscow Choral Synagogue has a *yeshiva* (school) for rabbis, cantors and readers of the Torah. There's a kosher cafe, too.

Since the church was all but openly persecuted until quite recently, little is known about the number of believers, church weddings and the like. However, if random polls are anything to go by, about a quarter of the population (around 40 million) believes in God.

In any case, one thing is certain: never in the history of Soviet Russia has the Church experienced such popularity as after its official comeback in 1988, when the first millenium of Christianity was celebrated. Churches are packed on Sundays; tens of thousands have accepted Baptism; church activities get extensive press and TV coverage. The downfall of communist ideology left a void which people seek to fill —

Next on the list are the Catholics, the assorted Christian sects (Old Believers, Evangelists, Seventh Day Adventists, Molokans and so on), and the Buddhists.

Viewed as part of the cultural revival now taking place in the country, religion is without doubt an unfailing tourist attraction. A visit to an Orthodox church, for example, can be quite an experience. The solemnity, the beauty of ceremonial attire, the ageless icons in the candle-lit interior are a unique setting for the student of Russian character.

Christmas is the greatest religious holiday. The Orthodox church celebrates Christmas every January 7 with a solemn "cross procession" around the church (the disparity between Catholic and Orthodox Christmas has to do with the 12-day difference between the "old" and "new" calendars). Then comes an all-night vigil. There are no seats in our churches, and one has the choice between standing or kneeling all night, which shows that our believers are serious about their faith. As an example, I'd like to cite Somerset Maugham's account of religion in turn-of-the-century Russia (it also includes a character study I thought you would find interesting):

"No one can make excursions into Russian life or Russian fiction without noticing how great a place is taken by an acute sense of sin. Not only is the Russian constantly telling you that he is a sinner, but apparently he feels it, and he suffers from very lively pangs of remorse. It is a curious trait and I have tried to account for it. Of course we say that we are miserable sinners in church, but we do not believe it; we have the good sense to know that we are nothing of the kind; we have our faults and we have all done things that we regret, but we know quite well that our actions have not been such as to need any beating of our breasts and gnashing of our teeth … The Russians seem different. They are more introspective than we are and their sense of sin is urgent. They are really overwhelmed by the burden and they will repent in sackcloth and ashes, with weeping and lamentation, for peccadillos which would leave our less sensitive consciences untroubled. … The Russian is not a very great sinner. He is lazy and infirm of purpose; he talks too much; he has no great control over himself so that the expression of his passions is more lively than their intensity warrants; but he is kindly on the whole and good-humoured; he does not bear malice; he is generous, tolerant of others' failings; he is probably less engrossed in sexual affairs than the Spaniard or the Frenchman; he is sociable; his temper is quick, but he is easily appeased."

Much of this still holds true today.

SPORT IN RUSSIA

Russia is the home of some of the world's greatest athletes. Along with the now-de-

funct East Germany, the now-defunct USSR used to run a conveyor belt producing Olympic and world champions.

Football (the European kind) is the national sport, and watching football on TV is the national pastime. While the national team and such leading clubs as Moscow Spartak and Kiev Dynamo fare reasonably well in world and European tournaments, the level of the majority of our professional teams remains surprisingly low, especially considering the number of kids the selection coaches can choose from. Recently, things

were further complicated by the migration of our best players to Europe (mostly Italy).

The sport that comes a close second to football is dominoes. It is, in fact, more than a game—it is a ritual. God help anyone who disturbs Russians playing dominoes (even if they are playing during working hours). The game is too intricate for me to understand, but from the way some of the players I've seen slammed dominoes down on the table, I'd say it has a great future.

Also popular are such sports as track-and-field, hockey, volleyball, basketball, and weightlifting.

We take our sports seriously: there are phys-ed colleges in Moscow and Petersburg (graduates become coaches or schoolteachers). Moscow also has a scientific research institute of physical culture.

Of the sports peculiar to Russia, there's wrestling and assorted winter sports. We are a nation of skiers. No high school student

OPPOSITE: Buddhist datsan;
ABOVE: learning the ABC's of the millenium-long Orthodox tradition.

can (theoretically) graduate without first proving that he or she can cover several kilometers of snow-covered cross-country on skis within a certain time limit. There's also mountain skiing in the Caucasus and the Kola Peninsula near Murmansk.

Some sports remain out of reach for ordinary people. They constitute the pleasure of the elite. Being able to hire a tennis court in winter takes a lot of clout, and getting to play on the country's only golf course in Moscow, which was opened by Sven Juhansson and has since seen the likes of Pele, is a privilege reserved for a handful of my compatriots.

RUSSIAN CUISINE

Historically, Russia never amounted to much in terms of cuisine, although there are several interesting dishes. "Squalor is inventive," says the Russian proverb, and this first of all concerns food. A classic example is borscht, a soup prepared from ingredients that are always available and affordable: beets, cabbage, onions, carrots, potatoes and such more expensive options as sweet peppers, tomatoes, meat, frankfurters, etc. Other dishes highlight foods that you gather in a forest or catch in the river — mushrooms, berries, honey, fish (even though sturgeon is expensive today, well-to-do peasants could easily afford it in the past century). In short, Russian cuisine is peasant cuisine. This does not mean that the variety of dishes included in our cookbooks is not large, merely that most of them were exported from Europe or the Orient together with the chefs, who flocked to the courts of the great emperors by the hundreds.

Before I suggest a few dishes that it would be a mortal sin for you not to try during your stay in Russia, I would like to apologize for the sorry situation with food, which is bound to affect your gastronomic explorations. In fact, some of the dishes from our national cuisine are to be found only in the homes of the more conscientious housewives. (Although few and far

between, they still exist, thank God. "Imagine!" an American friend told me after a visit to such a household. "She cooks mayonnaise herself!")

Another thing you should bear in mind is that Russians customarily drink when they eat, so every change of dish is usually preceded by a toast and a shot (or two or three) of vodka.

The first thing you have to try is the famous Russian pie. There are small, two-bite sized ones and very large ones called *kulibiaka* (strictly non-restaurant fare, alas!), baked or fried in boiling oil with a variety of stuffings: meat, liver-and-heart, fish-and-rice, cabbage-and-egg, potatoes, mushrooms, steamed sauerkraut, stewed carrots and other culinary delights; my grandmother, who came from Siberia, could cook a triple- or even quadruple-layered kulibiaka (cabbage on top of mushrooms on top of roast chicken fillet) — umm!

The next is *pelimeni* (a kind of small ravioli), which are cooked with at least two kinds of meat, pork and beef (the ideal combination is veal/pork/mutton). Any other kind is an ignoble forgery, as are the *pelimeni* that are not boiled to readiness in rich beef bouillon. *Pelimeni* are dipped into melted butter, sour cream or vinegar to add spice.

Blinces date to pre-Christian times, when these round, thin pancakes that symbolized the sun were an inalienable part of pagan festivals. There are different kinds, but the ones you should try are the large, thin ones. You eat them with caviar, salted salmon, sour cream, or jam.

Finally, there are the mushrooms. Mushroom hunting has evolved into a national mania in the last decade. As I hope you'll find out, Russians know what to do with them, too. And don't worry about being poisoned — we know our mushrooms well.

Oh, yes — don't drink too much. At least don't try to keep up with your local hosts (if you are invited somewhere). One foreign correspondent based in Moscow actually recommended sitting next to a potted plant, so that when you feel you've had enough, you can share whatever it is in your glass with it.

Now who was it that said you can't have a quick hamburger in Russia?

Moscow

MOSCOW

Leningrad Prospekt

Byelorussky Railway Station

Dostoyevsky Street

Olimpiisky Prospekt

Schepkin Street

Durov Street

Central Puppet Theatre

Sadovoye Ring

Mayakovsky Square

Sukharevskaya Square

Peking Hotel

Tverskaya Street

Pushkin Square

Petrovka Street

Rozhdestvenka Street

Hertzen Monument

Operetta Theatre

Lubianskaya Square

Church of the Ressurection

Vosstania Square

Tverskoi Boulevard

Nezhdanova Street

Intourist Hotel

Council of Ministers

Teatralny Lane

Maroseika Street

Hertzen Street

Povarskaya Street

Conservatoire

Staraya Square

Polytechnical Museum

Pokrovka Street

US Embassy

National Hotel

RED SQUARE

Nikolskaya Street

Varvarskaya Square

Solianka Street

New Arbat

New Arbat

KREMLIN

Ilyinka Street

Razin Street

Varvarskaya Square

ILINSKY GARDEN

Arbat Street

Volhonka Street

Rossiya Hotel

Smolenskaya

Gogol Boulevard

Starokonushenny Lane

Pushkin Museum

Kremliovskaya Quay

Moskva River

Borodinsky Bridge

Smolenskaya Square

Ministry of Foreign Affairs

Kropotkinskaya

Belgrade Hotel

Smolensky Boulevard

Prechistenka

Dostoyenka Street

Kadashevskaya Street

Lavrushinsky Lane

Tretiakov Gallery

Piatnitskaya Street

Prechistenka

State Gallery

Bolshaya Yakimanka Street

Krymsky Bridge

Krymsky val

Oktiabrskaya Square

Trinity Church

Monastery of the Savior

Paveletsk Railway Station

Komsomolsky Prospekt

Frunzenskaya Quay

Moskva River

Leninsky Prospekt

Dobrynins kaya

Serpukhovskaya

Markhlevskaya Street

Artists' Union

Moskva River

GORKY PARK

Donskoi Monastery

1 Bolshoi Theater
2 GUM
3 Maly Theater
4 Metropol Hotel
5 Ivan Fedorov Monument
6 Lenin Museum
7 Historical Museum
8 St.Basil's Cathedral

0.3 miles
500 m

N

WHAT can one say about a town which started as an obscure wooden fort, was burned either through malice or negligence with metronomic regularity every 25 years or so for seven centuries, was pillaged, plundered and put down by nearly every conquest-bent European neighbor, suffered epidemics of every lethal disease known to man save probably AIDS (we keep our fingers crossed), was deserted by its populace twice in the last two hundred years — yet miraculously, came back every time and eventually emerged as the

ably erroneously regarded as the founder of Moscow) invited his Seversk ally Svyatoslav Olgovich to what was a small village on Borovitsky (Forest) Hill — 300 steps from one end to the other. The place had all the makings of a future metropolis, but, more importantly, it was almost ideal for people whose chief preoccupation was survival: it had several waterways (used for transportation, defense, fishing), a hilly terrain (a fortifier's dream) and lots of timber (construction material and firewood — no small thing in a place with a mean annual temperature of 3°C (38°F).

capital of a territory larger than South America?

Like most large cities, Moscow has something for everyone. Whatever you may be looking for — history, architecture, the fine arts, big-city entertainment, loud sports festivals, pompous military parades, rock concerts and so on and on and on — Moscow won't let you down.

BACKGROUND

Slavs lived here in the seventh century. In 1147, the year Moscow was first mentioned in the chronicles, what Suzdal overlord Yury the Long-Armed (traditionally, but prob-

The Prince of Suzdal evidently considered Moscow important enough to merit some added protection: in 1156, the village got its first walls (of timber). In an age when even peasants wore chain mail when they ploughed (surprise attacks by neighboring potentates were not unheard-of), living near a fort had a life-or-death significance: even though they were not permitted to build their huts within its perimeter, and lived just outside the walls in *sloboda's* (unprotected villages), which were customarily looted and put to the torch by their enemies, they could at least count on a greater measure of

Russian troops led into combat by Prince Dmitry Donskoi.

personal safety, and freedom, (selling prisoners to the slave-traders was another of the time's charming customs).

Moscow's geographical situation was an extremely fortunate one. It stood at the junction of major trade routes from Novgorod to Ryazan, from Kiev and Smolensk to Rostov, Vladimir, Suzdal, and several other towns.

As soon as the village started to grow, however, it became an attractive booty for the assorted feudal vultures who filled the land in the thirteenth century. The first of these to try his luck against Moscow was my namesake, prince Gleb of Ryazan, who looted and burned Moscow in 1176. Muscovites quickly rebuilt the walls of their *kreml* (fortress), and successfully weathered the next attack (by Izyaslav of Ryazan in 1209). Moscow was now secure against military intervention by their brother Slavs. Then, in 1237, the Mongols came.

OPPOSITE: St. Basils, Moscow's monument to the final victory over the Tartars in 1552.

THE MONGOL INVASION

"There have come peoples, about whom no one knows anything for certain — who they are, whence they come, what tongue they speak, what tribe they belong to, what faith they preach," wrote the chroniclers in bewilderment. "The end of the world is at hand."

They came from the boundless steppes of Central Asia — the best fighters the world had ever seen. Their leader, Genghis Khan, remained illiterate to the end of his days. But literacy meant little in thirteenth-century Mongolia, the nomad state with a surprising amount of centralized control, whose warriors were reputed to "drink dew, ride the wind, and devour human flesh on the battlefield." In the course of Genghis Khan's lifetime, the Mongols conquered Siberia, Kirghizia, half of China, Turkestan with its ancient forts of Merv, Bukhara and Urgench, Iran, Azerbaidzhan, Georgia, the Crimea and Armenia. In 1223 they came to the southeast borders of the Russian land, gave the Russians a terrible thrashing, and... left.

The most impressive thing about the Mongols (known as "Tartars" among Russians) was their army, structured along totally novel principles. The basic unit was the hundred, which was made up of tens; the hundreds were united into thousands and ten-thousands. Every unit answered for each man: if one in the ten fled in battle, the other nine were executed. There were no foot-soldiers: every fighting man had at least two horses. They were also incredibly well-armed for hand-to-hand combat — their arrows, for example, could penetrate chain mail. As the Russians soon learned, the Mongols' greatest strength lay in their knowledge of human nature combined with utter ruthlessness. During siege, they rarely resorted to all-out assault, but had an unerring knack for finding traitors in every city they came to. Another favorite trick was to drive local dwellers, women and children included, before their troops when they did attempt to scale the walls or enter via a hole made with catapult machines they brought with them from China.

In Russia, which was rendered almost totally helpless by feudal rivalry, the Mongols skillfully fueled internal strife by recruiting allies from among the Russian princes, and then turning on the traitors at the first opportunity. Such tactics, however, were something of an overkill, because the hopelessly fragmented Russians could do nothing against an enemy numerically much stronger than what any one principality could put together.

In 1237, Batu Khan, Genghis Khan's grandson, came to the Kama River at the head of a vast army. Terrified by the advance of "an army so great that it darkened the skies and made the Earth tremble under horses' hooves" towards his city, Prince Yury of Ryazan pleaded with his "brothers" in Vladimir and Chernigov for help. But it was each man for himself in Russia, and Ryazan fell on the sixth day of siege, followed

by Kolomna, Moscow, Tver and Vladimir. The Mongols pressed on towards Novgorod, but it seemed that this time, they got more than they bargained for: the Russians put up a resistance so fierce that Batu was finally forced to turn back (his advance got bogged down in the famous mid-Russian marshes anyway) and give his depleted armies a much-needed rest in the steppes back home.

Two years later, they came back, took Kiev and continued towards Poland, Hungary and the Balkans. After suffering a major defeat in Czechia, they stopped. "Russia's endless plains sapped the Mongols' strength and stopped their advance at Europe's very edge; the barbarians did not dare leave the enslaved Russia in the rear, and returned to the steppes of the Orient. Thus fledgling Enlightenment was saved by plundered, mortally wounded Russia," wrote Alexander Pushkin, the national poet, in the nineteenth century.

The country was in for more than two centuries of Mongol domination.

During the fourteenth century Moscow emerged as a successor to Vladimir. Strange as it may seem, Moscow owed its rise to the Golden Horde, the state established by the Mongols on the Volga. The Mongols granted the title of Grand Prince to Yury Danilovich of Moscow in 1318. In 1328, his successor, Ivan I (who was known as *Kalita* — moneybags) obtained the khan's patent to rule Vladimir through "shrewd diplomacy" (i.e. bribery).

Ivan I also went out of his way to woo Metropolitan Peter out of his arch-rival Michael's Vladimir. The head of the Orthodox church spent a lot of time on an extensive building program inside the Kremlin (the famous Church of the Dormition was begun in 1327). Peter died in December of that year, and was buried, in accordance with his will, in the still-uncompleted cathedral. This laid the groundwork for the shift of the metropolitan see to Moscow.

The stage was set for the "gathering of the Russian lands" (as the chronicles put it). One by one, the principalities recognized Moscow's supremacy. Once internal strife was out of the way, Russia turned to the east: in 1380, it scored its first victory against the Mongols, and in 1480, stopped paying tribute to the now-shaky and fragmented Golden Horde. The days of the "Mongol yoke" were over.

The sixteenth century became a time of empire-building. Ivan the Terrible conquered Kazan in 1552. In those days, it was quite a prize — we have St.Basil's cathedral in Red Square to prove it. Today, the people of starving, crime-ridden Kazan (home of Russia's own youth gangs) would probably welcome any foreign invader in exchange for a little food and clothing. By 1583, Ivan's domain engulfed Khan Kuchum's Western Siberia. Yet territorial expansion seemed to be of no help at all when it came to solving Russia's domestic problems. The greatest of these problems was the half-mad czar himself. Torn between piety and a lust for blood which earned him his famous nickname, Ivan proved least fortunate when it came to family matters. Several of his wives were forced to take the veil, two or three were clandestinely poisoned, and one publicly executed for "excessive whoring". Then, three years before his death, Ivan killed his son and heir and put an end to the old Moscow dynasty. In a time when the existence or absence of centralized power was life or death for hundreds of thousands, Ivan the Terrible's senseless act could spell only one thing — trouble.

The following six decades are known to historians of Russia as just that — the Troubles (see page 21). The suspicious demise of three year-old Prince Dmitry, Ivan the Terrible's sole surviving heir, resulted in a power struggle between the top Boyars. Boris Godunov came out on top. His reign as czar was an extremely unfortunate one for Russia, with famines, bad harvests, unemployment and peasant revolts. It was widely rumored that infant Dmitry escaped death at the hands of Czar Boris, that he was safe in Poland. The Poles, itching to get back at Moscow for Ivan the Terrible's Livonian war, used these rumors to their advantage. They found one Grigory Otrepiev, a fugitive monk from a Moscow monastery, to play Dmitry's role. At the head of an army of malcontents, the Pretender took Moscow (Czar Boris was dead, and his son was clearly no match for False Dmitry) in 1605. By 1606, he was dead as well. The throne passed from the hands of one Boyar to another. After a bloody two-year-long peasant uprising, there appeared False Dmitry II, who would have taken Moscow but for the heroic defense of the Trinity-St.Sergius Monastery. But the beleaguered Seven-Boyar government had nothing left to fight with. In 1610, they chose the Poles over the "Brigand" (the second pretender's popular name), and surrendered the city.

It is difficult to say what would have happened but for the Orthodox church. Headed by Patriarch Germogen, the nation stood up against the invaders. By that time, King Sigizmund of Poland had conquered Smolensk, and the Swedes seized Novgorod. This time, it was the Volga Region that helped. Led by Kuzma Minin and Prince Dmitry Pozharsky, a sizeable militia from several Volga towns ousted the Poles and the Swedes and called upon the Boyars to elect a czar from their midst. In July 1613, Michael Romanov was crowned in the Kremlin as Michael I. The Romanovs seemed poorly equipped to govern a realm of such unlimited savagery. The only exception, before the coronation of Peter I, was Michael's son and Peter's father Alexei (the Quietest).

In Peter's time, Moscow embarked on a long downward journey towards near-provincial decline. There was no love lost between Peter and Moscow, where the young czar had nearly been killed on more than one occasion. Instead, Peter the Great concentrated on his wars, on his ships, and on his beloved "window into Europe" — St.Petersburg, the town which humiliated Moscow by taking its status of capital city away for more than two centuries.

The next momentous page in Moscow's history came in 1812, when the greatest army in the world, headed by the invulnerable Napoleon himself, took Moscow without so much as a skirmish. They say that Napoleon waited for the better part of the day for the "Boyar deputation," as he put it, to present itself on the Hill of Bows with the keys to the city. Yet no one came. The city beneath his feet was all but deserted. Napoleon's campaign ran against his opponent Kutuzov's ingenious engage-and-avoid tactics and an incredibly powerful patriotic upheaval in Russia, which spawned an all-out guerilla war against the invading armies. Supplies became scarce, the French were demoralized and quickly degenerated from disciplined fighting force to a band of marauders.

It was against the rules! In all his previous wars (with the possible exception of Spain), the taking of the largest city had always

meant the end of the war (and usually a humiliating peace for the vanquished). Yet Napoleon's repeated requests for negotiations were left unanswered. Realizing his plight, he finally decided to abandon Moscow. There was little enough of the city left at that point, but all is fair in love and war, and Napoleon, who'd come to Russia to "return it to civilization's embrace" gave the order to blow up the Kremlin and everything in it. But God finally intervened: most of the structures inside the citadel survived the blast (even Ivan the Great which, given its height, was clearly the most vulnerable of the lot).

Dancing outside Moscow's most prestigious cemetery in the Novodevichy Convent.

Realizing that the Smolensk Road by which he'd come could not possibly sustain his armies during the retreat, Napoleon pressed on towards Tula, but was stopped cold by Kutuzov's army, which was growing numerically stronger by the hour, at Malo-yaroslavets. Napoleon had no choice but to retreat via the plundered, scorched earth of the Smolensk Road. Then the famous Russian winter gave a hand to Kutuzov's better-supplied (and warmly-dressed) soldiers. In the end, a mere 30,000 French troops crossed the ice of the borderline Berezina River — all that was left of a nearly 600,000 strong Grand Army.

Even in defeat, Napoleon was almost too much for the Russians with their notorious lack of coordination and, in many cases, shortsighted strategies. He managed to escape, and Alexander I had no choice but to pursue him. The Russians entered Paris on March 30, 1814. Europe was liberated of Napoleonic tyranny.

Moscow prospered in what remained of the nineteenth century. It has never again fallen into an invader's hands.

But the coming twentieth century was to teach Moscow a lesson it will remember for a long time to come.

"Beat your own, and scare the stranger:" the old Russian proverb (it loses much in my translation) may well serve as the slogan for the first half of this century. Together with the rest of Russia, Moscow went through the revolution of 1905, World War I, two revolutions in 1917, the Civil War, the war against Finland at the end of the 30s, the terrible purges of 1937 and 1938, World War II, and more purges in the 1940s. Measured in human lives, the toll of these cataclysms is staggering. Historians say that in World War II alone, from 28 to 34 million had been lost. Add another 20 to 25 million GULAG victims, and you can see how terrible the twentieth century had been to a country whose population numbered just over a hundred million in 1914. To this day, the army has serious problems trying to draft the required number of recruits each year because most of the victims were men. Our army is much too

Kalinin Avenue became New Arbat after the statue of Mikhail Kalinin, Stalin's puppet prime minister, came down in the heady days of the August, 1991, revolution.

large, it is true, but it is also a sign of an unbalance in the men-to-women ratio of the population — the lethal breath of the past.

I'd love to say something nice about the years of Soviet rule in Moscow. In fact, I was driving along the Kremlin Embankment one day, and heard someone trying to do just that over the radio. The person being interviewed was obviously a Communist and a World War II veteran (it was in those not-too-distant days when we still had a Communist Party). "Yes, there were drawbacks," the man was saying, "but we scored major victories, as well!" At this point, my brother turned off the radio in obvious disgust and continued where the man on the radio left off: "… We scored a victory over culture! Over material interest! Over food and clothes! No foreign army in the world could have so successfully killed as many of our countrymen as we did in the 30s alone!"

He forgot architecture.

When Stalin had firmly installed himself in the Kremlin, he decided, among other things, to do something about the "village layout" of Moscow. He felt that it lacked scale and grandeur, that it failed to reflect the "triumphant march of socialism". To straighten things out, he embarked on what would have been the costliest construction program in any other country on earth. Stalin, however, had a vast army of practically free labor (GULAG prisoners), which made the program cost-effective.

The first phase of the project involved liberal amounts of TNT. Hundreds of buildings were demolished all over town, the most famous of them being the Church of Christ the Savior in Volkhonka Street. The triumphal arch was moved from its old site near Byelorussky Station to the newly-built Kutuzovsky Prospekt. Tverskaya Street was "straightened out". Entire quarters of old Moscow ceased to exist.

When the dust settled, a "General Plan for the Reconstruction of Moscow" was adopted (it is still in force, by the way). The towering Moskva Hotel was erected a stone's throw away from Red Square. The city got seven pseudo-Gothic "high-rises," of which the largest is probably the new university build-ing on Sparrow Hills. Also built were several dozen apartment houses, in the same style. Most of them are located in Kutuzovsky Prospekt and the old part of Leninsky Prospekt. Solzhenitsyn remembers in his *Gulag Archipelago* how he worked on the apartment house in what is now Gagarin Square as a prisoner. Moscow also got the so-called Exhibition of Economic Achievements (which Muscovites call *Ve-De-En-Kha*, the Russian abbreviation). The collection of souvenirs from the Soviet era in or near the exhibition includes Mukhina's Worker and

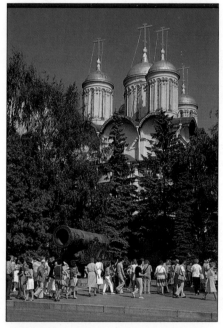

Peasant Girl, a monument to the space conquests in the shape of a rocket sitting on its blast-off trail, and the Ostankino TV Tower (the latter two were added after Stalin's death).

I'll say one thing for Stalin's housing: it was certainly much better than what they build today. As for its architectural value… but judge for yourself. Any trip you take around Moscow is certain to include at least a glimpse of these relics of what, hopefully, is a by-gone era.

GENERAL INFORMATION

Your best source of information in Moscow is the service bureau of the hotel you're staying

---

Czar Cannon: the Mongol deterrent.

at. In fact, even if you're not staying at a hotel, don't hesitate to call on the service bureau at any major Intourist hotel. The people who work there are very helpful, especially if you offer them a small gift (a couple of packs of cigarettes should do nicely). Here are the phone numbers of a few of them:
KOSMOS (217 91 91; 217 91 93; INTOURIST: (203 40 08; SAVOY: (929 85 00.

The address and phone number of the central Intourist office is: 16 Marx Prospekt, (203 69 62 or (203 63 50.

For specific travel inquiries:
AEROFLOT (domestic flights and reservations on other air-carriers): Central Offices: 4 Frunzenskaya Naberezhnaya, (245 00 02; AIRPORT: (155 09 22; DOMODEDOVO INTOURIST: (234 86 55; VNUKOVO INTOURIST: (436 29 67.

CAR RENTAL

Car rental (with or without driver plus gas coupons and emergency service):
BUSINESSCAR (231 82 25 (Toyotas at $52 without driver)
INNIS (927 11 87; 928 78 64 (Nissans at $51 to $65 without driver)
MOSRENT (248 36 07; (248 02 51 (Mercedes $56 to $79 without driver).
INTOURSERVICE (203 00 96 (with driver only, $10 to $13 per hour, or $30 per hour for a Lincoln limosine).
ROZEC CAR (241 78 18; (241 53 93 ($ 45-80 without driver).
EUROPCAR (253 13 69; (253 24 77 ($46 to $0.95 plus $0.29 to $0.75 per kilometer).

OTHER TRANSPORTATION OPTIONS

TAXI (927 00 00; (927 20 18 (same day reservations). (227 00 00/40 (advance booking).
METRO 1 rouble.

PASSPORT

Keep your passport with you at all times.

WHAT TO SEE

There's so much it would take weeks — and then some. But no matter how much time , **Red Square** and the **Kremlin** are a must.

THE EPIDEMIC OF RENAMING

A history as long as ours was bound to produce a bucketful of absurd misunderstandings, nonsensical oddities and funny incongruities, which never fail to present themselves when the conscientious bureaucrat forces his clinical vision of an orderly world on a people whose loathing of orderliness is legendary. The mess with street names is a case in point.

It all started with Christian names. Since the Bolsheviks were bent on eradicating religion, they opposed church baptisms. Instead, people were encouraged to invent "revolutionary" names of their own. Here are a few of them: Revmira (revolution and peace); Oktiabrina; Vladlen (Vladimir Lenin); Kim (Communist International); Industria and even Dazdraperma (a charming girl's name abbreviated from "Long Live the First of May!"). But that, I repeat, was just for starters. "The deeper into the forest, the more firewood" says the Russian proverb…

"Dear Editor," went a letter to a national daily, "help! I live in Vtoroi Pniovy Pereulok (Second Stump Alley). That the name is terrible is only half the problem. The other half is that there isn't a First (or a Third) Stump Alley either in my home town or, to the best of my knowledge, anywhere else in the country!"

"Dear Editor," went another letter, "I live on one of the most interesting streets in the Soviet Union. For three centuries, it was known as Alexander Nevsky Street. The name was quite appropriate, since the great general was born in our town. In 1925, the Bolsheviks renamed the street to … I'm willing to stake my last rouble that you won't guess… It's Clara Zetkin! Imagine: Alexander has lived together with Clara for 65 years!"

Finding your way about Moscow is difficult without a knowledge of Russian. But the people are helpful, and usually know enough English to understand what you are looking for. But now, there is another problem — they may not know where it is! When Mayor Gavriil Popov's new Municipal Council decided to rename over fifty streets and squares in midtown Moscow, little thought was given to the consequences. The deputies certainly meant well—most of the streets that are now getting their old names back still boast signs with last names of either recognized criminals (Stalin's cronies), or of people who will soon be recognized criminals (Brezhnev's cronies). The problem, however, is that most Muscovites don't remember how these streets were called before Lenin's revolution opened the way for Stalin's epidemic of renaming.

Starting in the late 20, it became fashionable among the party bureaucrats, secret-police chiefs and top technocrats to have their names "awarded" to factories, streets, schools, towns and cities. Khrushchev recalled how they judged each other's importance in accordance with the number of places bearing their names. In the late thirties, a macabre picture emerged.

Every town had a Lenin Street (or avenue if it was big enough). Every town but Moscow had a Moskovskaya (Moscow) Street.

Every town had a Stalin Street, a Molotov Street, an Ordzhonikidze Street, and so on down to the last member of the Politburo.

Petrograd was renamed Leningrad. Tsaritsyn was renamed Stalingrad. Nizhny Novgorod was renamed Gorky, in honor of the writer who gave us "socialist realism." Regional capitals suffered the same fate (Frunze, Ordzhonikidze, Sverdlovsk).

Somebody proposed to rename the Moon "Stalin," and the papers gave the matter serious consideration.

It was also fashionable to give places the names of Marx and Engels, prominent foreign revolutionaries (living and dead), Russian military leaders starting with Suvorov and Kutuzov, highway robbers who chanced to lead peasant revolts in centuries past, musicians and composers, schoolteachers, cosmonauts and foreign politicians such as Indira Gandhi.

One collective farm was given the name of Lope de Vega: they are still wondering down there who he or she might be. Then they started naming places after events (24th CPSU Congress Street), dates (Fiftieth Anniversary of Great October Revolution Square), and, worst of all, other places (Orchestra named after Factory named after Stepan Razin).

I swear that all of it is true. If you don't believe me, just take a taxi to Sharikopodshipnikovaya (Ball-Bearing) Street, but don't forget to tell the cabbie which one you want — there are three of them in Moscow!

One can go on and on, but the best thing for me to do is to give you a list of places in Moscow which have been, or will soon be, renamed. Here it is:

FORMER — CURRENT/IMPENDING
25TH OCTOBER — NIKOLSKAYA
50-TH ANNIVERSARY OF OCTOBER SQUARE —
    MANEZHNAYA SQUARE
ALEKSEYA TOLSTOGO — SPIRIDONOVKA
BOGDANA KHMELNITSKOGO — MAROSEIKA
BOLSHAYA KOLKHOZNAYA SQUARE —
    BOLSHAYA SUKHAREVSKAYA SQUARE
CHERNYSHEVSKOGO — POKROVKA
CHKALOVA — ZEMLIANOI VAL
DIMITROVA — BOLSHAYA YAKIMANKA
DOBRYNINSKAYA SQUARE —
    SERPUKHOVSKAYA SQUARE
DZERZHINSKOGO — BOLSHAYA LUBIANKA
DZERZHINSKOGO SQUARE — LUBIANSKAYA
    SQUARE
ENTHUSIAST SHOSSE (ROAD) —
    VLADIMIRSKOYE SHOSSE
REVOLIUTSII SQUARE — VOSKRESENSKAYA
    SQUARE
FRUNZE — ZNAMENKA

GORKOGO — TVERSKAYA
ILYICHA SQUARE — ROGOZHSKAYA
    ZASTAVA
KALININA PROSPEKT (AVENUE) — NEW
    ARBAT PROSPEKT
KARLA MARKSA — STARAYA BASMANNAYA
KIROVA — MYASNITSKAYA
KOMMUNY SQUARE — YEKATERININSKAYA
    SQUARE
KOMSOMOLSKAYA SQUARE —
    KALANCHIOVSKAYA SQUARE
KRASNAYA PRESNIA — BOLSHAYA
    PRESNINSKAYA
KROPOTKINSKAYA — PRECHISTENKA
KUIBYSHEVA — ILYINKA
METROSTROYEVSKAYA — OSTOZHENKA
NOGINA SQUARE — VARVARSKAYA SQUARE
OKTIABRSKAYA SQUARE — KALUZHSKAYA
    SQUARE
PROSPEKT MARKSA — MOKHOVAYA
PROSPEKT MARKSA — OKHOTNY RIAD
RAZINA — VARVARKA
SOVETSKAYA SQUARE — SKOBELEVSKAYA
    SQUARE
SPARTAKOVSKAYA — YELOKHOVSKAYA
SVERDLOVA SQUARE — TEATRALNAYA
    SQUARE
TCHAIKOVSKOGO — NOVINSKY BOULEVARD
VOROVSKOGO — POVARSKAYA
ZHDANOVA — ROZHDESTVENKA

... and for LENIN ... er,
    ST. PETERSBURG:
DEKABRISTOV SQUARE — SENATSKAYA
    SQUARE
DZERZHINSKOGO — GOROKHOVAYA
GERTSENA — BOLSHAYA MORSKAYA
KANAL KRUSHTEINA — ADMIRALTEISKY
    KANAL

KARLA MARKSA PROSPEKT — BOLSHOI
    SAMPSONIEVSKY — PROSPEKT
KHALTURINA — MILLIONNAYA
KIROVSKIY BRIDGE — TROITSKY BRIDGE
KIROVSKY PROYEZD (LANE) —
    KAMENNOOSTROVSKY PROYEZD
KRASNAYA — GALIORNAYA
KRASNOGO FLOTA QUAY — ANGLIISKAYA
    QUAY
LITEINY BRIDGE — ALEKSANDROVSKY
    BRIDGE
MIRA SQUARE — SENNAYA SQUARE
NARODNY BRIDGE — POLITSEISKY BRIDGE
NEKRASOVA — BASSEYNAYA
OSTROVSKOGO SQUARE —
    ALEKSANDRINSKAYA SQUARE
PETRA LAVROVA — FURSHTADSKAYA
PROFSOYUZOV BOULEVARD —
    KONNOGVARDEISKY BOULEVARD
PUSHKINSKAYA SQUARE — BIRZHEVAYA
    SQUARE
RAKOVA — BOLSHAYA ITALIANSKAYA
REVOLIUTSII SQUARE — TROITSKAYA
    SQUARE
SALTYKOVA-SCHEDRINA — KIROCHNAYA
SHOSSE (ROAD) REVOLIUTSII —
    POKROVSKOYE SHOSSE
SOYUZA SVIAZI — POTCHTAMSKAYA
STACHEK PROSPEKT — NARVSKOYE ROAD
STACHEK SQUARE — NARVSKAYA SQUARE
STROITELEI BRIDGE — BIRZHEVOI BRIDGE
SVERDLOVSKAYA QUAY —
    POLIUSTROVSKAYA QUAY
TRUDA SQUARE — BLAGOVESCHENSKAYA
    SQUARE
VOSSTANIA SQUARE — ZNAMENSKAYA
    SQUARE
ZHELIABOVA — BOLSHAYA
    KONNIUSHENNAYA

Moscow's most famous square is also its largest — its cobblestones cover an impressive 73,000 sq m (18 acres). The cobblestones, by the way, come from a quarry near Lake Onega. They are held together with tar and are fiendishly difficult to poke out of their sand bed, although people try every year, with sad results as you can imagine.

One side of the square is the Kremlin wall, and the granite structure near it is Lenin's Mausoleum. When Lenin died, his body was embalmed and placed in the mausoleum (the original was made of wood) for all to see, despite the protests of his wife Nadezhda Krupskaya. The mausoleum is still open to the public (from 10 am to 1 pm on weekdays; from 10 am to 3 pm on Sundays; closed Monday and Friday), so you are welcome to go inside, provided you like that sort of thing. Just stand at the end of the line which usually starts somewhere near the Tomb of the Unknown Soldier. The ceremonial changing of the guard takes place every hour on the hour when the clock chimes.

Red Square reflects what nineteenth-century Russian intellectuals called "the Asiatic strangeness" of Russia in a nutshell: Lenin is still admired throughout the land, yet the obvious, even glaring impropriety of mummifying his body or of making a stand for Sovietdom's highest officials atop his tomb passes unnoticed in a country which insists on calling itself European and developed.

Another of Red Square's little oddities is the **mini-cemetery** near and, of all places, in the Kremlin wall. Aside from the absurdity of it being there in the first place, there's the added absurdity of the motley collection of people whom Soviet power considered worthy of being buried there as national heroes over the years. Here you find Stalin near Lenin (they even shared the mausoleum for several years before Khrushchev's famous Secret Speech); John Reed, the adventuresome American journalist who witnessed the October revolution and wrote about it in *Ten Days That Shook The World*, near Konstantin Chernenko, truthfully described by Newsweek as Brezhnev's "chief pencil sharpener and bottle opener"; Yuri Gagarin, the first man in space, near Felix Dzerzhinsky, the founder of the KGB...

The jewel of Red Square, the **Cathedral of the Virgin of the Intercession** (also and perhaps better known as St.Basil's), is universally regarded, together with the brown bear, as Russia's "trademark."

Actually, it isn't one church, but several. The eight smaller churches twined round the tent-roofed **Pokrovsky** (the ones with the famous multicolored onion cupolas) are named after saints on whose days Russia scored major victories in the most successful of its wars against the Mongols (the cathedral itself commemorates the taking of Kazan and Astrakhan, two of the Mongol strongholds on the Volga). Late in the sixteenth century, another small church was added to the cathedral. It was built over the grave of Basil (Vasily), the celebrated "God's fool" of Moscow (such people were revered in old Russia), and eventually gave the entire structure its present name — St. Basil's.

Another interesting thing about the church that's really several churches is that

it isn't a church at all. Its cramped interior was never intended for religious service because what Ivan the Terrible wanted his two top architects Barma and Postnik to build, was a monument to his great victory.

St.Basil's is the earliest example of "monumental" architecture in Russia that I know of, and while it may not be the first, it is certainly the most famous. It is open from 9:30 am to 5:30 pm every day (there's a lunch break between 1:15 and 2 pm), except on Tuesdays and the first Monday of the month.

The plaque on the **monument** in front of the cathedral reads "To Citizen Minin and Prince Pozharsky from Grateful Russia, 1818." It was a gratitude well-earned: Kuzma Minin and Dmitry Pozharsky recruited,

equipped and headed the army of volunteers which ousted the invading Poles and Lithuanians from the Kremlin and, eventually, from the country. Ivan Martos, who worked on the sculptures for 14 years, portrayed himself making a gift of his three sons to his country on the frontal bas-relief.

Not far away, there's the circular **Lobnoye Mesto**, from which the Czars purportedly addressed Muscovites in the old days. On the other side of the square, there's the **Historical Museum**, which was built between 1874 and 1881 by Vladimir Sherwood. If you have the time (the museum is open between 10 am and 6 pm, 11 am and 7 pm on Wednesdays and Fridays, and closed on Tuesdays and the first Monday of the month), you can join the

two million or so who visit the place every year.

The fourth side of the square is formed by the largest department store in Moscow, known as GUM's among the English-speaking community (even though GUM is not a person, but an abbreviation of Gosudarstvenny Universalny Magazin — State Department Store). There's hardly anything on sale there these days, but hope dies last and you can join the 350,000 who try their luck there every day.

Crowded interior of the Moscow Kremlin. The last residence in the Kremlin grounds belonged to one of Catherine the Great's favorites and passed on to the crown after his death.

TOWERS OF THE KREMLIN

You'll be passing **Senatskaya** (Senate) **Tower**, which is behind the mausoleum, Nikolskaya Tower (1491, by Pietro Antonio Solari), and one of the Kremlin's three corner towers, **Arsenal Tower**. The 60 m (197 ft) tower survived, with nary a dent, the explosion that utterly demolished the Arsenal building during Napoleon's retreat from Moscow. As you see, the masons who'd built the Kremlin knew their business well. Recently, when a mains pipe had to be installed in Alexandrovsky Garden, a part of the old Kremlin wall was unearthed; it blocked the way and was targeted for demolition. Several broken sledgehammers later, the construction workers realized that nothing short of TNT could do the job. So they just reburied their find and made a detour around the piece of stonework held together with mortar whose ingredients were kept secret but were rumored to contain egg yolks.

As you walk up from Kutafia Tower towards the 80 m (262 ft) **Troitskaya** (Trinity) **Tower**, tread softly: the bridge connecting the two towers dates to 1516; it was built on the site of Moscow's first stone bridge, erected in 1367 over the Neglinnaya River (which you can't see: it runs through a pipe now).

A short walk away (through Alexandrovsky Garden) is my favorite tower — **Borovitskaya**. It was built (again by Solari) in 1490 at the foot of Borovitsky (Forest) Hill, chosen by Yury the Long-Armed as the site for the original Kremlin. The tower has a drive-through gate (the other automobile entrance to the Kremlin is through the Spasskaya Tower), which is used by Mikhail Gorbachev and assorted other dignitaries to the dismay of hundreds of exasperated Moscow drivers: the traffic cops are in the habit of stopping the normal flow of traffic well before some VIP or other is scheduled to whizz past in the usual black limo (or four limos, in Gorbachev's case) with the standard entourage of black Volga sedans.

At the next corner of the Kremlin is the **Water-Raising Tower**. Built in 1488, the tower housed a special machine (installed in the 1630s) which raised water from a nearby well and pumped it through lead pipes. The machine was designed by Christopher Galloway, a British engineer. Unfortunately, Galloway's pressurized waterworks (the first in Russia) had been all but destroyed in a fire late in the seventeenth century; several years afterward,

Peter the Great had the pipes removed to St.Petersburg.

The Tainitskaya (Secret Storage) Tower is the oldest in the Kremlin. It dates to 1485. The tower was used as a hush-hush supply store in times of siege, hence the name.

It was also one of the two towers with a well in it (the other is the Arsenal Tower).

The round **Beklemishevskaya Tower** was built in 1487 (by Marco Ruffo of Italy), near the Kremlin estate of Beklemishev, the Boyar whom Grand Prince

Soldiers sightseeing inside the Kremlin.

Vasily III had had executed for "high-mindedness."

If we follow the wall as it turns away from the river towards Red Square, the first tower on our way will be **Konstantino-Yeleninskaya**, built by Solari in 1490. The tower owes its name to the church of Constantine and Helen, which used to be nearby. The tower had a drawbridge and a drive-through gate, which is half-covered with earth today.

The next, **Nabatnaya Tower** was where the alarm was sounded in the old days. It had a huge bell which never failed to gather the people of Moscow in times of trouble, before it became a troublemaker itself in 1771, the year of the plague riots. Outraged that the bell was used to assemble a mob near the Kremlin, Catherine the Great had the bell punished: its clapper was taken out. The bell is now on display in the Armory.

The smallest tower — **Tsarskaya** — huddles near the Spasskaya Tower. Legend has it that it was built for Ivan the Terrible, who liked to watch executions and similarly entertaining events in Red Square.

And finally, there is the **Spasskaya** (Savior's) **Tower**, which by all accounts is the most impressive of the lot. Its clock, six meters (20 ft) in diameter, was installed in the middle of the last century. The tower itself was built in 1491 by Solari, and served as the main entrance to the Kremlin. It was customary to take your hat off and bow to the icon of the Savior; people who failed to do so were quickly shown the error of their ways, and forced to bow fifty times by the indignant guards. It measures 71 m (233 ft) from foundation to star tip.

The stars may look small, yet each weighs over a ton and spans 3.75 m (12 ft) between the end points of its ruby rays.

INSIDE THE KREMLIN

A ten-minute stroll from Red Square (past the Historical Museum and to the left, past the eternal flame) is Kutafia Tower, through which you can enter the Kremlin grounds. As you walk, take a good look at the walls and towers (see cameo at left).

Before you actually pass through the Kutafia Tower, it is a good idea to go down into Alexandrovsky Garden and buy admission tickets to the Kremlin museums (about 4 roubles per person for all of them).

Once inside the Kremlin, take a good look at the cathedrals. The largest, with white walls and five golden domes, is the **Uspensky** (Assumption or Dormition) **Cathedral**. To me, it's the greatest church in the world, perhaps because its name coincides with my family name. The cathedral, whose outward modesty underscores its glittering interior, was built between 1475 and 1479 by Aristotle Fioravanti (another Italian architect). Uspensky Cathedral was the number-one church of Muscovy: here, Czars were crowned and patriarchs were buried. It is also known for its holy relics, including one of the nails used in the crucifixion of Christ. The nail is kept in a golden ark. It is 6 cm (2.5 in) long. The cathedral is open from 10 am to 6:30 pm except Thursdays.

Its nine-domed neighbor, **Blagoveshchensky** (Annunciation) **Cathedral** is known for its icons (Rublev, Feofan the Greek) and frescoes (Theodosius). In the seventeenth century, the floors of the church, which had by then become the family chapel of the imperial family, were laid with red jasper from the Urals. It is open to visitors from 10 am to 6 pm and closed Thursdays.

There are a lot of distinguished tombs in the **Arkhangelsky** (Archangel's) **Cathedral** (46, to be exact). In the summer of 1963, several were opened by anthropologists. As the result of this rather gruesome event, we now know what Ivan the Terrible looked like. He had a thin, long nose, a drooping

mouth, a low forehead, and big eyes. It all adds up to a rather nasty face. For his time, Ivan was tall — 178 cm (5 ft 9 in) — and heavy — 80 to 90 kg (170 to 190 pounds). He was also very strong physically.

One of the buildings in the square is lined with stones faceted like diamonds —

hence its name, **Granovitaya** (faceted) **Chamber**. Built by the splendid team of Ruffo and Solari (between 1487 and 1491) as Moscow's largest assembly hall (500 sq m. or 600 sq yds), it endorsed one of Russia's most ancient and best-loved traditions — that of pulling the wool over foreign eyes. It was here, amid the glowing splendor of the Czar's court that foreign ambassadors presented their credentials — and, as a rule, generous gifts from their sovereigns — and were sometimes allowed to see the Czar, in jewel-studded ceremonial attire, in conference with his Boyar elders (who also wore their best for such occasions); meanwhile, just a few hundred yards away in Red Square, the Czar's hapless subjects tried to exchange the more attractive of their rags for enough food to get them through the day. But people cared little, if at all, for social justice in the Middle Ages. Celebrations were another story. For example, Ivan the Terrible presided over three days and three nights of merry-making when Kazan fell to his armies in 1552.

Gone are the czars and their Boyars, yet the tradition remains: official receptions still take place here, and being invited to the Granovitaya Chamber is akin to getting an invitation to the White House (yet, unlike the White House, it is off-limits to tourists).

The tallest structure in the Kremlin (and, in the old days, in the entire city) is the octagonal **belfry** of Ivan the Great (81 m or 266 ft). Its lower part dates to the early

---

ARISTOTLE FIORAVANTI

The chronicles said that Fioravanti's compatriots called him Aristotle because of "the shrewdness of his wisdom." This is not true. The future architect came from a family with a mania for antiquity. His name was a tribute paid by his parents to the great philosopher, and, perhaps, a bid that Aristotle would someday rival his famous namesake.

He was popular and sought-after. But Turkey and Western Europe, where he was repeatedly invited, failed to spark his imagination. He was then at an age when he was still adventurous enough to travel somewhere off the beaten track.

So when an envoy from Muscovy, who was impressed with Aristotle's accomplishments as a silversmith asked the Duke of Venice for Aristotle to be "loaned" to Muscovy, Fioravanti did not hesitate.

He arrived in Moscow in 1475 — and was immediately sent to Vladimir to see the cathedral there.

It took four years to build a near-replica on the site of the Kremlin's old Church of the Dormition.

When it was finished, Fioravanti, the "patriarch of Russian architecture," pronounced his toasts at the celebration in Italian — he did not speak Russian...

sixteenth century. The belfry was very useful in those days, serving as an observation post and alarm tower. The inscription just below the cupola says that the cathedral was built in 1600, during Boris Godunov's reign.

Weather permitting, pose for a picture near the **Czar Bell**, which took Ivan (the father) and Mikhail (the son) Motorin two years to make (1733 to 1735). They made it, but they could not lift it. The bell just stayed where it was, losing an 11.2-ton piece in a fire (water was rather rashly poured over it

manias — that for things gigantic. The latest addition to that line in the Kremlin is Nikita Khrushchev's Palace of Congresses, which was proclaimed "the world's largest building with a theater stage." The building in front of it is the **Arsenal** (1702–1736), and the large yellow building with the flag on top (the flag never hangs limply because there are special fans under the flagpole) is where Catherine the Great's Senate used to meet. The building now belongs to the Council of Ministers (if we still have a council of ministers). The largest building

when it was red hot, and the temperature difference produced the crack), until Auguste Montferrand, the brilliant French architect (of St. Petersburg fame), came to the rescue and installed it on the platform you see today.

While you're at it, don't miss the **Czar Cannon**, cast by Anton Chokh in 1586 (in the cannon foundry that used to be where the Children's World Department Store now stands). Designed to protect the Moskva River crossing near Savior's Tower, the cannon was never used and probably won't be unless Genghis Khan comes back.

The enormous bell that never tolled and the colossal cannon that never fired are symptoms of another of Russia's ancient

in the Kremlin — it faces the Moskva River — is the **Grand Palace** built in the middle of the nineteenth century by Konstantin Thon, who also designed the adjacent **Armory Chamber** (the museum inside is a treat, particularly for first-time visitors. It is open from 9:30 am to 5 pm except on Thursdays). The Kremlin's government buildings, by the way, are closed to the general public.

Russia is an incredibly rich country. This may sound funny, tottering on the brink of starvation as we Russians are, but I'm sure

OPPOSITE: a panorama of Moscow shows what 75 years of socialism can do to a city skyline.
ABOVE: Inside the Granovitaya ("Faceted") Chamber of the Kremlin.

you'll think so after a visit to the **Diamond Fund**. On the museum's heavily-guarded premises, gold nuggets weighing 36 kg (80 lb) are displayed side by side with the crown jewels of the Czars and other assorted fairy-tale treasures. Check with your service bureau, because tickets may be a problem. The place is open from 10 am to 6 pm except on Thursdays.

After the glitter of gold clears from your eyes, you will probably see that as national shrines and symbols of empire-building go, the Kremlin and Red Square are just fine. Yet

they stand apart from the rest of Moscow, which is, after all, only a large village as we Muscovites call it. Let us then partake of its simple, homely pleasures, for it lies just outside the wall.

MIDTOWN MOSCOW

On the map, it's a bow of streets and squares with the Moskva River the string. Though it may not look like it to you, **Tsentr** (Center), as most locals call it, is one of Russia's more cosmopolitan urban areas and as such, is appreciated by most Muscovites as a pleasant change of scene from their over-standardized residential districts in the city's "bedrooms."

Walking is the best way to get around here. If you start in Red Square, say, you're in for several architectural treats — such as **N°18 Razin Street**, which is a typical house …of a typical sixteenth-century Boyar. Alas, you are also bound to notice (for the simple reason that they are impossible to overlook) such Soviet-spawned monstrosities as the **Rossiya Hotel**. God help you if you are staying there: with accommodations for six thousand and restaurant space for forty-five hundred (yes, gigantism again), "the second largest hotel in Europe," in addition to the usual sloppy service, is a fire trap. It has had two serious fires in the twenty or so years of its hapless history. I know this sounds too "heavy" for a guidebook, but I will rest easy now that I've warned you.

To see how the now-outlawed Party used to live, you only have to go down Razin Street, turn left as you reach the square known as **Staraya** (Old) **Square**, and go uphill through the surprisingly quiet and shady (in summer) **Ilyinsky Garden**. When you reach Ilyinskiye Gates, and the monument to Russian soldiers killed at Plevna (in the 1887 war against Turkey for the liberation of Bulgaria), turn left. The first thing that you are bound to see will be several uniformed policemen: "the mind, honor and conscience of our epoch" (as the communists modestly described themselves) liked to be well-protected, and so do their successors from the Yeltsin administration.

The architectural fruit salad up ahead is the **Polytechnical Museum**. It was built by four architects in at least two styles — modern and Old Russian. If you want to see for yourself, you'll have to go all the way around the building, which isn't small. I suggest you don't waste time and press on, for there, in **Lubianskaya Square**, is the headquarters of the fearsome organization known under various names in the seventy-odd years of its existence and presently referred to (and known to the whole world) as the **KGB**.

Until August 23, 1991, the statue of "Iron" Felix Dzerzhinsky, the Polish-born father of the KGB, used to adorn what used to be "his" square. Recently, original names have been returned to several dozen locations in Moscow, and this plaza is once again called Lubianskaya.

There is a story about the statue. Rumor has it that it is made of … solid gold, which had purportedly been hidden by the Nazis and captured by the Red Army in 1945. They say that Lazar Kaganovich, the nonagenarian member of Stalin's Politbureau who died quite recently, had reported to Mikhail Gorbachev that Stalin had intended the statue for the party's rainy-day fund. When Felix came down after the August coup fell through, the statue was taken away some-

"As future fighters at the ideological front, comrades," she said as we reached old Felix, "you'll understand that it's best not to reveal the location of the KGB to the foreigners you'll be working with."

"But what if they point a finger at the building and ask what it is?"

"Just tell them it's an office building."

What would you expect — a month or so later, one dear old American lady did ask. She pointed at the KGB HQ and said to me, "This is the conservatoire, isn't it?" "Yes, ma'am," I gasped in a heroic attempt to stifle

where. Who knows, maybe they've already sawn it apart?

Three of the buildings in the square (it's not difficult to single them out, for all three make you think of prison) belong to the **Committee for State Security** (the oldest is the one in the middle, where Stalin's archrivals were interrogated and executed). Today, glasnost has made a dent in the KGB's iron-hard hide. Until recently, it had not been wise even to talk about its whereabouts: when I was a student in the seventies, we had to work a summer for Intourist as part of our college program. On the first day, the instructor ushered the lot of us into a bus for a model tour of Moscow.

a laugh. "And the statue you see over there is Tchaikovsky."

Now the KGB has a public-relations office (they even promise guided tours of the premises, although their innocent-eyed spokesmen insist that the famous death cells and underground torture chambers don't exist), but the public is loath to accept such wolf-in-sheep's-clothing masquerade: demands to turn KGB property over to orphanages are made in parliament and

The Durov Animal Theater OPPOSITE is a good choice, particularly if you've brought children along. For details, refer to the THE GARDEN RING section. ABOVE: Vladimir Ilyich Ulianov (Lenin) giving highly important instructions to revolutionary sailors and soldiers in 1917 (by M.Sokolov).

recently, a memorial stone was installed in the square in honor of the millions of victims of the KGB.

Not far away, where Nikolskaya Street (formerly 25th October Street, formerly Nikolskaya Street — see what havoc an epidemic of renaming can wreak?) joins the square, there's the exquisite facade of the **Archive Institute**. It is flanked on the right by the **Slav-Greek-Latin Academy**, the first higher school in the country, and on the left — by the **Slaviansky Bazaar Restaurant** (☎ 921-18-72), which attracted such fans of

Russian cuisine as Anton Chekov and Leo Tolstoy. That was at the turn of the century, and today food is scarce, but I suppose you can still get a bowl of good borscht there. The avenue that starts in Dzerzhinsky — sorry, Lubianskaya — Square was known as Marx Prospekt before it was re-renamed into the original **Teatralny Proyezd** (Theater Lane), **Okhotny Riad** (Hunter's Row), and **Mokhovaya Street**. The first building on this avenue is the **Detsky Mir** (Children's World) **Department Store**. I strongly advise against your going inside, unless, of course, you want to find out how it feels to be a parent in Moscow, where survival-of-the-fittest is much closer to its Darwinian sense than in other parts of the world (meaning you have to fight tooth and nail to buy a bicycle here).

The monument across the street is to Russia's first book printer, **Ivan Fedorov** (his first book, *The Apostle*, came out on March 1, 1564). Soon afterwards the unfortunate publisher was forced to abandon his home in Moscow (the Czar orchestrated a "show-

ing of popular discontent," in other words, unleashed a bloodthirsty mob on the hapless printer), becoming the first man of letters to be persecuted in Russia by the powers that be, a tradition that's still with us whatever they may say (after all, Solzhenitsyn is still in Vermont).

The house on the corner at the end of the street is the **Metropol Hotel**, recently redecorated by a Finnish contractor. There's a famous restaurant inside with a main hall of 500 sq m (600 sq yds) (☎ 927-60-39), and, around the corner, a ticket office selling rail/air tickets to international destinations. The **dark-red wall** just behind the Metropol is what's left of Kitai Gorod after Stalin's "renovation" of downtown Moscow. You can see another piece of this wall near the Rossiya Hotel. Built in 1538, it was over 2.5 km (1.7 miles) long and had 12 towers; the fortress was supposed to guard the inner approaches to the Kremlin from the east, where the absence of a river made a surprise attack easier.

The stone next to the wall used to serve as a foundation for the statue of Yakov Sverdlov, Lenin's aide-de-camp and the first head of the Bolshevik government. It is said that Sverdlov had given the order to execute the Czar and his family, although no one knows for certain (he did keep news of the execution under wraps for as long as he could). After the statue came crashing down in late August 1991, the word "Regicide!" promptly appeared on the foundation.

Up ahead, behind the former Revolution Square metro station (now called Teatralny Proyezd), there's the **Lenin Museum**. Before 1917, the building belonged to Russia's first parliament — the State Duma (from the verb *dumat*, "to think"). Our ancestors clearly believed that elected legislators must use their heads for the benefit of their country, a notion that seems lost on most of our MP's today.

Admission to the Lenin Museum is free. There's hardly a person in Moscow who hasn't visited it at least once (until recently, ceremonial admission to the ranks of communist organizations for children, Young Pioneers and Young Communist League, was conducted at the museum).

When Abraham Lincoln said that it's impossible to fool everyone all of the time, he couldn't have imagined how far authoritarianism can go in a country that craves religion. To this day Lenin is more popular than Jesus Christ — not in the least owing to the Lenin Museum, its affiliates in eight cities, and the 25 memorial museums established in places where the Great Leader stopped — or may have stopped — for lunch. Recently, Moscow's new mayor announced his plans to move his offices to the Lenin Museum. This produced a series

Wagner performed here with his orchestra in the last century, and shocked his distinguished audience (the theater was not affordable to commoners) by facing the music (literally), and not the public, as was customary at the time. Rakhmaninoff, who conducted the Bolshoi orchestra from 1904 to 1906, endorsed this novelty and had the conductor's stand installed in its present place.

As you've realized by now, if the Bolshoi is in town, you must go to the Bolshoi, if only for a single performance. Even though the theater is going through hard times, a whisk

of save-the-museum demonstrations. The issue was still open at the time this book was being written.

To get your thoughts away from this sad subject, I suggest you look at the **Bolshoi** (Large) **Theater** with Klodt's spectacular Apollo's quadriga on top. It's always a breath of fresh air, to me at any rate. Built in 1780 of wood, the theater burned down in 1805, was rebuilt by architects Bove and Mikhailov in 1825, burned down and was rebuilt again by Kavos in 1856, was hit by a German bomb during the war, rebuilt, and finally reconstructed in November 1958.

There are a million stories about the Bolshoi. One is about the time Richard

of its special atmosphere goes a surprisingly long way.

The Bolshoi building forms the northwest side of Moscow's most charming square. On the east, there's the **Maly** (Small) **Theater**, and on the southwest — the **Children's Music Theater**. The square (understandably enough called **Teatralnaya**) is open on the Mokhovaya Street side.

ABOVE: Bolshoi Ballet: still going strong despite the hard times. OPPOSITE: Books were a luxury in the Middle Ages, even after Ivan Fedorov's printing technique made them cheaper to produce. Nevertheless, literacy was widespread and virtually any free person could send children to monastery schools.

Most guidebooks have at least a few words of warning for women traveling alone. Well, women have nothing to fear in Teatralnaya Square: it is the men who have to be on their toes here. The place is a favorite hangout of Moscow's hard-pressed gay community. So think twice if a bench near the fountain looks appealing to you after a night performance in the Bolshoi: it may be wiser to opt for **Tverskaya Street** and the **National Hotel** with its night bars. (I'm only kidding, of course. Moscow streets and parks are perfectly safe after 10 pm — one of the things that Muscovites take pride in). On your way, you'll be passing the smart six-columned **House of Unions** (formerly the Assembly of the Gentry), built by Kazakov in the 1780s. It is a place of rather gruesome fame, among my generation at least. The House of Unions, you see, was chosen as the place where the bodies of deceased party bosses lay in state for all to see. For example, whenever a member of Brezhnev's septuagenarian Politbureau died, the body was exhibited in the Column Hall. Every time, an endless flow of "grief-stricken mourners" was promptly organized. On the surface, everything was, of course, "spontaneous" and "voluntary" (these, and several dozen other words, acquired an antonymic meaning in Stalin's newspeak). The "volunteers" were appointed by party bosses and KGB officers at every work place. As with many other things in Russia today, the cynicism of those people was often appalling ... and funny. When Yury Andropov died a mere 12 months after Brezhnev's pompous funeral, a friend of mine was summoned by his boss.

"Be on the corner of Gorky Street and Tsvetnoi Boulevard tomorrow at nine," he was told.

"But I've so much work to do," my friend protested, "and besides, why should I go twice in a row when others haven't been once? I went last year!"

"You did at that, didn't you," came the reply. "Oh well, you may skip this one, but remember — the next time you're definitely going" (everyone knew that Konstantin Chernenko, the last of the "three stiffs" as the three general secretaries who'd died in the course of less than three years were lovingly referred to by their subjects, was ailing and could not possibly last much longer).

Besides the House of Unions, Pushkinskaya Street is famous for the **Operetta Theater** (N°6) and its fur shops.

Tverskaya Street

As you continue along Okhotny Riad Street, past the canyon formed by two more hulking relics of Stalin's day — the Council of Ministers and the Moskva Hotel — you reach one of the most "in" streets of Russia — Tverskaya (formerly Gorky) Street. Its attractions are numerous.

At N°3, there's the **Intourist Hotel**, famous for its pricey top-floor suites offering spectacular views of the Kremlin and downtown Moscow — and for its ladies of the night who, not unlike the Bank of Foreign Trade, take nothing but freely convertible currency.

There's Russia's first **McDonald's** (probably the most besieged of the world-wide chain — on an average day, you'll have to wait in line to get served, despite the price hikes) on the boulevard corner.

There's **Pushkin Square** with the poet's statue and the famous lanterns, which has of late become a kind of Speaker's Corner of Moscow. Here, assorted radicals congregate and air their plans to build a better Russia in all of ninety days. They do so in defiance of the national law on demonstrations, which in turn violates the Constitution's freedom-of-assembly provisions in that it specifies that permits are required for rallies, manifestations, and so on.

Also in Pushkin Square are the offices of *Moscow News*, one of our more honest papers.

In N°14, there's Gastronom N°1 — the food store that Muscovites stubbornly call Yeliseev's after the famous pre-revolutionary food-chain owner. After the prices went up nearly 300 percent in April 1991, and were "released" entirely in January, 1992, food was reported sighted at the store which proudly offered live oysters and fresh artichokes before the revolution. Now, for 250 roubles, you can buy a tin of red caviar there — a good price considering the current exchange rate of the dollar.

Finally, there's **Byelorussky Railway Station**, Moscow's gate to the western Europe (it's a 60-hour ride to Paris, provided that you get tickets).

There's much to see in Tverskaya Street. Take a walk, browse through the bookstores and gift shops, go to the **Aragvi Restaurant** (☏ 229-37-62) for traditional spicy Georgian shashlik.

There's a problem with Tverskaya, however. Hardly anyone you'll see there is a native Muscovite. Hopelessly outnumbered by the two million visitors who come every day, local residents prefer to keep to the side streets just off the main thoroughfare. If you are keen to observe their daily routine, try ducking into any of the several delightful little lanes going off to the west (left if you walk uptown from the Kremlin). This is where the writers, artists, musicians, actors, top bureaucrats, nouveau-rich Mafia types — in other words, the cream of Soviet society — hang their hats. A single-bedroom apartment here sells for as much as $30,000 (the average monthly wage, converted into dollars at the black-market rate, is $9). I suggest you try my favorite — **Nezhdanovoi Street**.

To get there, just look for the archway in N°9 — the apartment house lined with the red granite which was purportedly captured from the Germans who'd planned to use it for a victory monument in the center of Moscow after the 1941 blitzkrieg. The moment you pass through the archway, you're in another world. After all the noise and the crowds, the quiet is almost eerie.

The street was named after Antonina Nezhdanova, the Bolshoi diva who lived in N°7 (before that, it was known as Bruce Lane, after Jacob Bruce, one of Peter the Great's aides-de-camp). There's something about the place that actors find irresistible. Among its residents were such theater greats as Meyerkhold, the outspoken director whom Stalin's henchmen had arrested in 1939, Kachalov and Moskvin, the famed actors of the Khudozhestvenny Theater, and Sergei Yesenin, the romantic poet better known abroad for his marriage to Isidora Duncan.

As you reach the crossroads with Yeliseevsky Pereulok (side street), be sure to visit the **Church of the Resurrection** (1629). If you're in luck, you might be in time for mass (in Old Slav language, which no one understands) and a sermon (in Russian) by Father Vladimir, one of the most interesting clergymen I've met in Moscow. Feel free to ask him about anything you may fail to understand — he speaks English and Italian and will be glad to help. Then light a candle for your loved ones and, as is the Orthodox custom, another for Mother Russia — you'll find it an experience difficult to forget, even if you're not religious.

Walk straight ahead after you leave the church. At the end of the street, take a look at what I consider one of Russia's architectural marvels — the Conservatoire building. The house, with Mukhina's talented monument to Tchaikovsky in the front garden is, in my view, what "music in stone" is all about. In any event, I envy you the experience, particularly if the day is sunny.

Heading west down **Hertzen Street**, you'll pass the sprawling army HQ (General Staff) buildings on both sides.

The circus is a good start for a night out on the town.

Up ahead, across Gogol Boulevard, you'll see the semi-circle of the Praga Restaurant — the beginning of Arbat Street.

Arbat Street

She couldn't have been more than seventeen. Everything about her had the characteristic garishness of the cheap streetwalker. She approached me (evidently I looked sufficiently foreign, and therefore safe, to her) and said in heavily-accented high-school English, "I love you. Give me fifty dollars!"

"If you love me, give me fifty dollars," I replied almost automatically, failing to put the right amount of sarcasm into the joke, because there was really not much to laugh about. I remembered how the city fathers promised to transform the shabby and noisy traffic trap that Arbat Street was just a few years ago into a pedestrian-only "zone of culture and recreation." Recreation, indeed! Somehow, traffic was not the only thing that Arbat Street lost. It is no longer the place that "singing poet" Bulat Okudzhava called "my religion." Like the face of that young whore, the face of Arbat Street is overdone. A piece of old Moscow had been killed to create little more than a five-and-dime tourist attraction. Still, it's nice on a sunny afternoon, when you can mill with the crowd, look at paintings exhibited by artists who hope to sell them right off the fence (and obviously they do, for why would they be there if they didn't?), have an ice-cream or an espresso as you listen to an amateur street band do a spin-off of the latest top-of-the-charts pop hit. If you plan your trip to the Arbat just before lunch, there's a place you can try on the second floor of the building opposite the Foreign Ministry. It offers real Siberian food, including the best pelimeni in town (in fact, it isn't much of a place, and the service is, as usual, nothing to write home about, but the pelimeni — the Russian version of ravioli — are clearly worth it).

Arbat Street ends near another leftover from the era of Big Brother — one of Moscow's seven pseudo-Gothic towers.

This one houses the Ministry of Foreign Affairs.

We've reached the Sadovoye (Garden) Ring. As you've probably realized by now, Moscow has a circular layout, with the Kremlin directly in the center of the city's three major rings — the picturesque Boulevard Ring (the perimeter of the now-extinct White City), the historic Sadovoye, and the functional Circular Motorway — the official boundary of the capital.

THE GARDEN RING

The **Sadovoye** is a major traffic artery; almost every time you take a taxi, you'll either cross it or follow it for at least a part of your route. It is too long for a comfortable

You can find anything you want — from hashish to a Matrioshka Doll — in Arbat Street.

walk — over 16 km (10 miles), but if you're game, you can choose an off-peak hour and try the trolley — N°10 for a part of your way or N°Б for the entire route.

Smolenskaya Square where the Ministry of Foreign Affairs faces the twin towers of the Belgrade Hotel, is formed by Sadovoye Ring (going to the left and right if you stand with your back to the ministry) and Smolenskaya Street, which leads to the west and ends at Borodinsky Bridge over the Moskva River, beyond which you can see the outlines of Kiev Railway Station on the left.

Let's make a right turn here and walk north. The first thing you'll see is the **Smolensky Gastronom** (food store), where you can get your hands on a greater variety of foodstuffs than elsewhere — provided, of course, that you are willing to sacrifice two or even three hours of your life waiting in its assorted lines (the only thing that you can get relatively quickly there is liquor. If none is exhibited on the counter, the more experienced of my countrymen usually go round the building to where supplies are delivered, and ask one of the blue-robed load-handlers for a butylka (bottle). If you come on naturally enough to suit them, they'll promptly bring you what you ask — at a price, of course. It can be quite an experience if you've never done it before).

The passage to the right leads to **Smolenskaya Metro Station**. Up ahead, you'll see the Aeroflot globe — the trademark of **Novy** (New) **Arbat Avenue**. On your way there,

SIEGE OF THE "WHITE HOUSE"

You are now in the perfect spot to see where it all happened. If you face the US Embassy from the middle of Sadovoye Ring, which is quite wide in this place (unfortunately, the traffic will probably make it impossible), you'll find yourself in the exact spot where two armored personnel carriers stood on the memorable night of August 20/21 1991. Even though the military governor of Moscow imposed a curfew several hours pre-

as to climb onto the fender (Heaven only knows how she managed it — she was what is politely termed "very stout"), and started to work the driver over with her umbrella (it was raining, on and off, all night). The young man, who'd seconds before tried to explain, in what I suppose was his best official manner, that no, their guns were not loaded, and no, they could not possibly shoot at civilians, and no, they were not there to storm the White House, was clearly caught off-balance

viously, it was neither observed nor enforced, and the Sadovoye Ring was littered with small groups of people. Many of them gathered around the two vehicles, talking to the soldiers, youngsters who looked like they would have given a lot to be elsewhere. The crowd was giving them what had already become the usual treatment since the morning of August 19: "Will you shoot? We could be your mothers! Aren't you ashamed of yourselves?!" And so on. One middle-aged lady even went so far

by this latest development. Instinctively, he raised his Kalashnikov over his face to ward off the merciless umbrella. It was a very funny scene, and everyone there laughed, relieving the tension.

From the bits and pieces of conversation I'd picked up here and there, I put together the picture of what had happened in the previous two hours. (If you stand with the US Embassy on your right, you will perhaps find it easier to understand). Up ahead, about 400 m away, is the crossroads with New Arbat. (The Sadovoye Ring, on which you stand, runs underneath New Arbat). At around 10 pm, a barricade of trolleys, assorted

Lenin made his speeches from an armored car. Yeltsin prefers a T-72 tank.

debris, bus stop shelters and even two shiny Mercedes buses, was made on this side of the tunnel. Meanwhile, several mechanized infantry vehicles broke off from a large group (there were several tanks there, too), which was positioned in front of the Foreign Ministry, and entered the tunnel from the other side. Now, since the White House is to your right, this means that there is no way the infantry carriers could get anywhere near it via the tunnel. Nevertheless, as soon as they were inside, another barricade, mostly of street-cleaning trucks, was formed on the other side of the tunnel. The soldiers were blocked under New Arbat Avenue. Apparently, the group commander (or whoever) had given the order for a passage to be cleared into the tunnel from the side they had come from. One infantry carrier smashed into the line of cleaning trucks, breached it with ease, and retreated to the main group. This is what happened before midnight.

The telling of what happened next is simpler, because I saw most of it with my own eyes.

The section of Novy Arbat to the right of the crossing (are you still standing with the US Embassy on your right-hand side?) was filled with people. Mostly, they stood in chains, elbows hooked. Some moved about (it was only on the succeeding night, as they tell me, that all movement was prohibited). For the most part, the people who were unwilling to form chains were young. Many were drunk. Some carried bottles with rags sticking out of them. Others had sections of pipe and rods of metal of the kind used to reinforce concrete.

We (it was my Godfather and his wife who brought me there) walked towards the crossing. When it was about a hundred yards away, we heard the sound of machine-gun fire. Now, if you take a good look at the square in front of the Foreign Ministry, you'll see that its practically level with the section of Sadovoye Ring in front of the US Embassy's commercial office: both places are higher than the crossing itself, which sort of dips down a bit. This means that there was a clear line of fire between the two spots. Needless to say, this immediately became apparent to almost everyone there (except us, because we were new arrivals). I watched with astonishment as people around us got on their hands and knees and crawled towards the walls of houses on either side of the street (it was a long crawl, you know). Others ran. Yet no one was hurt. The reason was that the fire did not come from the main group of tanks. It came from the tunnel.

As eyewitnesses reported later, several young men from among those I'd seen walking around with Molotov cocktails tried to stop the next vehicle to move through the breach in the barricade. They managed to set it ablaze from the top of the tunnel wall, jumped down, and attacked the soldiers (whose unprotected heads were sticking out of the hatches, which shows that they expected nothing of the kind), very probably with their iron rods.

The soldiers went berserk and started shooting. It was a perfectly human reaction — they'd probably known their comrades for at least a year, and besides, they couldn't have been older than twenty, clearly not the best age for sagacious conduct. Three civilians were killed, and they showed a bloodied pant leg lodged in the tracks of an infantry carrier the next day on TV.

It was a crucial moment. Who knows what may have happened next but for the quick thinking of, presumably, the group commander. Whoever he was, he started firing tracer bullets from a heavy machine-gun on top of his tank. He fired straight up in the air, but if you've ever seen a line of tracer shells at night, you'll know that it was quite enough for everyone to realize that it was the last warning. The crossing cleared of people in a few seconds. There was no more shooting from the tunnel. The bloodshed was over.

you'll pass a side-street, where you'll find a beautiful neo-classic mansion built in 1900 by Mart and Adamovich with, of all things, an American flag on a huge pole. This is where the US Ambassador lives. (Mr.Matlock, the former resident of **Spaso House**, was something of a celebrity on the social scene. He used his excellent Russian in TV appearances to advise the 100 million or so Soviet citizens living below the poverty line not to apply for immigration to his native land but rather, "to solve their problems at home.")

plate on N°6 — the "cupboard house" as its famous inhabitant called it. It is open between 11 am and 6 pm (from 2 to 9 pm on Wednesdays and Fridays), and closed Monday and the last day of the month (☎ 291-61-54). Do make a point of dropping in.

Up ahead on the left side of the crossing with Tverskaya Street, opposite the Satire Theater, is the **Peking Hotel**. It has a restaurant (reputedly a favored KGB hangout) where you can have a good breakfast, brunch or lunch (if you like Cantonese). I wouldn't recommend dinner, though — the

The section of New Arbat between Boulevard Ring and Sadovoye Ring was created between 1962 and 1967 by a team of architects headed by Posokhin. There's little of interest there save for the **Dom Knigi** (House of Books), where I buy all my Lenin posters (great gifts for foreign friends). *Lenin is Today More Alive Than All Those Living!* is my favorite.

After you cross New Arbat you'll see the hapless US Embassy on the left (the building caught fire in March 1991) with the usual line of would-be emigrées in front.

One of the highlights of Sadovoye awaits on the right just beyond Vosstania (Uprising) Square with yet another Stalin skyscraper. "**Dr.Chekov**" reads the name-

place is too noisy. Even though it's expensive and never crowded, reservations are always a good idea (☎ 209-24-56).

As you cross Mayakovsky Square (where the Peking Hotel is situated) and Tverskaya Street, look to the left. There, half a mile or so up ahead, you'll find the only other theater besides the Bolshoi that you can enjoy without knowing the language — the **Central Puppet Theater** (N°3 Sadovaya-Samotechnaya Street). The theater is known to Muscovites as "Obraztsov's Theater" (after the name of its late founder Sergei Obraztsov who entertained five or six generations of grateful Moscow kids — Obraztsov was very well-liked). For tickets, check with your service bureau.

Another great place to go if you've brought your kids along is **Durov Corner**, a theater of animals managed by the famed Durov Family of animal trainers (just turn left under the Samotiochnaya Overpass and look for N°4 Durov Street). Your service bureau should help you with tickets, but just in case, here's the phone number: ℂ 281-29-14.

As you continue your journey by trolley, it'll be a while before you see another place worth visiting. You'll be passing **Kursk - Railway Station**, a 600-m (2,000 ft) tunnel, **Paveletsk Railway Station** (shiny and new

The name dates to the time when the Crimean Khan had his embassy here on the Crimean Shallow.

Across the Sadovoye from Gorky Park is the huge expo hall of the Artists' Union. Together with the Tretiakov Gallery, it exhibits Russian painting and sculpture.

ART GALLERIES

The Golden Age of Art is not coming back to Russia. This sad news was announced

after recent restoration), and another two tunnels before you get to **Gorky Park**. It's a nice place, even though it's officially called "Park of Culture and Rest." And, contrary to the impressions you may have derived from Smith's famous book, you won't get killed here. The park is actually a lot of fun, particularly if you buy a ticket to one of the small boats ("river trams" we call them) that go up and down the Moskva River from Luzhniki Stadium to the Kremlin Embankment and the Rossiya Hotel (tickets are sold on the wharf on the river side of the park from May to October).

As you wait for the boat, you can admire the view of the Krymsky (Crimean) Bridge.

late in 1990 by the USSR's first non-bureaucrat Minister of Culture, Gubenko (he is a professional actor). What culture is there to speak of, the minister queried, when state per capita allocations amount to 3 kopecks (0.05 cents) a year?

As often happens, when there's nothing to look forward to in the future, we turn to the past. In the time of Catherine the Great's and Alexander I's enlightened monarchies, museums flourished. The private

Moscow Metro (Subway) OPPOSITE is easily the most astounding achievement of socialism. It also has one of the world's cheapest fares.
ABOVE: "So how about it — I'll trade you my dog for your 'cello?"

THE LAST ATTACK

In the reign of Fyodor, Ivan the Terrible's son whose favorite pastime was listening to church bells, the affairs of state were left in the hands of the czar's brother-in-law, Boris Godunov. All was quiet, until one day, there came the terrible news: Kazi-Ghirei, the fearsome khan, was marching on Moscow with a Turkish fighting force. Kazi-Ghirei had been assured by the King of Sweden that Moscow was empty of troops (as was indeed the case). In anticipation of such easy pickings, the Crimeans hurried on, not even bothering to plunder the villages and small towns in their path. Ghirei, as the chronicles report not without sarcasm, climbed Sparrow Hills to admire the golden domes of Moscow. But he could hardly have liked what he saw. The endless walls of the White City bristled with cannon. A second wall of wood towered beyond the natural barrier of the Moskva River. The line of fortified monasteries, five in all, looked like it meant business. The only unprotected gap between the roads to Tula and Kaluga was filled with troops positioned around the movable fort that Muscovites referred to as the "Walking Town."

Meanwhile, the Kremlin was boosting morale. A small tent-cloth chapel was quickly set up in the rear echelons. The Icon of the Don Mother of God, which had seen the taking of Kazan, was solemnly installed therein. Czar Fyodor did what he could: "with warm tears and unshaken faith he prayed" before the image.

That night, a terrible racket was raised in Moscow. Huge bonfires erupted on the towers of the Kremlin and the White City. Almost every soldier was given a blazing torch and told to move about as much as possible. Meanwhile, Boris told a number of Muscovites to give themselves up for purposes of disinforming the enemy. They told the khan that a mighty force was due from Novgorod and several other towns; as soon as they would reach Moscow, they were bound to attack.

Terrified at the prospect, the khan made a quick, if less-than-graceful, exit. His troops, seeing their leader's sudden departure, followed suit "stepping one on another."

collections of Russian aristocrats were talked about in Europe. Artists received imperial scholarships to study in the home country of Raphael and Leonardo. Architecture blossomed, and theater became a passion. In short, a spectacular foundation for future growth had been laid.

Private patronage has always played a key role in artistic development. In fact, both art galleries in Moscow owe their origins to wealthy Maecenas.

TRETIAKOV GALLERY

The Gallery was started by the Tretiakov brothers, Pavel and Sergei, who had the money of one of Moscow's wealthiest merchant families behind them. Pavel Tretiakov embodied a rare combination of good taste and enough money to buy practically any painting that appealed to his connoisseur's eye. From the very beginning, it had been his self-confessed goal to found a museum of national painting.

The first paintings were purchased in 1856. In 1873, his house opened its doors to the general public. His initial acquisitions were mostly works by such democratic-minded contemporaries as Vasily Pukirev, Konstantin Flavitsky and Vasily Vereschagin.

As Tretiakov grew older, he became more systematic. The idea was to show the progress of Russian art. A separate hall was filled with works by early masters of the portrait genre — Levitsky and Borovikovsky. He also bought portraits by Tropinin, Venetsianov and Briullov.

Next came the historical (Ge, Repin, Kramskoi) genre and landscapes (Levitan, Shishkin). The house was too small for the growing collection. Tretiakov built an additional 25 halls in 1905.

In his will, Pavel Tretiakov left his gallery, together with the paintings collected by his brother, to the city of Moscow.

Whenever I visit the Tretiakov Gallery, I feel that nineteenth-century Russian art somehow got cheated out of the world renown it clearly deserves — and I'm sure you'll agree with me after you see our more famous paintings in Moscow and Petersburg.

It's a place you come back to throughout your life, for it has something for all ages, tastes and outlooks. It lifts the veil of secrecy, which so effectively keeps the Russian soul hidden from prying eyes to such an extent, that it would be madness for any foreigner to miss it. In addition, it is one of the few places left in Moscow where you can forget about everyday trivia, and discover, not without surprise, that, for example, the almost tangible line of hatred in the czar-strelets duel of the eyes in Surikov's *Morning of the Execution of The Streltsy*, strikes some deep note of compassion and admiration for the doomed man with the candle ... that the glittering ode to life in Briullov's The Mount makes you remember the first time you'd been in love... that the melancholy sunshine in Serov's *Girl With Peaches* gives you a feeling that life is, after all, worth living even if it is sad sometimes .... In short, the place makes you a better person, and believe me, Moscow is very grateful to the Tretiakov brothers for their precious gift.

The Gallery is closed for repairs at the writing of this book. It is scheduled to re-open late in 1992, but I wouldn't bet on it. Check with the service bureau at your hotel. The address is 10 Lavrushinsky Pereulok (☎ 231-13-62).

PUSHKIN MUSEUM OF FINE ARTS

The first exhibits of this museum, founded in 1912, were plaster casts of world-famous sculptures. The building itself was finished in 1912 (architect Klein); its construction was started in 1898 and financed with public donations.

The museum's first important collection was assembled by Golenischew, the prominent Egyptologist. Then came 1917 and a new way to expand the exposition — confiscation. Many items from the collection of French Impressionists had been owned by Shchiukin and Morozov. The museum owns several Rembrandts. There is no Russian art in the Pushkin Museum. Be sure to visit the place which is in Volkhonka Street. It is open from 10 am to 8 pm, Sundays 10 am to 6 pm, and closed on Mondays.

Sometimes there's a long line standing before the gates, which means that there's an out-of-town exhibition. You'll need to contact your service bureau to get in without waiting.

THE MONASTERIES

"If you want peace, prepare for war": the Latin saying worked as well in fourteenth-century Russia as anyplace else. And because Muscovy's most terrible enemy had been alien to Christianity, the Orthodox Church took an active part in the struggle. This should give the visitor a notion of why Moscow's monasteries look more like well-engineered fortresses than places of religious refuge.

ANDRONIKOV MONASTERY

Founded in 1360, Andronikov Monastery was named after its first father superior, a disciple of St. Sergius of Radonezh. Most of the walls, turrets and the Holy Gates were restored in the 1950s. Between 1795 and 1803, Kazakov built a 72-m (236-ft) belfry, which the communists demolished in the 30s. The monastery has Moscow's oldest existing stone structure — the Cathedral of the Savior (1425–1427), which stands in the center of the grounds.

What Andronikov Monastery is best known for, however, is not its architecture (however impressive), but the work of one of its monks. Icon painter Andrei Rublev worked and probably died here in approximately 1430. His works are to be found in the Cathedral of Annunciation in the Kremlin, in Vladimir churches and, of course, in the Tretiakov Gallery (which has one of his best icons, the *Holy Trinity*).

Today, there's the Andrei Rublev Museum of Early Russian Art in the monastery. It's open between 11 am and 6 pm except Wednesdays and the last day of the month.

NOVODEVICHY CONVENT

You can get here by the subway — take the orange line to Sportivnaya Station, south exit to Frunzensky Val Street, which leads right up to the convent. The place was founded by Czar Vasily III in 1524. Most of the nuns there were traditionally of high birth (and some even of imperial blood — Irina Godunova, Czar Boris' wife and Czarina Sofia, Peter the Great's power-hungry half-sister).

Since most of the nuns were not there of their own free will (it was Ivan the Terrible who started the charming — and afterwards popular — tradition of confining his wives to convents whenever he grew tired of them), they could hardly have been expected to embrace the ways of the Lord. When the sweeping Luzhniki construction project was launched in the 50s near the monastery, dozens of infant skeletons were unearthed by the astonished workers — evidence of convent sin.

As any other Moscow convent, the Novodevichy convent is a veritable fortress with high walls and 12 towers. The oldest (and to me, the most beautiful) structure of the convent is the Cathedral of the Virgin of Smolensk (1524–25), which was modelled after the Assumption Cathedral (the onion domes were added in the seventeenth century). Another thing the place is famous for is the necropolis, with the graves of Nikolai Gogol, Anton Chekov, Samuil Marshak (the poet and brilliant translator of Shakespeare), Konstantin Stanislavsky, Sergei Prokofiev, Valentin Serov, Nikita Khrushchev (don't miss the tombstone by Ernest Neizvestny), and Stalin's second wife Allilueva.

If the graveyard proves too much for you, go and check the bargains at the Beriozka Shop at Luzhnetsky Proyezd, Nº25 (across the street from the convent).

DONSKOI MONASTERY

Stasovoi Street; open between 11 am and 6 pm Closed Mondays, Saturdays and last Thursday of the month. Founded in 1591, the year when the Khan of Crimea besieged Moscow.

Many believed that victory came to the troops of Boris Godunov through the miraculous intervention of the Don Virgin, which Dmitry Donskoi carried into battle against the Mongols in 1380. Mind you no one felt grateful to Boris or to his envoys who'd fooled the khan at the cost of their own lives. But then, the Russian people never did think much of their leaders.

The monastery was built in the spot where the chapel had stood during the siege over a relatively short period of time (1684–1733), and therefore is architecturally

whole. The eighteenth century was the monastery's time to shine: it possessed some 7,000 serfs in the 1760s. After secularization in 1764, it was all downhill, and the lowest point was reached when the Bolsheviks added insult to injury and opened an Anti-Religious Museum there. Today, you can hardly find a cross in the monastery's acropolis — all were broken by the "Red Godless Youth" of the 1920s.

Caught unawares by the sudden religious upsurge, the Orthodox Church is expanding its network of religious schools and academia; ABOVE a student of the Sergiyev Posad Spiritual Academy. The walls of the New Convent of the Virgin (Novodevichy) OPPOSITE made a pretty cage for many a *Czaritsa* who had the misfortune to earn the wrath of a monarch husband.

There are two churches on the grounds, but the monastery's greatest attraction is its cemetery. After the 1771 plague, Catherine II forbade burials within city limits. For some reason, the monastery was chosen by the nobility as the "vogue" burial ground. Famous names on the tombstones include Osip Bove, the architect of the Bolshoi, Piotr Chaadayev, the nineteenth-century Hussar-philosopher, and representatives of almost every noble family in the land.

MUSEUM ESTATES

KOLOMENSKOYE

In 1532, a tent church was built near Grand Prince Vasily's summer residence; the chronicler hailed it as "a marvel of stature, beauty and lightness as yet unseen in Russia." Needless to add, they drank for three days to celebrate the completion of the church.

In addition, you can attend a mass at the Kazan Church, and see what remains of the "eighth wonder of the world," the wooden palace which decayed after a hundred years and was taken apart in Catherine the Great's time. There is a model of the palace, made in the previous century by Dmitry Smirnov, near the entrance.

It's also a great place for a picnic — but don't drink for three days. 31 Proletarsky Prospekt; open 11 am to 5 pm except Tuesdays and last Monday of month.

NEW JERUSALEM

Founded by Patriarch Nikon in 1656, the **Monastery of the Resurrection in New Jerusalem** was meant to show off the power of the Orthodox church. The huge **Cathedral of the Resurrection** (1685) is a replica of the Church of the Holy Sepulchre in Jerusalem, no less. When I was there in September 1991, they promised to finish restoring the cathedral sometime in the summer of 1993 (the dome, at any rate, was just about finished).

The monastery is 56 km (35 miles) along the Volokolamskoye Shosse in the town of Istra, from Moscow dial 8 (tone) 231-44375. Open 10 am to 5 pm except for Mondays

and the last Friday of the month. It belongs to a very poor museum now which consists of a collection of churches, cathedrals, the Patriarch's Cell, and so on. Other attractions include a beautiful if totally uncared-for park and an assortment of wooden structures from nearby villages. You'll see for yourself what they are; I just want you to remember that the only tool used by the carpenters in those days was the axe. Nails were unheard-of (except when they made them of a harder wood), which is the reason why the peasant's dwelling has such an intricate roof. The restorers also tell me that when the need arose to change some of the huge logs used in the walls of the house, they couldn't find any around Moscow — such trees just don't grow here any more (the new logs are from beyond the Urals).

There's a souvenir shop on the grounds, which offers clay toys, earthenware, embroidery and knitwear.

When you've finished with the monastery, go see the shops in the town of Istra — it should be a fascinating experience.

ARKHANGELSKOYE

Arkhangelskoye derives its name from the Church of Michael the Archangel (1667). In 1703 the estate passed to the Golitsyn family, who built a chateau and laid out a garden in the French tradition. Eighty years later, the sorry state of the estate prompted Prince Golitsyn to hire the services of de Guerney, a Frenchman, and Trombara, an Italian. When the place was about to be reopened in 1810, it was bought by one of the richest men in Russia, Prince Yusupov. It was money poorly spent, however, because between the French occupation in 1812 and the subsequent revolt of the local serfs, the estate very nearly ceased to exist. It was restored for the second time by a team of architects headed by Osip Bove (of Bolshoi Theater fame).

The terraces, park and statues provide for a nice change of scene. There is also a souvenir shop.

Arkhangelskoye is 26 km (16 miles) along Volokolamskoye Shosse (don't miss the turn-off). Open 11 am to 5 pm. Closed Monday and Tuesday. Attention! The museum is undergoing restoration. Please consult your Intourist service bureau before you go there.

IZMAILOVO

Believe it or not, but they grew grapes here three hundred years ago. The favorite hunting reserve of Czar Alexei the Quietest, Izmailovo was also the place where his son, the future founder of St.Petersburg, spent several years as a child. Izmailovo is also the home of Peter's "mock regiments," which later on became the backbone of

The hotel, built for the 1980 Olympics, accommodates 10,000 in its five buildings. It is the largest hotel in the world, not in the least because it would be sheer lunacy to build something of the sort in a normal market economy.

The open-air flea market, which was officially "allowed" only a few years ago, has recently been relocated to the unfinished Izmailovo Stadium (just take a left turn after you exit from the Izmailovsky Park metro station and go past the hotel). To me, the flea market has been a kind of a barometer of

the unbeatable Russian army (Semionovsky Regiment, Preobrazhensky Regiment, and Izmailovskiye Guards — all three now have Metro stations named after them).

Of the buildings that survived, there's the Bridge Tower, the Ceremonial Gates and the church-cum-hostel built in Peter's time for army veterans (who served for 25 years and often had no homes to return to).

Today, Izmailovo is famous for three things: the park, the hotel and the flea market. The first two are symptoms of that familiar disease, gigantism: the entrance to the park from the Izmailovskaya Station is adorned with a sign claiming that the park is "the largest in Europe." In fact, it is large, but it's more of a forest than a park.

democracy. In its early days, the hawkers would offer you a Brezhnev *matrioshka* doll only if you looked safe enough to them (and still, they held it under a half-raised coat lapel — a habit of marijuana pushers in New York's Greenwich Village). Now the dolls are exhibited for all to see, and the "line of tolerance" has shifted to foreign currency. Needless to say, the prices are so high that most of the buyers are foreigners; yet it is still against the law for Soviet citizens to accept dollars, so every time you want to buy something, you have to take part in the traditional (sometimes whispered) conversation about exchange rates and so on.

Kolomenskoye is a nice location for a picnic.

Another thing about these *matrioshkas*: after the August coup, they served, to me at any rate, as a litmus test of Gorbachev's waning popularity. Whereas before August, the most expensive doll had been Nicholas II inside Lenin inside Stalin inside Khrushchev inside Brezhnev inside Yeltsin inside Gorbachev, after the abortive attempt to "set things right" by a junta many regarded as being composed of Gorbachev's close friends, it was already the Gorbachev inside Yeltsin doll that had the highest price tag.

The beautiful green **church** next to the metro station is dedicated to the resurrection of Christ. Another interesting building near the metro is the **fire tower**, from which Moscow was observed in the nineteenth century for signs of trouble. The truly amazing thing about the building, however, is that after all the reshuffling and relocation of municipal services after the revolution, this one stayed with the fire department. There's no one up in the tower anymore, though. Metro Station: Sokolniki.

Although the flea market is not the safest place in Moscow (hold on to your purse!), I advise you to go and have a look. On a good day, it's fun.

Oh yes, there is a fourth attraction in Izmailovo — myself. I've lived here for 20 years. Metro Stations Izmailovsky Park or Izmailovskaya.

SOKOLNIKI

This is the place where the czars went falcon-hunting in the seventeenth century (*sokolniki* means "falcon hunters"). Today, there is a huge park, a museum of wax figures, and a "palace of sports."

WHERE TO STAY

You don't have much of a choice, I'm afraid. It's not that there aren't enough hotels in Moscow, it's that there aren't enough quality hotels. Until recently, the ones with the best service (or maybe I should say "least bad") were controlled by Intourist, the state-owned travel agency. The problem with Intourist, however, is that you never know at which of its hotels you are going to wind up. Asking your travel agent for a specific hotel doesn't always help, either, because the Intourist bureaucratic machine is too unwieldy to be bothered with such trifles (even if you ask a couple of months in advance).

Things have changed with the appearance of two or three non-Intourist hotels. Yet even there, service is rarely on a par with what you would usually expect at the price (they are expensive) anywhere else in the world, so be warned!

EXPENSIVE

If you can afford the prices, I recommend that you stay at one of these hotels. The difference between expensive and medium-range can be considerable.

to the joint-venture hotel line... Good cafe. Singles start at DM 480, doubles at DM 570.

Savoy 3 Rozhdestvenka Street. (929 85 00. Bookings can be made through Finnair. Restaurant, small casino. Excellent location in midtown Moscow. Single rooms start at $130.

Cosmos 150 Mira Prospekt. (217 86 80; 217 91 93. Built by the French for the 1980 Olympics, it has a swimming pool and sauna, a bowling alley, and an assortment of bars and restaurants (mostly for hard

Metropol 1/4 Teatralny Proyezd. (927 60 96. Lenin stayed here (he must have liked the location, as you will). Singles start at $244, doubles at $290 and this is at 1991 introductory prices).

Mezhdunarodnaya 12 Krasnopresnenskaya Naberezhnaya. (253 13 91. Shopping mall, swimming pool and sauna, several restaurants (some for hard currency, some for roubles) and bars. Single rooms start at $150.

Pullman-Iris 10 Korovinskoye Shosse. (488 80 00. Health club, saunas and swimming pool, limousine service, French restaurant. Singles start at $260, and doubles, at $300.

Moscow Olympic Penta 18/1 Olimpiisky Prospekt. (971 61 01. The newest addition

currency), some with variety shows. Doubles start at $120.

Intourist 3 Tverskaya Street. (203 40 08. The hotel is over two decades old. It has several restaurants and a variety show Moscow Lights. The best thing going for the place is its location in midtown Moscow (you can get a suite with a view of the Kremlin). Singles start at $100.

Slavianskaya 2 Berezhkovskaya Naberezhnaya. (941 80 20. Expensive (singles start at $180) but easily the best for service and business facilities. Good location, too.

Moscow's State Circus ABOVE and Operetta Theater OPPOSITE offer two more ways to get around the language barrier for a night of entertainment.

Sovetskaya 32 Leningradsky Prospekt.
(250 72 53; 250 72 55. Favored by Winston
Churchill, it has one of Moscow's best restaurants and — surprise, surprise! — room
service. Consult your travel agent — the
hotel is currently closed for repairs, and
scheduled to reopen in early 1993.

MEDIUM RANGE

Belgrade 5 Smolenskaya Square. (248 67
34; 248 16 43.
Budapest 2/18 Petrovskiye Linii. (924
88 20.
Ukraina 2/1 Kutuzovsky Prospekt. (243
30 30.
Saliut 158 Leninsky Prospekt. (438 65 65
Leningradskaya 21/40 Kalanchiovskaya
Street. (975 30 08.

INEXPENSIVE (YOUTH HOSTELS)

Molodiozhnaya 27 Dmitrovskoye Shosse.
(210 45 65.
Orlyonok 15 Kosygina Street. (939 88 44.
Sputnik 38 Leninsky Prospekt. (938 71 06.

A final note to newcomers: after you
check in, you will be given a hotel pass
(which is surrendered in exchange for room
keys in some hotels). Try not to lose it,
because you may find it difficult getting into
your hotel without it.

WHERE TO EAT

Even though HOW NOT TO STARVE would
have been a more appropriate title for this
section, the surprising thing is that you can
eat reasonably well in Moscow. All restaurants are inexpensive, given the current
exchange rate of the dollar. A lavish meal
at the best rouble restaurant with caviar,
champagne and the most expensive Soviet
alcoholic beverage, brandy, would cost
roughly 1,200 roubles per person. At the
time of writing, the price of one dollar on the
"black market" was 300 roubles. For the
past two years, however, the dollar
seemed to follow the rouble (meaning
that if a bottle of champagne cost 20 roubles in 1990, it cost one dollar because the
exchange rate was 20 to 1; if it costs 420 rou-

bles by the end of 1992, it will still be one
dollar, because the exchange rate will be 420
to 1). So thank God you have convertible
currency in your pocket, and try not to think
of the less fortunate Russians whose skimpy
wages make restaurants as unattainable as
the Moon.

The restaurants which take convertible
currency (all major credit cards are accepted) are in the medium range by European standards. A meal at the Japanese
restaurant in the Mezh would set you back
by about $80 (with wine).

Some restaurants offer food for roubles
and drink for dollars (again, you can pay by
credit card).

It is always wise to make reservations; if
you want to be absolutely sure, come in
person and leave a deposit (200 roubles for
a meal for two should do nicely). If your
reservation is confirmed, the table will be set
at the appointed hour.

Many things have been said about our
restaurants, few of them nice. As a veteran
restaurant-goer, I want to give you some
advice, which will come in handy, I hope.

The best way to deal with the maitre'd
is to discuss everything in advance (the
menu, the wine, the price, whether he will
accept dollars "under the table" even
though the bill will be made out in roubles,
and at what rate). Remember: when you
offer to pay in dollars at the black market
exchange rate, you are not breaking any law
that I know of, and you are doing the man a
big favor.

If you cannot do that for some reason,
talk to the waiter who approaches your
table. When the price is settled, look him
straight in the eye and say, "I'll throw in an
extra five (ten, fifteen) bucks if you do
everything quickly." With the negotiations out of the way, I guarantee that you
will get excellent service. Of course, if you
have a Russian friend along, things will be
easier.

Following is a list of restaurants I would
go to myself.

Arlekino (Italian) 15 Druzhinnikovskaya
Street. (205 70 88. All right except when
there's a bunch of drunken Italians there.
Delhi (Indian) 23b Krasnaya Presnya
Street. (255 04 92. There are two halls — one

for roubles, one for dollars. Please stay away from the rouble one.

Kropotkinskaya 36 (Russian) 36 Kropotkinskaya Street. (201 75 00. They charge dollars for drinks.

Praga (Czech) 2 Arbat Street. (290 61 71. Ask for a *kabinet* — a separate dining room. It should cost an extra 500 roubles, but it's worth it. One of the best restaurants in town.

Tren-Mos (American) 21 Komsomolsky Prospekt. (245 12 16. For the homesick. Credit cards only.

Razgulai (Russian) 11 Spartakovskaya Street. (267 76 13. The place to go for Russian cuisine. Good service.

Sakura (Japanese) 12 Krasnopresnenskaya Naberezhnaya. (253 28 94. Entrance through the Mezh. The food is Japanese, although the waitresses are not.

Sovetsky (Russian) 32 Leningradsky Prospekt. (250 74 49. Built on the site of the famous pre-revolutionary Yar Restaurant, the place is famous for its fish. The other feather in its cap is that they have vegetables, even in winter.

Pullman-Iris (French) 10 Korovinskoye Shosse. (488 80 00. Foreign currency only. Jazz quintet Sunday through Wednesday, 7:30 pm until midnight.

The Little Mermaid (Danish Sea Food)/ **Glazour** (Russian) 12/19 Smolensky Boulevard. (248 44 38. Hard currency only. A lunch there will set you back by about $30.

U Pirosmani (Georgian) 4 Novodevichy Proezd. (247 19 26. Hearty but satisfying. The place to go for *basturma*, *shashlik* and *satsivi*. I hope they have wine when you are there. If not, bring your own.

Vienna (German) 18/1 Olimpiisky Prospekt. (971 61 01. Brunch served every Sunday between 10:30 am and 2:30 pm at DM 45 per person (half price for children under 12). I do not go into gastronomical details here, because the selection of dishes offered by our restaurants never varies by more than five or six items; it is also very small. The places I put on my list are very good; but they may very well seem terrible to you if you forget your sense of humor and the fact that the country is groping its way out of seven-and-a-half decades of socialism.

Following is the average menu of a very good cooperative restaurant.

HORS D'OEUVRES Cold cuts (canned ham, two or three kinds of salami, sliced roast pork or beef, smoked chicken or pork lard, boiled sliced tongue); cheese (Russians never eat cheese for dessert); sauerkraut, pickled cucumbers, olives, tomatoes, carrots (a Korean dish); smoked salted salmon or similar fish; sliced sturgeon (if you're lucky); *Beluga* (black) caviar; salmon (red) caviar; fresh vegetables (tomatoes, cucumbers, sweet peppers, garlic, onions, dill, parsley, celery) if you're very lucky.

SOUPS Borscht; *Solianka* (the soup that's got everything in it, including sliced frankfurters and green olives); mushroom noodle; *kharcho* (Georgian lamb stew with rice and tomatoes).

MAIN COURSE two or three kinds of meat; chicken; two or three kinds of fish; *pelimeni* (a kind of ravioli); mushroom souffle; meat, fish, cabbage pies (if you're lucky).

SIDE DISHES Potatoes (even French fries); green peas.

DESSERT Honey; ice cream; fruit preserves; cake (rarely) ... and that's about it.

Every restaurant does have a speciality, of course, but I'll leave that for you to discover on your own.

If you're in Russia with a group, be warned that the breakfast and lunch that you are served is probably included into the price of your tour; if you want something that's not on the menu, you have to pay extra — if they find it for you. *Bon appetit!*

TAKE-OUT

McDonald's charges a five-dollar fee for orders under $50, (200 16 55; **Pizza Hut** delivers for roubles and hard currency (ten percent), (229 20 13 (Tverskaya Street) or (243 17 27 (Kutuzovsky Prospekt); **Pettina**, a large menu and free delivery, (286 52 17; **Baku-Livan** sells sandwiches for roubles, regular restaurant fare for dollars (takeouts) at 24 Tverskaya Street.

The Land of White Stone

A VOYAGE to the Land of White Stone is a voyage into another time. The land itself no longer exists. We are left with the relics — churches and cathedrals, monasteries and fortresses — which have preserved, in the traditional limestone of Ancient Russia, the soul of a bygone era. You can see most of the towns described in this section as daytrips out of Moscow. Some of the towns, such as Sergiyev Posad, are an hour's drive out, while others, such as Yaroslavl, may be 300 km (160 miles) away. Getting there is not a problem — just book the Intourist Golden Ring tour (there are various options available).

SERGIYEV POSAD

The fourteenth century was a time for monasteries. Christianity was taking root, and dozens appeared throughout the land. Sergiyev Posad is where it all started. Legend has it that the first (wooden) church in the monastery was built by two brothers, monks from Radonezh, one of whom, Sergius, eventually became its father superior.

Sergiyev Posad ("village of Sergius") is certainly legend material, with an impressive history of wars, spectacular sieges, and Gospel-grade miracles. The Russian equivalent to Jerome K.Jerome's pub where every queen and king of England seemed to have stopped at one time or another, Sergiyev Posad is the place everybody who was anybody in Russian history made a point of visiting.

In 1380, for example, Moscow's Prince Dmitry ("Of-the-Don") and Serpukhov's Prince Vladimir ("The Brave") stopped at the Trinity Monastery on their way to Kulikovo Field (and easily the most dramatic battle in Russian history). Prince Dmitry received the blessing of Sergius. This was more important than might seem, for Russia in 1380 was still a breeding ground for fratricidal strife (two Russian princes fought on the invader's side), and the support of the man many regarded as a living saint was tantamount to getting, if temporarily, carte blanche in the struggle for supremacy. It is difficult to say what Dmitry's future would have been had he lost. But he won the gruelling sixteen-hour battle, which brought together over a quarter of a million Russian and Mongol fighting men. After the victory, Sergius' prestige soared. His spirit seemed to hover over the town, which became, almost overnight, a place of pilgrimage and prayer for Orthodox believers as soon as he died.

Another famous moment in the town's history came in 1608, when the monks went through 16 months of siege by the Poles (who, by the way, never managed to take the citadel).

WHAT TO SEE

The monastery, first and foremost. Recently restored to its original, if somewhat erratic, splendor, the Trinity–St. Sergius is a delightful mixture of architectural styles and schools spanning six centuries. It is one of the best places for taking pictures that I know, especially if the weather is right.

Then there's the interior of the monastery's churches and chapels: the iconostasis by Andrei Rublev and pupils, which once boasted Rublev's chef-d'œuvre, The Trinity (until the Bolsheviks stole it from the fifteenth-century Trinity Cathedral). The icon, dedicated by Rublev to "the pleasure of Sergius," is now in the collection of the Tretiakov Art Gallery in Moscow.

Finally, there's the atmosphere of the place. Once inside, make a point to look at the faces. People come from hundreds of kilometers away, often on foot, to pray over the remains of St. Sergius for private miracles of their own — children for the childless, health for the crippled or the terminally ill, safety for faraway loved ones. Less serious "requests" are made at the Chapel of the Well. The water flowing from the fountain under the ornate roof is

OPPOSITE: the carpenters of yore were magicians who built their unique churches without a single nail.

said to possess wishing-well properties. They say that all you have to do is wash your hands and face … (An American friend from a major publishing company asked for an exclusive interview with a high-placed Soviet politician whose book she was promoting back in the States. Her wish — certainly one never made there before — came true. What would you expect?)

Another place you should visit is the icon shop, where all attendants are monks. The shop, which has signs calling for visitors to be "reverent and God-fearing," offers an unusually wide variety of icons, and prices are way below Arbat Street standards. Good hunting!

WHERE TO STAY

Actually, you don't have much of a choice. There is a small Intourist hotel with a restaurant. Since Sergiyev Posad is within easy driving distance from Moscow, there's little sense in staying, unless, of course, you want to stick around for two or three days. If you do, check with the service bureau at your hotel in Moscow, or call Intourist Information (225 68 83.

WHERE TO EAT

There's a very nice place on the way, about 50 km (30 miles) along the highway. When I go to Sergiyev Posad, I usually stop by and book a table (look for the highway sign saying **Skazka Restaurant**). A meal there will set you back by five dollars tops, brandy and champagne included.

In the town itself, there's an Intourist restaurant within walking distance from the monastery. It's cheaper, but not as good as Skazka. Make a point of reserving a table.

HOW TO GET THERE

The town lies 71 km (44 miles) from Moscow on the road to Yaroslavl. You can also get there by suburban train (from the Yaroslavsky Station in Moscow, Komsomolskaya Metro Station).

CHÂTEAU IN ABRAMTSEVO

On your way, make a quick detour to the chateau in Abramtsevo (take a left turn at the 62 km) — if you feel like it, that is. The place is a famed "literary nest" (Gogol, Tiutchev, Turgenev, Granovsky). Its last owner was Savva Mamontov, the celebrated turn-of-the-century patron of the arts. Mamontov's hospitality appealed to some of our best artists of the time — Repin, the Vasnetsov brothers, Levitan, Vrubel, Serov, Polenov, Korovin — whose paintings you are bound to notice in major Russian-art museums.

Open 11 am to 5 pm, except for Mondays, Tuesdays and the 30th of each month. English, French, German spoken.

VLADIMIR AND SUZDAL

BACKGROUND

A twelfth-century Insider's Guide to Russia would start with these two. Along with Chernigov, Ryazan, Novgorod and several other towns of historic fame, Vladimir and Suzdal had been of tremendous import for the political and cultural goings-on in those distant times.

The Vladimir-Suzdal Principate, or Suzdalia, rose to ultimate authority during the reign of Vsevolod ("The Big Nest") between 1177 and 1212. Don't let his nickname mislead you — Vsevolod had other interests besides family ones. He was a shrewd military leader (somewhat poetically, the chronicles claimed that his soldiers could "empty the Don with their helmets") and a patron of the arts.

After the rise of Moscow in the fourteenth century, Suzdalia sank into drab provincial oblivion. Sadly, it remains there to date.

The curious thing about Soviet provinces is that, probably because they are denied their past, they seem to have little or no present, and certainly not much of a future. Yet even in this, they are Soviet, and, as such, packed with brain-twisting paradoxes and oddities which make you want to laugh, or cry, or, not infrequently, both. An example? The Vladimir Kremlin. I walked around its walls twice, yet could not find a way in. Finally, I noticed a plaque near the gates which said, "USSR Committee of State Security. Vladimir Department." It's true that the democratic press describes the KGB as "under siege," but

When Valdimir Monomakh founded his capital city of Vladimir in 1108, he wanted it to rival the mighty Kiev in architectural beauty and military strength. His strategy certainly paid off with the Golden Gates (1164) and the Uspensky Cathedral (1160). Lavishly decorated with stone carvings, gilt and frescoes, it became the model for its twin cathedral in the Moscow Kremlin. The church burned several times, and the decor had to be restored. One of the last times this was done, Andrei Rublev and Daniil Chyorny had taken a

they're taking it a little too literally in Vladimir, don't you think?

What to See

Architecturally, Suzdalia is easily on a par with Moscow, Smolensk or Novgorod. The czars of Moscow wanted Suzdal to become the keeper of the Orthodox tradition, and poured enormous amounts of money into monastery construction there. Since the czars were too far away for minute (and restrictive) supervision, the architects were left pretty much to their own devices. The result: a series of Russia's most harmonious ensembles in white stone.

hand. You can still see some of the frescoes by Russia's two greatest icon painters there.

As for Suzdal, it is small enough for a walking tour. This is definitely the case when you have to discover it all on your own. The best way to go about it is to leave Moscow in the early afternoon, see Vladimir (and maybe have a late lunch there), drive to Suzdal, spend the night at the local Intourist Motel, and start out on a tour of Suzdal first thing in the morning.

ABOVE: souvenirs of a savage epoch: more than anything else, our monasteries resemble fortresses.

The Land of White Stone

Of the hundred or so architectural monuments in Suzdal, the Spaso-Yevfimievsky Monastery is the one I love best, because that's where the bells are.

There are nineteen of them, from small chimes to baritone biggies, atop the seventeenth-century belfry of the monastery. They say that when the belfry had finally been restored, it turned out that no one could actually work the bells. Three people were sent to Rostov the Great to learn the basics and the fine points of this ancient art.

The last time I visited the monastery, there had been about 200 children there, more noisy and unruly than usual, as it was August and their summer holidays. They made the place look more like a playground, and the few stray adults there, mostly foreign tourists, raised their eyes beseechingly to the Heavens, silently praying for a little peace and quiet.

Suddenly, with the first resounding boom of the great baritone bell, their prayers were answered.

It was the centuries talking, and believe me, everyone listened. Not just listened — every man, woman and child there was mesmerized, responding to the mellow magic with every fiber of their beings. With a conscious effort of will, I tore my eyes away from the top of the belfry where the two bellmen sat amidst a veritable spider's web of ropes and lines, and looked at the faces around me. It was a sight unseen in Russia for the last 70 years. There was deep concentration. Inspiration. Bewilderment, certainly. And the realization that, almost in spite of themselves, the magic of the bells had penetrated into some remote recess of their souls, which they probably hadn't even known existed.

Another, um ... interesting thing about the Spaso-Yevfimievsky Monastery is that it served as a prison for the better part of the last two centuries. The czars used the monastery's grisly cell block as a political prison from the 1810s to 1905. Shortly after the October coup in 1917, the place became a kind of Bolshevik Bastille, and quickly filled up with highly-placed opponents of the new re-

gime. If you care for that sort of thing, "go to jail" and get all the gruesome details in the small museum of the former cell block.

Of the permanent exhibits on the grounds, don't miss the one with the "amateur revolutionary art," particularly the earlier items. The paintings provide a unique insight into the psychological aura of the October Revolution and, of course, the mentality of the people who made it.

If you still have time after your tour of Suzdal, try going to nearby Bogoliubovo to see the Pokrov-on-Nerl. The church, which dates to 1165, is of world-wide — and, in my opinion, well-deserved — fame.

WHERE TO STAY

In **Vladimir**, there's **Hotel Vladimir** (74 Third International Street, ☎ 30 42). I do not recommend it.

In **Suzdal**, there's the so-called "**Tourist Complex**" (hotel/motel, ☎ 2 17 57). Built less than two decades ago with a sauna and swimming pool, it is a perfect example of what socialism can do with a good idea. The only other hotel in town is called **Pokrovsky Monastyr** (13 double rooms in a stone building and accommodations for 32 more in wooden *izba's*).

If you go by car, a word of warning — make sure you have enough gas for the return trip. It is in extremely short supply in Suzdal.

WHERE TO EAT

Again, the choice isn't large.

In **Vladimir**: **Traktir Restaurant**, a small one built in the form of a peasant's cottage, with decent Russian dishes (2 Ulitsa Sovetov, ☎ 67 53); U Zolotykh Vorot (11 Third International Street, ☎ 34 55); and the largest, **Russkaya Derevnia** (5a Moskovskoye Shosse, ☎ 9 71 32). In Suzdal, there's a huge restaurant in the motel, and three more in

Troika of cupolas in Ipatievsky Monastery shows off the best of the local school.

town — **Gostiny Dvor** in the building of the former marketplace, **Suzdal** at 3 Kremliovskaya Street, and Trapeznaya at Nº20 on the same street. Then there's a small restaurant in Pokrovsky Monastery (provided they have enough food to serve you there. The last time I went to Suzdal, I offered an exorbitant sum for a table, but they said they couldn't serve "outsiders," since they first had to take care of the board for the guests of the small hotel in the monastery).

If you are lucky to get a table, though, be sure to ask for the standard fare, which includes mushrooms, meat cooked in ceramic pots according to a traditional local recipe, and large glasses of **medovukha** — a mildly alcoholic honey beverage.

OTHER TOWN MUSEUMS

PERESLAVL-ZALESSKY

Founded by Yury the Long-Armed in 1152 on the site of the ninth-century Slav fort on the banks of Lake Plescheevo, the town has several things for you to see. First, there's the **Spaso-Preobrazhensky Cathedral** (1157) with the monument to Alexander Nevsky, who was born here, not far away. Then, there are the three monasteries, built mainly in the sixteenth and seventeenth centuries.

ROSTOV THE GREAT

Should be your next stop. It is first mentioned in the chronicles in 862. Whenever I visit the place, I always admire the way the towers and cupolas of the Kremlin are reflected in the waters of Lake Nero. The Kremlin took thirty years to build (starting in 1665). In August, 1953, Rostov was attacked by a hurricane of unbelievable force. Every church lost its cupolas. You can see the now-restored sixteenth-century **Assumption Cathedral**, the **Church of St.John the Apostle** (1683), the single-domed **Ascension Cathedral** (1566), the **Odigitry Church**, and the rest of them. Be sure not to miss the **bell arcade** (1687). It

has thirteen bells; the largest is the 32-ton Sysoi, which can at times be heard 20 km (12 miles) away.

YAROSLAVL

It stands where the Volga meets the Kotoroslya River. The skyline on a good day is breathtaking. Yaroslavl is famous as the place where the oldest work of Russian literature — *Slovo o polku Igoreve* (Tale of Igor's Regiment) — was found. Another interesting thing about this town is that it is probably the only one in Russia where peasants built their houses of stone.

You can admire the interiors of the churches in the **Monastery of the Savior** (May through October). Then there's the museum of architecture, which is open 10 am to 5 pm except for Mondays and the first Wednesday of each month (2 00 69). The **museum of art** (the works of Aivazovsky, Savrasov, Perov, Repin) is open 10 am to 5 pm except for Fridays (2 24 57).

The telephone number of the Intourist representative in Yaroslavl is (2-12-58.

KOSTROMA

Another Volga town. Its emblem is a sail ship, because this is where most of Western Europe used to get its sails from. Fan-shaped Kostroma is one of those rare cities that have kept their original layout. The **Ipatievsky Monastery** in the heart of the city was founded in the fourteenth century. Its fortunes are connected to the Godunov family, which had two czars among its members. An unforgettable view opens from the five-storied belfry — if they let you up there. If they do, you'll get a bird's eye view of the nearby museum of wooden architecture with peasant *izba's*, barns, bath houses, mills, and churches, all collected in outlying villages.

Sergiyev Posad is the Mecca of the Orthodox world.

St. Petersburg

POLITICALLY, it was the center of an empire and the cradle of Russia's enlightened monarchy. Geographically, it was "a window into Europe," the Venice of the North, the City of White Nights. But for St.Petersburg, the silver lining came before the cloud. It turned out that the wages of empire-building is revolution. That enlightenment easily gives way to total cultural collapse. That a city built on such a quick-tempered river as the Neva has no choice but to contend with periodic — and disastrous — floods, and that the near day-like transparency of summer nights can quickly turn into Stygian blackness as soon as the Arctic winter comes.

St.Petersburg — Petrograd — Leningrad — St. Petersburg is probably the most famous victim of the "epidemic of renaming". Yet curiously enough, the four names reflect, if roughly, the eras of its illustrious history.

The seed had been planted by Czar Peter I ("The Great"), who somewhat immodestly decided to name his creation after his patron saint. Yet the decision to found the city on the Baltic has been endorsed as the most fortunate one of his life, by the city's spectacular and swift subsequent growth.

Then, in the second half of the nineteenth century, the empire and its capital city entered a phase of decline, which was appropriately, if entirely inadvertently, consummated by Nicholas II's decision to rename St. Petersburg.

The Germanic "burg" gave way to the Slavonic "grad" because the last czar thought it fitting: there was, after all, a war with Germany going on. So when the Bolsheviks decided to re-baptize Petrograd after their deceased-but-still-unburied leader' pseudonym, they were really only picking up where Nicholas left off. The Soviet era of the town's history they'd ushered in, by the way, brought Leningrad untold sufferings and, in the days of World War II, very nearly killed everyone in the place.

Then Leningrad's flamboyant mayor Anatoly Sobchak finally coaxed parliament into giving back his town its original name in the fall of 1991. Hopefully, this latest renaming will open a new and better chapter in the life of the second-largest city in Russia.

And hope there is, for the half-starved, crumbling metropolis, which is plagued by a million problems ranging from an acute shortage of housing to rampant crime, still has people such as the old lady I saw last year on TV during the 24-hour fund-raising telethon. "I have lived here all my life," she said, "I lived through the Blockade. I am old. I have nothing to give except my wedding ring. I give it gladly so that my city can live."

But it's certainly going to need a lot of wedding rings.

BACKGROUND

The eighteenth century dawned on a Russia which made Prince Hamlet's rotten state of Denmark a paradise by comparison. The policies of forced centralization conducted by the half-insane Ivan the Terrible and the ensuing Troubles left the economy in ruins; in addition, half of Europe seemed to regard Russia as ridiculously easy pickings for any invader willing to hack off a piece of its territory. Moscow was racked by a series of uprisings of the streltsy (the czar's guards). The ruling Boyar Duma (assembly of top aristocrats) was entirely occupied with petty feuding and palace intrigues. In short, things were black indeed.

Yet there was a glimmer of hope. It lay in a rudimentary nationwide market, created largely through the efforts of industrial enterprises operated by the crown and a budding private sector. Another thing going for Russia was the hyperactive, obstinate and often cruel will of its monarch.

The first stone was laid by the czar personally on May 16, 1703, into the foundation of a fort on tiny Hare Isle. Legend has it that after an inspection of the island, Peter took a bayonet from a guard, cut two chunks of topsoil and, having laid them out in the shape of the cross, said, "Here will be a city." He then proceeded to dig a trench. An eagle appeared overhead and soared above the czar. When the trench became about four feet long, a stone container was placed therein and sprinkled with holy water by the clergymen in the czar's attendance. The czar placed a golden ark with the holy relics of Apostle Andrew the First-Called, and

CZAR PETER I

"Peter was a most unconventional man and ruler. Almost seven feet tall and weighing 240 pounds, he nonetheless retained qualities of a small boy who revelled in noise, buffoonery, and horseplay and combined tenderness and devotion with vicious cruelty. He was curious, a keen observer, and possessed an excellent memory; obstacles and reverses left him undiscouraged. Like his contemporary, Frederick William I of Prussia, he embodied the concept of the ruler as first servant of the state. In everything he insisted on 'going through the ranks' and doing things himself. He learned many manual skills and a dozen trades, setting an example for the gentry of firsthand knowledge and hard work. Peter hated ceremony, luxury, and artificiality; he disliked subterfuge and expected honesty from his subordinates. Although sincerely religious, he scorned and even made fun of the hidebound Orthodox clergy. Unlike his predecessors, who generally had remained esconced in the Kremlin, he wandered restlessly around Russia, open to new ideas and ready to experiment. These qualities helped determine his iconoclastic, innovative policies as czar."

(From *A History of Russia and the Soviet Union* by David MacKenzie and Michael W.Curran)

covered it with a stone lid, which had the following engraved on top: "On the 16th of May in the year of our Lord 1703, the capital city of St. Petersburg was founded by the great sovereign, Czar and Grand Prince Peter Alekseevich, lord of all Russia."

May 16 is now celebrated as the city's birthday.

The following year, Peter moved the capital from Moscow to his new town; understandably, the court took several years to move to what in effect was still little more than a collection of mud-huts. Meanwhile, the war with Sweden continued. Russia needed ships. That's how the Admiralty Wharf came into being.

After Peter's death, it was touch and go for his creation: his successors apparently did not cherish the idea of living there. St. Petersburg owes its continued development to Peter's niece, Anna, who firmly established the royal court in the northern capital during her reign in the 1730s.

Then came Elizabeth and Catherine the Great. The empire Peter I dreamed of was now reality. Catherine spared no expense to invite the cream of European talent, including such grandees of architecture as Rastrelli and Cameron, to the new capital. After Catherine's reign, the city was for the first time called "the Venice of the north."

Two centuries of relatively untroubled growth followed.

The twentieth century kicked off with Bloody Sunday, the shooting of a worker manifestation out to petition the czar in Palace Square on January 9, 1905. The era of revolutions was here.

Soviet historians loved to call St.Petersburg "the cradle of three revolutions," meaning the unsuccessful one in 1905, the February revolution in 1917, which brought the Romanov empire to an end, and the Bolshevik revolution in October, 1917.

Terrified at the prospect of being taken prisoner by the armies of Yudenich, a general of the White Guard who operated out of nearby Poland and Finland, Lenin moved the capital to the relative safety of Moscow 700 km (430 miles) deeper into the mainland. This set the stage for subsequent rivalry between the Moscow and Leningrad Bolsheviks, culminating in December 1934 with the assassination of Leningrad party boss Sergei Kirov (probably orchestrated by Stalin). The "brutal murder of our beloved Comrade Kirov," as Big Brother chose to phrase it, provided a welcome cue to start the purges of 1937–38 and 1948. Thousands of Kirov's supporters faced KGB firing squads even as dozens of factories, streets, bridges, stadiums and kindergartens across the land were given Kirov's name. Yet in a way, Stalin's hatred of Leningrad was also a blessing: the northern capital escaped the fate of Moscow, a third of whose historic monuments were ruthlessly destroyed under Stalin's "reconstruction programs," because the Father of Peoples considered it beneath him (or maybe because he was too far away to care).

Then came World War II, which started with a series of deafening defeats for the Red Army. Before you could say "Long Live Stalin!" the German tanks were at the outskirts of Moscow and Leningrad. It is said that the Nazis brought along statues of Hitler for installation in the conquered cities. In Leningrad's case, they'd have done better to erect a monument to Voroshilov, the civil war derelict who extolled "cavalry warfare" (meaning the horse-and-sabre variety) well into the 1950s and who'd managed to commit so many blunders on the Leningrad Front that the city was practically sealed off from the rest of the country by September, 1941 (the war started in June).

The Blockade lasted for 900 days and nights, taking at least 650,000 lives. But Leningrad persevered.

Mikhail Gorbachev's *perestroika* ushered in an era of hope. The city is now under democratic control. Anatoly Sobchak, the democratic candidate who'd made it to the mayor's office on a wave of anti-Communism, plans to move into Smolny, the former institute for daughters of nobility that the Bolsheviks used as their Leningrad headquarters since 1917.

It is certainly a far cry from what Peter the Great planned; yet every day, the grateful descendants of his subjects lay flowers near his monument in the Peter and Paul Fortress.

GENERAL INFORMATION

You can find the Intourist representative at 11 St. Isaac Square. (315 51 29. Other Intourist offices are at the air and sea ports, railway stations and all major hotels.

Specific travel inquiries:
Aeroflot 7-9 Nevsky Prospekt 211 79 80; 006 (general information).
Pulkovo Airport (293 99 11 (domestic flights); (291 89 13 (international flights).
Emergency Fire: (01; Police (02; Ambulance (03.

Telegraph (066.
Telephone International: (07; information: (09.
Weather (001.
Medical 85 Bolshoi Prospekt, Vasilievsky Island. (217 02 82 (adults and children). 14 Komsomola Street, (216 52 98 (adults); 6/8 Lva Tolstogo Street. (234 57 72 (adults and children); 87 Moskovsky Prospekt. (298 45 96 (adults and children); 25 Mytninskaya Street. (274 43 84 (children); 25 Liteyny Prospekt. (272 59 55 (eye injuries); 30 Bolshaya Podiachevskaya Street. (310 45 25 (bone fractures); 12 21st Line of Vasilievsky Island. (213 55 50 (dental); 34 Mayorova Prospekt. (314 25 65 (dental for children).
Car rental Sovinteravtoservis (292 12 57 or (292 17 45.
Taxi Bookings in Russian (312 00 22.
Railways General information (168 01 11; International (274 20 92; Domestic (162 33 44.
Sea Terminal 1 Morskoi Slavy Square. (355 19 02 (Intourist (355 13 30).
US Consulate 15 Petra Lavrova Street. (273 21 04.

I again remind you to keep your passport with you at all times.

WHAT TO SEE

"When everything else fails," says Murphy's Fourth Law, "read the instructions." The instructions for the newcomer to St. Petersburg are, in my opinion, quite simple: begin at the beginning. Let us then proceed to the Peter and Paul Fortress, where it all started.

PETER AND PAUL FORTRESS

At 3 Petropavlovskaya Krepost, (238 45 40, the fortress is open from 11 am to 6 pm (to 5 pm on Tuesdays). Closed Wednesdays and the last Tuesday of the month.

Originating as a fighting fort with earthen ramparts, it was supposed to protect the mouth of the Neva River from the Swedes. But they never came in force, not in the least, perhaps, because they'd been informed of its might. Like the Czar Cannon in Moscow, the fortress exemplifies an early attempt to implement the doctrine of

Mutual Assured Destruction; as it were, except for a couple of tentative tries by the Swedes in the 1700's, no one dared (or bothered) to attack the place from the day of its foundation.

But some use had to be found for it, and it became — what would you expect? — a political prison. In 1718, Peter the Great's son was imprisoned in one of the bastions, and eventually died there. He became the first in a 150 year-long line of political conspirators to see the cells of the fortress from the inside: Alexander Radischev,

members of Kerensky's ill-fated Provisional Government ....

There is a special atmosphere to the place. If you are not in a hurry, go to the **Mint**, founded in Peter's time. It is a place of interplanetary fame: the pendants which Soviet spaceships delivered to the Moon, Venus and Mars were manufactured here.

Another place in the fortress that you can't miss (because its the tallest building in Petersburg — 122 m or 400 ft) is the **Peter and Paul Cathedral**, built by one of the town's earliest architects, Domenico

author of *Voyage from Petersburg to Russia*, an anti-serfdom pamphlet which earned him the fame of Russia's first dissident; a thousand or so of the ill-fated Decembrists; Petrashevsky (Dostoyevsky's spiritual mentor) and the renowned author of *The Idiot* himself; Nikolai Chernyshevsky, the radical revolutionary democrat; Bakunin and Kropotkin, the famous anarchists; assorted terrorists from organizations such as "People's Will," who declared open season on czars and high-placed state officials in the second half of the nineteenth century (Lenin's brother Alexander was one of them); representatives of "proletarian" revolutionary groups; Maxim Gorky, the founder of socialist realism;

Trezzini. Trezzini was a master of early Baroque, but he obviously was not acquainted with Benjamin Franklin, who could have told him that a building of such height could not possibly last long without a lightning rod. Nor did it: the spire was repeatedly hit by lightning, until a particularly nasty bolt set it ablaze in 1756.

The golden angel on the top, by the way, is the fourth since Peter's time. The first, placed there in 1724 when the cathedral was still under construction, was destroyed by lightning in 1756. The second, put in place two decades later, was the most unfortunate of the lot: he was torn down by a hurricane after a short three years in his high post. The third lasted for 79 years, but was substituted in 1856 when the spire was renovated. The one you see up there today is made of gold-plated beaten copper, and turns in the wind despite his two meter (seven-foot) height. When the statue was taken down for restoration in November, 1991, it was displayed in the fortress, attracting thousands who wanted to see the "fallen angel."

The cathedral contains the remains of all Russian czars starting with Peter himself.

NEVSKY

Banks, shops, hotels, cafes, a flea market, street bands, beggars, tourists, gypsies, prostitutes, soldiers, Soviet yuppies, and artists with their paintings add up to a kaleidoscope of colors, sounds and smells that form the unique character of the place. It is, in the words of Somerset Maugham, "dingy and sordid and dilapidated." Yet every house in it is a treasure; every palace, a legend; every statue, a masterpiece.

Leningrad's main street is nearly five kilometers (three miles) long. It starts by the Admiralty on the Neva and ends near the Alexander Nevsky Monastery, from which it derives its name.

The **Admiralty** started out as a fortified shipyard. What you see today was built by Andreyan Zakharov early in the last century. The golden sail ship atop the spire may be familiar — it is generally regarded as the symbol of the city. The best view of the Admiralty is from the city side. You cannot see it from the river anymore, because the view is blocked by profit houses erected there in the second half of the nineteenth century (the permit must have cost someone a fortune in bribes). If you walk along Nevsky away from the river, look at **N° 13/8**. Piotr Tchaikovsky died here of cholera after drinking unboiled water. Take heed!

Five minutes away, there's **Kazanskaya Square**. The huge 96-column cathedral with a Latin cross-shaped layout there gets its name from the Kazan Icon of the Mother of God, the famous miracle-working image lavishly decorated with 1432 uncut diamonds, 1665 diamonds, and 638 rubies.

During his foreign travels in the days of his youth, Emperor Paul I visited Rome and was astonished by the beauty of St.Pe-

ter's. Early in his reign, he decided that Petersburg needed a cathedral similar to Bernini's creation. A contest was announced for the best project. Charles Cameron won, and was about to get down to the numerous details inevitably involved in such a huge undertaking, when the emperor suddenly changed his mind and commissioned another architect.

Evidently, Paul "bought" Stroganoff's idea of an out-and-out, all-Russian project (laborers, architect, decorators, materials — all would be Russian, Stroganoff said).

But Paul still wanted a colonnade. On the other hand, what Russian church can do without a belfry? Stroganoff proposed to add one, together with a residence for priests, to the cathedral. The emperor's answer was sarcastic: "Even St.Peter's in Rome does not have a belfry, so who are we to stick our necks out! As for the priests, they'll take care of themselves, don't you worry." (And they did, by the way, establishing their residence in N°25 on Nevsky).

OPPOSITE: The Peter and Paul Fortress is one of Petersburg's architectural symbols.
ABOVE: The Comedy Theater is one of the best in the country.

ANDREI VORONIKHIN

His life is an eighteenth-century success story. Born as a serf of the wealthy Stroganoff family (known for their love for art and the inventiveness of their chefs, who came up with Beef Stroganoff), he studied architecture first in Moscow (possibly, under the great Vasily Bazhenov himself), then in Petersburg, and eventually abroad (he was still in his teens when young Count Paul Stroganoff took him to France as his "personal painter").

He became a free man in 1786. But the favors of his former master did not stop there: the old count went out of his way to procure lucrative orders for the young architect. In 1797, he became a member of the Academy of Arts, despite sneers from aristocrat snobs, who claimed that Voronikhin was "a born shoemaker."

I don't know how good a shoemaker he would have made, but the spectacular creation now standing in Nevsky highlights, for me, Voronikhin's unique gift — that of blending his buildings into a townscape, tying them in with their surroundings with such incredible skill as to attain the illusion of what is known in the art as "concentration of space."

Unfortunately, the southern colonnades were never built: Voronikhin, called a "master greater than his glory" by twentieth-century architect L.Ilyin, died in 1814.

Paul's aversion for the clergy and the church in general was shared by the twentieth-century city fathers, who added the insult of establishing a museum of atheism in the Kazan Cathedral to the injury of

OPPOSITE: For many foreigners, a trip to the Russian Museum is their first opportunity to discover Russian painting and sculpture of the eighteenth and nineteenth centuries, which is almost unheard-of in the West.

stopping religious service there. In November 1991, Mayor Sobchak gave the cathedral back to the Orthodox Church.

The two statues in front of the cathedral honor the commanders of the Russian armies in the 1812 war, de Tholly and Kutuzov (who is buried inside the church).

The **House of Books** (N°28) is across the street, . The building was commissioned by the Singer Sewing Machine Co. in 1902. On the second floor of the shop, there's a section where you can find interesting St Petersburg postcards plus, of course, assorted items for your Lenin collection (I hope I've convinced you to start one back in Moscow).

I won't bother you with minute descriptions of the houses in Nevsky (although some of them are worth it. See the *Benn Blue Guide* for painstaking detail). Rather, I would like you to take in what Somerset Maugham described so well at the turn of the century:

"Petrograd. Towards evening it can be very beautiful. The canals have a character all their own, and though you may be reminded of Venice or Amsterdam, it is only to mark the difference. The colors are pale and soft. They have the quality of a pastel, but there is a tenderness in them that painting can seldom reach; you find the dreamy blues, the dying rose, of a sketch by Quentin de Latour, greens and yellows like those in the heart of a rose. They give the same emotion as that which the sensitive soul obtains from the melancholy gaiety of the French music of the eighteenth century."

The **Square of Arts** (up ahead on the left) is a case in point. The strategically placed statue of Pushkin (by Anikushin) seems to pull the surrounding buildings together. Behind Pushkin, there's the Russian Museum.

Nevsky ends at the gates of **Alexander Nevsky Monastery**. It was founded by Peter the Great in 1713 on what he erroneously believed to have been the site of Prince Nevsky's famous rout of the Swedes. By the end of the century, the monastery was elevated to the rank of "lavra" (senior monastery).

Apart from having another of Trezzini's churches (to the left of the entrance), the place is famous for its necropolis. Its occupants include national heroes and top aristocrats:

Generalissimo Alexander Suvorov ("Here lies Suvorov" says the epitaph); Ivan Martos, the sculptor of Red Square fame; the great builders of St. Petersburg — Starov, Voronikhin, Quarenghi, Zakharov, de Thomon, Rossi; writers Karamzin and Dostoyevsky; sculptor Piotr Clodt (nearly every statue of a horse you saw in both capitals is his work); Petipa the choreographer and many other people who influenced the nation's history.

As in any necropolis, you find amusing epitaphs. The best ones here are in the merchants' sector. "Here lies, my goodly children," says one, "your mother who has left for your remembrance her last will: live in friendliness … and don't forget that her name was indeed Irina, that she was in marriage bound to Petersburg merchant Vasily Krapivin for 19 years, and lived for 44 years, 10 months, and 16 days; and to my and your immeasurable sorrow parted from your company, leaving you in peace and with her blessings." There are also the three wives of the good Colonel della Scari, who, as the inscriptions on the tombstones testify, were buried in the course of nine months (it's interesting that the Petersburg Bluebeard did not even bother to have them buried at different cemeteries).

Both sections of the necropolis are a museum (1 Ploschad Aleksandra Nevskogo. (274 25 45). The museum is open 11 am to 6 pm, except for Thursdays and the last Tuesday of the month.

PALACE SQUARE

Freedom has come to Petersburg. I realized that the last time I visited Palace Square and saw a bunch of teenagers on roller skates (an absolutely impossible sight under the communists. Compare how smoking is still prohibited in Red Square, not because they worry about your health, but because it is a "national shrine"). There was, however, a decidedly Russian twist to the city's newly won liberty: brandy was on sale by the paper cupful at a small hamburger stand near the corner of the Winter Palace …

Every time I see Palace Square, I decide to move to Petersburg. Then I remember about the climate — and resolve to stay in Moscow.

THE RUSSIAN MUSEUM
At 4 Inzhenernaya Street, (214 73 54, the museum is open from 10 am to 6 pm except on Tuesdays and December 31.

Built as the Mikhailovsky Palace by Carlo Rossi between 1819 and 1825, the mansion was turned over to the first public museum of Russian art by Czar Nicholas II (opened in 1898).

The Russian Museum (with an inventory of 260,000 items) is larger

than the Tretiakov Gallery in Moscow. In fact, while the latter is closed, you have to make a point of visiting the museum in Petersburg. Beyond the collection of icons and nineteenth-century realist art, the museum offers a glimpse of budding Russian impressionism. But for the revolution, the works of Valentin Serov and Mikhail Vrubel would have started an impressionist school that could have easily rivaled the one in France. You have only to see Serov's portrait of Ida Rubinstein, the controversial ballet dancer, to see what I mean.

Also of interest are paintings by Kuindzhi (the master of the night landscape) and Vereschagin (the battle-scene painter who drowned together with Admiral Makarov in a naval battle against the Japanese in 1905).

Even a brief acquaintance with the exposition will give you a better understanding of Russian history than a dozen guidebooks ever could. Please go there.

It is a tradition of the St. Petersburg school of architecture (if we may speak of one) to use as many statues as the construction budget (and human reason) allows. Perhaps it is a minor one, but it is a tradition nevertheless. If you remember the Admiralty as you look at the facade of Rastrelli's Winter Palace, I'm sure you'll agree with me.

Our version of the Nelson column is the 700-ton **Alexander Pillar** (put in place by the genius of Auguste Montferrand, the creator of St. Isaac's). Across from the Baroque Winter Palace is the classical **General Staff** building by Carlo Rossi. It is interesting in two ways. The first is that it opened the way to the Palace Square for the Epidemic of Renaming: after Uritsky, Dzerzhinsky's right-hand man in Petrograd, was assassinated there in 1918, the square was promptly renamed in his honor. The second is the story

about the archway with the equestrian group on top. When Rossi submitted his plans to the czar for approval, someone said that the archway would not support its own weight, let alone a heavy statue. Evil tongues leaked the word to the press, and the ensuing campaign enraged the quick-tempered Italian to such an extent that when the archway was finally completed, he climbed into Apollo's chariot and jumped up and down (he was 54 years old at the time) with the ceremonial crowd looking on.

The third side of the square is the **Guard Corps** headquarters by Alexander Briullov. The street running between that building and the Winter Palace is the former Millionnaya. **Millionnaya Street** did not escape the fate of Palace Square: it was renamed, too. And they couldn't have found a more appropriate person to name it after, either. Stepan Khalturin was a founding member of the Northern Union of Russian Workers, a terrorist group similar to the notorious People's Will. He spent the better part of 1879 building a huge bomb under the floor of the main gala hall of the Winter Palace (he transported the bomb into the palace, where he worked in the stables, piece by piece on his person). Finally, in February 1880, the charming fellow very nearly blew half of the palace apart, but his target, the czar, was not there. Khalturin did not have a long time to live, for he was hanged in Odessa for assassinating the military prosecutor there the following year. Naming the street on which the Winter Palace stands after the man who all but destroyed it was certainly an novel idea.

THE HERMITAGE

At 4-6 Dvortsovaya Naberezhnaya, (212 06 32, the Hermitage is open from 10:30 am to 6 pm (10 am to 5 pm between May 26 and September 15). Closed Mondays.

Many people come to Petersburg with the sole purpose of visiting these three buildings stretched out along the waterfront, buildings which now house the largest museum in Russia. The largest is, of course, the **Winter Palace** of the Romanovs.

Commissioned by Empress Elizabeth in 1754, the palace became Bartolomeo Rastrelli's most famous creation. When its first

ABOVE: few visitors are left unmoved by the splendor of the Winter Palace.
OPPOSITE: Rastrelli's Winter Palace is an example of how facade ornaments can liven up even the dullest proportions.

BALL IN THE WINTER PALACE

"That evening, Emperor Alexander II wore an elegant military uniform, which was a perfect fit on his tall, lithe frame. The top of his uniform was a long white tunic, which stopped just above the knee and had gold tabs; the collar, cuffs and flaps were trimmed with Siberian blue fox; the side of his chest was sprinkled with the highest orders. He also wore tight sky-blue pantaloons, which terminated with graceful shoes. The Emperor's hair was cropped short over his regular forehead of agreeable form. His perfect facial lines could have come from a medal's gold or bronze. His blue eyes acquired a special hue on his sun-tanned face, darker than his forehead, which he usually covered during his frequent travels and regular exercise outdoors. The precise contours of his face were Greek, embossed work. His face bore the expression of grand yet never stony hardness, at times softened by an easy smile.

"The Imperial family was followed by high-ranking officers of the army and the palace guard, and men of state, each of whom offered his hand to a lady companion.

"It was a cornucopia of uniforms, gold braids, epaulettes, diamond-studded order planks and insignia decorated with enamel and precious stones, which formed sources of illumination on their chests. Several officials from the highest ranks of the hierarchy wore in their collars a very honorable order, which bespoke their friendship with royalty: the Czar's portrait set in diamonds; but such orders were few in number and indeed could be counted.

"As the procession moved, it was joined by new couples: some gentleman would separate from the row of spectators, offer his hand to the lady opposite him, and the new couple would be off, shortening or quickening their pace to fall in stride with those in front. Apparently, it wasn't all that easy to walk forth, touching no more than each other's fingertips under the scrutiny of a thousand gazes, which so easily became mocking; here, as under a magnifying glass, the slightest clumsiness, the smallest uncertainty of stride, the tiniest falling out of sync, were immediately detected. Men were saved by their military bearing, but what a trial for the ladies! The majority, however, rose to the occasion, and many could be described with the words, *"Et vera incessu patuit dea."* The women floated along under feathers, flowers, and diamonds, eyes cast demurely down-

wards or wandering about with an air of perfect innocence, controlling the waves of silk and lace with easy movements of the body or a click of a heel, and fanning themselves just as nonchalantly as if they were walking alone in a park. To walk with nobleness, grace and simplicity when you're being scrutinized from all sides! Even the great actresses of the stage at times found themselves unequal to the task.

"It is a distinction of the Russian court that from time to time, the procession would be joined by, say, a young Cherkes prince with a wasp's waist and puffed-up chest in elegant and decorous

Oriental attire, some Lezga chieftain or Mongol officer whose soldiers still carried bows, quivers and shields. Hidden under the white glove of civilization, holding the hand of a countess or a princess would be a small Asiatic hand used to playing with the handle of a dagger between its nervous dark fingers. Yet no one found this surprising. Why, what can be more natural than a Mahometan prince dancing polonaise with an Orthodox high-born lady from

flooded with light as if by magic. This abrupt transition from semidarkness to the brightest light imaginable was a genuine fairy-scene. Yet in our prosaic age, the workings of every wonder must be revealed: a pyroxylin fuse ran from candle to candle, whose wickers were saturated with a flammable substance; lit in seven or eight places, the flame conquered space instantly. A similar method is used to light the giant chandeliers in St.Isaac's, where pyroxylin

St.Petersburg? Aren't they both subjects of the Emperor of All Russia?

"A myriad candles filled candelabra or lined the friezes and contours of the arcades. In their whiteness, they stood out from the overflowing standard lamps, as so many pistils from flowercups, yet glittering patches of light did not yet flicker on their ends.

"The thunder of the approaching crowd was akin to the noise of a waterfall. The Emperor appeared on the threshold, and it was like *"fiat lux."* A barely discernible flame ran from one candle to another, all of them lit up at once at the speed of lightning, and the gigantic hall was

fuses hang over the heads of believers as so many spider webs. An analogous effect is yielded with gas lights, but gas was not used in the Winter Palace. Here, there were candles of natural wax. Only Russia preserved a way of life in which bees still contributed to indoor lighting.

"The Empress, surrounded by several high-ranking persons, walked onto the podium where a horseshoe-shaped table had been set. Behind her gold-plated armchair, a huge branch of a rosy-

ABOVE: The Hermitage is famous for its interiors; Andrei Stackenschneider's Pavillion Hall is a case in point.
OPPOSITE: "Having a ball?"

white camelia was plastered against the wall as some gigantic vegetative fireworks. A dozen tall Negroes, chosen from among the most beautiful representatives of the African race, dressed as Mamaliuks in white turbans, green waistcoats with golden cuffs and wide red sharovary tied with cashmere belts and embroidered with soutache along every seam, walked up and down the podium steps, handing dishes to the waiters or taking plates from them. The movements of the Negroes, even in service, were full of elegance and confidence which are so typical of Orientals. Forsaking Desdemona, these sons of the Orient carried out their duties with a grandeur that transformed what was essentially a quite European supper into an Asian feast in the best of taste.

"Places had not been assigned, and the guests were free to choose them at their discretion. At the head of the table, there were ladies in rich dresses embroidered with gold and silver, with figures or flowers, mythological scenes or ornamental fantasies. Candelabra were interspaced with pyramids of fruit and the taller pieces of tableware on exquisitely arranged tables. From upstairs, the glittering symmetry of crystal, the porcelain, the silver and the bouquets of flowers, made a better view than from floor level. Two rows of bosoms which protruded from their lacy beds and shone with diamonds reigned along the table covers, surrendering their secrets to the unseen eye, which was also at liberty to roam the parts in dark and blond coiffures among the flowers, leaves, feathers and precious stones.

"The Emperor passed from table to table, addressing someone he wanted to single out here, sitting down for a moment to take a sip of champagne there. Such attentions are considered a great honor."

occupant, Peter III, moved there in 1762, it was not yet finished. The exterior of the palace is textbook Baroque, and is very much the same today as in Peter's time. Rastrelli's interiors, however, were not to the liking of Catherine the Great, who assumed the throne after her husband Peter III died in a palace coup, and proceeded to make changes (Jegor Velten, Jean-Baptiste Vallin de la Mothe and Antonio Rinaldi created some of the earliest interiors; later on, several others were commissioned from Giacomo Quarenghi, Auguste Montferrand and Carlo Rossi). The main staircase remains as Rastrelli planned it.

The next building is the **New Hermitage** by von Klenze (the one with the Atlantes on the facade) plus the **Hermitage Theater** (by Quarenghi).

The third stands across the narrow Winter Ditch. It is called the **Old Hermitage** (by Velten) and the **Small Hermitage** (by de la Mothe). The **arched bridge**, which spans the narrow canal and the **Neva Panorama** behind it, are certainly worthy of a brisk stroll along Khalturin Street.

Whenever I go to the Hermitage, I get lost. Charts and maps are of little help, as one is constantly distracted by the beauty of an interior here, a brilliant painting there, an so on; things are further complicated by the maintenance work which never seems to end at the museum, so that every fifth or sixth room is always closed to the public, making the original route (charted in the plans) fiendishly difficult to follow. A word of advice: if you're in the Hermitage just for a couple of hours, don't worry about getting lost. Keep walking, look out the window (you can orient yourself depending on whether you see the river to the northeast, or Palace Square to the southwest), and try to absorb as much of the atmosphere of the place as you can.

Be sure to see the **Pavilion Hall** (Room N°205 in the Small Hermitage), a breathtaking airy environment of white, gold, and crystal created by Stackenscheneider one hundred and forty years ago; von Klenze's **Hall of Twenty Columns** (Room N°130) with its famous beams; Catherine the Great's "Rules" urging visitors to "leave all ranks at the door, along with hats and swords"

A riverside view of the Winter Palace.

(Room N°258); and the **Nicholas Hall**, which is one of the largest in the palace. It was here that the great balls were held in the old days. To help you feel more at home in these exotic surroundings, I yield the floor to Theophile Gautier, whose *Voyage en Russie* was published in Paris in 1867 (see cameo on page 102).

If, on the other hand, you've time to spare, pay more attention to the exhibits. Whether you're interested in Egyptian antiques, Scythian gold, Flemish painting or the Postimpressionists, you won't be sorry. But there's no need to hurry on this type of excursion, either: as some obscure statistician has calculated, you would need sixty years to see the entire inventory of the museum if you spend 30 seconds on each item.

A word of warning: if you plan to visit the museum in high season, it is best for you to book tickets (7 roubles plus 2 roubles for photo/video) through your service bureau. You'll pay 10 percent more, but this will save you the trouble of standing in an enormous queue which runs halfway around the Winter Palace. And only Intourist can help you with tickets to the so-called **Special Storage** (Osobaya Kladovaya), where some of the most expensive exhibits are on display.

St. Isaac's Cathedral

Located at Isaakievskaya ploschad, (212 22 76, the cathedral is open from 11 am to 6 pm (to 4 pm on Tuesdays). Closed Wednesdays and every second and last Monday of the month.

You shouldn't have any trouble finding St.Isaac's: on a good day, its 101 m (334 ft) high dome can be seen from 30 km (19 miles) away. The cathedral, dedicated to the Byzantine monk from Dalmatia, whose church day was May 30, the birthday of Peter the Great, was commissioned from a French architect by the name of Auguste de Montferrand in 1818 (he was 32 years old at the time). It took, literally, a lifetime to build — the architect died in the year the cathedral was consecrated, 1858.

The cathedral is too heavy, both artistically (in my opinion) and physically: it is sinking into the weak ground of the riverbank, presenting contemporary architects with the formidable problem of trying, if not

to stop it from sinking altogether, than at least to make sure that its heavy main building goes down at the same rate as the comparatively lighter colonnades.

A study in Russian gigantism, St.Isaac's has 48 granite pillars weighing 114 tons each. Fourteen thousand can comfortably pray under its 800 sq m (7,200 sq ft) ceiling adorned with Karl Briullov's greatest work, The Virgin Mary. The czar gates of the altar weigh 5 tons.

It is a miracle that the cathedral still stands, having gone first through Stalin's

war against churches (it was made into an anti-religious museum in 1931, but fortunately did not share the fate of Moscow's Church of Christ the Savior), and then through the blockade (you can still see scars left by shell fragments on some of the columns). In 1990, the authorities allowed religious service there on major holidays; hopefully, St.Isaac's will be returned to the Orthodox Church in the next few years.

One more interesting thing about the cathedral is its observation platform (if you feel up to climbing all those steps). Note also the statue of Montferrand himself, who kneels with a replica of St.Isaac's on the left side of the west portico.

As you leave the cathedral, walk towards the river. There, on the other side of the Square of Decembrists, stands one of the symbols of Petersburg, the equestrian monument to Peter dubbed "the Bronze Horseman" by Pushkin. The statue was sculpted by Etienne Falconet and Marie Anne Collot.

VASILIEVSKY ISLAND

The island, the largest in the delta of the Neva, derives its name from its first owner, Vasily Selezen of Novgorod.

as **University Quay**). You'll be passing a former warehouse which is now the **Zoological Museum** (complete with replicas of prehistoric dinosaurs, it's Petersburg's answer to New York's Museum of Natural History), the tower-topped **Kunstkammer** (Russia's first museum and observatory), and the old building of the **Academy of Sciences**.

Peter the Great organized government administration into 12 colleges (ministries); the twelve-sectioned building on your right was where all the top bureaucrats,

Peter wanted the island to be the center of his city, but its development was hampered by an absence of permanent bridges across the Neva, and it was eventually transformed into a port area. In the eighteenth century, the merchantmen would dock at the spit of Vasilievsky Island, where the two rostral columns now guard the way to the **Exchange** (the temple-like building by de Thomon was finished in 1810). Today, the columns light up only on holidays, but in the past, they did a full-time job as lighthouses and helped navigators negotiate the tricky waters of the Neva.

If you feel up to it, and if the weather is good, take a stroll along the embankment of the Neva (this particular piece of it is known

together with the Synod (ruling church council) and the Senate, sat in the eighteenth century. In the 1820s, most of the buildings were turned over to the University of St.Petersburg, the second oldest in Russia.

At some point along the quay, not far from the former Mary Magdalene Hospital (now Vera Slutskaya Hospital), there is a plate with records of water levels during the worst floods in the town's history.

Up ahead, past the **Menshikov Palace** (N°15), there's the old **Academy of Arts**, a

The Neva panorama of St.Petersburg frequently evokes comparisons to Amsterdam.

THE FLOODS

West wind always spells trouble for Petersburg. The isle-specked, branched sea estuary of the Neva ("newa" means "marsh" or "bog" in Finnish) is nearly seven times the width of the river's continental bed. The current is slow here. So when the winds start to push the Baltic waves against the current every autumn, the Neva stops and then turns back on a city which lies a mere two to four meters (six to twelve feet) above the water level.

To remedy the situation, Peter proposed to dig a series of criss-crossed canals on Vasilievsky Island. Catherine dug a special canal, as did Alexander I. These projects, when they were realized at all, were of little help. A more recent project involves the construction of a huge dam which is purportedly capable of shielding the estuary from the onslaught of the Baltic, but, environmentalist critics claim, is between the devil and the deep sea in the sense that it threatens to turn the lower reaches of the Neva (and possibly the entire Gulf of Finland) into an enormous bog.

Meanwhile, the floods persist. A typical one was described by an eyewitness who watched the action from a window above Yeliseev's store on Nevsky in November, 1824:

"Towering waves raced across Palace Square, which formed one huge lake together with the Neva, into Nevsky, which was one wide river all the way to the Anichkov Bridge. All channels, and the Moika River, became utterly indiscernible and joined the waters covering the pavements; flotsam, stray logs, and furniture floated everywhere. A dead stillness soon fell over the streets.

"Around two o'clock, Count Miloradovich, the Military Governor General, appeared on Nevsky in a twelve-oar cutter to give aid to, and raise the spirits of, the citizens. Several small boats traversed Morskaya Street, and a large barque with several people from all walks of life, who had been fished out of the Neva, dropped anchor near Kosikovsky's mansion. Not far from Smolensk Field, on the Petersburg Side and in lower places where there had been wooden houses, the water washed everything away without a trace, leaving the streets blocked with timber, firewood and even small cottages; damaged barques lay here and there; one large steamer from the Berd Factory found itself in Kolomna near the Catholic Metropolitan's residence. All the bridges across the Neva ceased to exist except for the Samsonievsky Bridge and the one linking Kamenny Island with the Petersburg Side. The stone and iron bridges remained intact, but the granite embankment incurred a lot of damage, with many blocks dislodged or overturned. In the third hour of the afternoon, the waters started to recede, and at seven people were already going about in carriages."

rather famous place if the memorial plaques on the facade are anything to go by. Before you read them, however, take time out to admire the **sphinxes** on Konstantin Thon's granite quay. The figures date to approximately 1450 B.C. — a souvenir from the times of Pharaoh Amenhotep IV of Egypt.

It is next to impossible to lose your way on Vasilievsky. Its streets (called Lines) are numbered; the avenues run from north to south at a normal angle to the streets.

So if you leave the quay along, say, Line 7 (with the **Academics' House** at the corner), and walk right along the first avenue (**Bolshoi Prospekt**) that comes your way, you'll eventually find yourself back on the **Spit**. Once you get there, take a look at the late **Classical Customs House** (4 Makarov Quay) to the right of the Exchange. Today, the place belongs to "Pushkin House," the popular name of the Institute of Russian Literature. This is where TV announcers used to get their training (Petersburg Russian is the standard for the entire country, much as Oxford English is for the English-speaking world). There is also a **Literary Museum** here. The museum is open between 11 am and 6 pm, except Mondays and Tuesdays.

SMOLNY

Its five domes can be seen in fine weather from Vasilievsky Island. The name comes from the Russian word *smola* ("tar"): it was here that tar was made for the shipyards in Peter's time.

Another famous place in the area is the **Smolny Institute for Daughters of the Nobility,** the first school for girls founded by Catherine the Great in 1764. Its troubles started in 1917, when the schoolgirls were chased out by Leon Trotsky's Petrograd Soviet of Workers' and Soldiers' Deputies. From here, Lenin orchestrated the events of October 24/25. It was in the Smolny that Sergei Kirov was assassinated. When the Communist Party was outlawed in the autumn of 1991, Mayor Sobchak announced plans to take the building over for his office.

The church, which is part of the **New Convent of the Resurrection of the Virgin**, was commissioned by Empress Elizabeth in 1748. It was to become Rastrelli's greatest masterpiece, very probably because Rastrelli did not get the chance to complete the project himself. Instead, his runaway Baroque fantasies were curbed by the down-to-earth Stasov, who finished the building almost a century later.

The most ambitious part of Rastrelli's project, a 140-m (459-ft) -high tiered belfry over the main entrance, was shelved (owing to lack of funding and the fact that it would have been most unwelcome as the highest structure in the city).

THE ENVIRONS

PETRODVORETS

It lies on the Peterhof Highway 29 km (18 miles) to the west of Petersburg. Take a suburban train from the **Baltic Station** to **Novy Petergof Station**, and a bus (N°350, N°351, N°352 or N°356) to the palace. In summer, go by hydrofoil from the Winter Palace.

ABOVE: Konstantin Thon's elegant quay is a good place to think about the sphinx.
OVERLEAF: The fountains of Petrodvorets: a dream restored (the palace was totally ruined by the Germans in World War II).

In point of fact, it is a miracle that there is anything to see in Peterhof at all. During the last war, the Germans burned down most of it, stole whatever survived the fire, and blew up what they could not steal. It took architects Savkov and Kazanskaya three years to prepare a master restoration plan. As it were, for all the money and efforts expended by thousands of people in restoring the interiors of the palace and the

museum collection, this task is not yet finished.

A word of warning: if you plan to spend most of your day at Peterhof, bring some food! There's only one decent cafe in the area of the palace (in Sovietskaya Street), but it is much too small for everybody, and it is difficult to make reservations. As for the rotund cafe in the park itself, it did not look safe to me the last time I went there in the summer of 1992.

The museum is open 11 am to 6 pm except for Mondays and the last Tuesday of the month. (257 44 25 or 257 95 27. It is a trip you have to take if you are there in summer. To save yourself a lot of time standing in at least three lines (for hydrofoil tickets, tickets to the Grand Palace, and return hydrofoil tickets), consult your service bureau.

Petrodvorets (meaning "Peter's palace") was born out of military necessity. Before it became a kind of eighteenth-century Disneyland, it served as Peter's operational base during construction on Kotlin Island (**Kronshtadt**, the fortress guarding the approaches to Petersburg, can be seen on a fair day some ten miles away to the northeast). With two major naval victories and a trip to Versailles (1717) behind him, Peter decided to make Peterhof a permanent summer residence, complete with the two parks, the fountains, the Monplaisir, and the Grand Palace (by Le Blond, completed in 1721). The **Grand Palace** you see today, however, was commissioned by Empress Elizabeth (Rastrelli added the third storey, the wings, and the Baroque cupolas).

PAVLOVSK

To get there, take a train from **Vitebsk Station**, and walk through the park to the palace (1.5 km or roughly one mile). I would highly recommend that you hire a private car with a guide from Intourist for this trip (talk to the service bureau at your hotel).

Fountains are fun!

Open 10:30 am to 5:30 pm except on Fridays and the first Monday of the month. (290 21 56.

Named after the unloved son and heir of Catherine the Great, Pavlovsk is the place where Pavel spent several years as Grand Duke. The palace was built by Charles Cameron (between 1782 and 1786), Catherine's favorite architect (it was rebuilt by Voronikhin early in the nineteenth century). Since Pavel hated both his mother and everything she stood for (he was an advocate of everything Prussian), he moved away from what he regarded as Cameron's rather frivolous creation, leaving behind his wife, Maria, and their son, the future conqueror of Europe Alexander I.

Pavlovsk suffered the same fate as Pushkin and Peterhof — it was occupied and looted by the Germans during the last

war. Today it is fully restored, and I hope that you'll enjoy the fine rooms on the first floor of the palace, and, of course, the huge park with its statues, temples, pavilions, ponds, bridges and even a column known as World's End. Another famous place in the park is **Stackenschneider's Vauxhall**, where Johann Strauss appeared with his orchestra several times, and where his less famous colleagues still perform today.

Pushkin

It lies 27 km (18 miles) to the south on Pulkovskoye Highway, just before Pavlovsk. You can take the train from **Vitebsk Station** to **Detskoye Selo**, and then a bus (N°371, N°382) to the palace. Open 10 am to 6 pm except for Tuesdays and the last Monday of the month. (290 76 88.

The place owes its origins to Elizabeth and Catherine II.

The **Grand Palace**, named after Catherine, the second wife of Peter the Great, was rebuilt in its final form by Bartolomeo Rastrelli (1756). In 1941, the Germans used it as a barracks, and little of it survived after they left. Restoration continues to this day, although some of the treasures from the palace, for instance, Rastrelli's Persian Amber Room (complete with the collection of amber Peter the Great bought in Prussia), disappeared without a trace.

The town was named after Alexander Pushkin, who went to school here at the prestigious **Tsarskoselskiy Lycee**. It is a major tourist attraction, although I wouldn't call the palace an architectural success. Where Smolny Cathedral illustrates all the

WHAT LITERATURE MEANS
TO RUSSIA

If we look at literature as a pastime, it has seen little competition from other intellectual diversions in a country where tape recorders are still a luxury, VCR's are so few and far between that they constitute the dream prize of every burglar, television is a bore, theaters are either too expensive or too far away, and the motion-picture industry keeps stepping on its own tail.

views, a philosophy which existed outside the official ideology, a kind word for the downtrodden and the oppressed of this world. In Russia, it has never been sufficient to merely hold the imagination of your reader with a deft plot or a fortunate metaphor; to measure up, you had to use whatever it is you were describing to make a U-turn to present-day reality; in short, you had to be a moralist.

Is it surprising, then, that whole outdoor stadiums fill up with poetry

But there's more to it than that. Of the two aspects of belles lettres — amusement and education — our literature invariably emphasized the latter. Where does one find truth if it is officially banned? Where does one find religion if it is persecuted? Why, in literature, of course. Even with censorship, Russian poets, writers and playwrights invariably managed to get across a system of

lovers? That "thick" literary journals sell millions of copies? That bon mots and even entire phrases from the better-known works become proverbs?

"Russia cannot be measured with the mind," wrote Fyodor Tiutchev, one of our master poets of the nineteenth century. Perhaps it can be understood through its literature.

best in Baroque, the palace in Pushkin shows how garish and gaudy Baroque can get when the architect oversteps the hairthin line of good taste. Still, the park and the ponds are wonderful, as is the town around the palace grounds.

WHERE TO STAY

Much of what I wrote about Moscow applies to Petersburg. There still aren't enough quality hotels there, although there

If you are intrigued, then you have come to the right place, because no other city in Russia could ever hope to contest Petersburg's literary laurels.

The museum in Pushkin House displays personal effects, manuscripts, and first editions of works by Leo Tolstoy, Ivan Turgenev, Nikolai Gogol, Mikhail Lermontov, Ivan Goncharov and Alexander Blok.

It may be also interesting for you to see the Dostoyevsky Museum (5 Kuznechny Pereulok. (212 50 49. Open 10:30 am to 6:30 pm except for Mondays and last Wednesday of the month).

If you have the time, you could ask about an excursion "Literary Petersburg" at your service bureau.

are more joint ventures than in Moscow, which means that there's a greater chance of finding yourself in the hotel you wanted to stay at from the start. In the last fifteen years, Intourist built several large hotels, which are fairly decent. The bad news about most of

them is that they are cut off from the mainland, which can be quite a problem in a city where bridges are raised every night. Be careful with traveling plans!

Following is a list of St. Petersburg hotels, starting with the most expensive. Please understand that prices may change — consult your travel agent.

EXPENSIVE

Astoria 39 Ulitsa Gertsena. (219 11 00; 210 58 66. The famous hotel has been enlarged

(it now incorporates the **Angleterre**) to accommodate 800. Hard currency only. Excellent location (near St.Isaac's). Single rooms start at $200-250, doubles at $400.

Okhta 4 Bolsheokhtinsky Prospekt. (227 44 38. The newest Intourist hotel in town. Single rooms start at $90.

Grand Hotel Europe 1/7 Ulitsa Mikhailova. (312 00 72. Reopened in December, 1991, it is the only five-star hotel in Russia. Most of the interiors of this pre-revolutionary hotel are protected by the state as a cultural heritage. Bookings through

OPPOSITE: The Saltykov-Schedrin Library. With characteristic wit, the great satirist named his study after Dr. Faustus. ABOVE: Dining room in one of Petersburg's newer hotels, The Peterburg.

Sweden's RESO Hotels (telex Sweden 14511). Good midtown location. Single rooms start at $240.

Peterburg 5/2 Vyborgskaya Naberezhnaya. (542 90 31; 542 91 23. Get a view of the *Aurora*, the cruiser that started the revolution. Seriously, the hotel is not bad for an Intourist operation. Transportation may be a problem, but taxi drivers are more cooperative in St. Petersburg than in Moscow. Single rooms start at $100.

Moskva 2 Ploschad Aleksandra Nevskogo. (274 20 51. Located near the Alexander Nevsky Monastery on the far end of Nevsky, it is a typical large "Intouristy" place. Single rooms start at $100.

Pribaltiiskaya 14 Ulitsa Korablestroitelei. (356 51 12; 355 04 02. A very large Intourist hotel on the Gulf of Finland. Apart from its location, it is commendable in terms of service, and has better-than-average restaurants. There's also a bowling alley. Single rooms start at $120.

Pulkovskaya 1 ploschad Pobedy. (264 51 00; 264 51 22; 264 51 45. Another big Intourist hotel. What it loses in location, it gains in novelty. Several restaurants and cafes. Single rooms start at $120.

Karelia 27/2 Ulitsa Tukhachevskogo. (226 57 01.

A pleasant enough Intourist hotel except for its location. Offers the standard set of Intourist services. Single rooms start at $100.

Olgino 5 Primorskoye Shosse. (238 35 51; 238 34 84. Situated 18 km (11 miles) from the city, Olgino is an Intourist-run motel. Run-down but relatively inexpensive. There are bungalows, camping facilities, and a bus service to midtown Petersburg (30 minutes away). Single rooms start at $60.

MEDIUM RANGE

Baltiiskaya 57 Nevsky Prospekt. (277 77 31; 314 45 84.

Vyborgskaya 37 Torzhkovskaya Ulitsa. (246 23 19; 246 91 41.

Gavan 88 Sredny Prospekt (Vasilievsky Island). (358 85 04.

Druzhba 4 Ulitsa Chapygina. (234 18 44.

Rossiya 11 Ploschad Chernyshevskogo. (296 76 49.

WHERE TO EAT

Everything from the Moscow section applies here, as well.

Most of the restaurants on the list offer traditional Russian cuisine. Following is a list of restaurants I would accept personal responsibility for.

Neva (Russian) 46 Nevsky Prospekt. (311 36 78. Snappy service, especially if you slip the waiter a five-dollar bill.

Troika (Russian) 27 Zagorodny Prospekt. (113 53 43. The place has the best floor show in town, which is probably why it stays open until 1 am. An average meal here will set you back by $50.

Literaturnoye Kafe (Russian) 18 Nevsky Prospekt. (312 71 37; 312 85 36. A great idea for lunch. Reservations essential. Very cheap, given the exchange rate of the rouble. Nicely decorated, with a classical-music room.

Metropol (European) 22 Sadovaya Ulitsa. (310 22 81. Saying that it's the oldest restaurant in Petersburg isn't saying much in this case. A good idea for lunch.

Kavkazsky (Transcaucasian) 25 Nevsky Prospekt. (311 45 26. A nice place if you like it hot and spicy.

Schwabsky Domik 28 Krasnogvardeisky Prospekt. (528 22 11. Hard currency only. Best beer in town. Open until 1 am.

Fortezzia Ulitsa Kuibysheva. (233 94 68. Good European food. You can pay in roubles, but they cheerfully accept hard currency, something you can resort to if they tell you the place is full.

Chaika (German) 14 Kanal Griboyedova. (312 21 20. The first hard-currency, privately-owned pub/restaurant in Petersburg. No credit cards. You pay on leaving when you present a card (which you are issued as you come in), into which a hole is punched every time you order. Phew!

Gino Ginelli 14 Kanal Griboyedova. An expensive ice cream place (several flavors).

Belye Nochi 41 Prospekt Mayorova. (319 96 60. If you don't mind seeing the local Mafia living it up, try this place for the food. You can dance, too (the music is too loud for talking anyway).

Na Fontanke (Russian) 77 Naberezhnaya Fontanki. (311 45 26; 310 25 47. A co-op. Small but pleasant. Reservations essential.
Tbilisi (Georgian) 10 Sytninskaya Ulitsa. (232 93 91. Another small co-op. Good service — and wonderful food when the manager's been lucky enough to find something to cook.
Zhemchuzhina (Azerbaidzhani) 2 Shki-persky Protok (Vasilievsky Island). (355 20 63. Drop by while touring Vasilievsky Island (if you like spicy food, that is).
Demianova Ukha (Seafood) 53 Prospekt Gorkogo. (232 80 90. Probably the only place where you will get fish — guaranteed. Inexpensive, too.

Every major hotel has at least one passable restaurant, usually with a floor show and a band. **Pribaltiiskaya** is famous for its restaurant. The joint-venture hotels naturally have the best (and most expensive) restaurants in town. All reservations should be made through your service bureau.

HOW TO GET THERE

Whether you are coming to Petersburg by air, sea, or land, remember that a visa is required if the city is not your first destination in Russia. In short, if you decide to come on the spur of the moment, make the necessary arrangements through Intourist first.

You'll be most probably arriving in Petersburg by train from Moscow. Most Intourist trains leave at around midnight, and pull into Moskovsky Station between 7 and 8 am. They are comfortable (sleeping compartments for two).

If you go by air, you'll be arriving at **Pulkovo Airport**. If you're not part of a group, book a transfer, and present the voucher to the Intourist representative at the airport. You may wind up paying a bit more than a taxi would cost, but at least you'll be safe. The airport for domestic flights (in case you're meeting someone) is **Pulkovo One**.

The **Passenger Port**, which is the sea gate to Petersburg, is conveniently located in **Morskoi Slavy Square**. The only way out of there, for the last year or so, has been by taxi: public transport does not stop there owing to roadwork.

It was about to turn green when the frost hit: capricious climate makes Petersburg a difficult place — even for traffic lights.

Kiev

"WHAT!" I can almost hear the nationalists scream, "Kiev in a guide about Russia! Is he out of his *moskal* mind?" (There are two things you should know about the word *moskal*: it means a non-Ukrainian from Moscow, and it is as racist as "spic" or "kike").

Yes. Kiev in a guide about Russia. The reasons are all too obvious: Kiev was the cradle of Slavonic statehood; Kiev was the gateway of Christianity into Ancient Russia; Kiev was a large city before there were either Russians or Ukrainians; Kiev was the geographical, as well as political, center of old Russia; last but not least, Nestor the Chronicler wrote that Kiev was the beginning of Russia.

Who am I to argue with Nestor?

BACKGROUND

"Whence did the Russian Land take its origins?" asked Nestor, the first known Chronicler, in his *Tales of Bygone Years.* "There were three brothers. One was named Kiy, the second Schek and the third Khoriv; Lybed was their sister. Kiy ruled on the hill which is now called Borichev, and Schek sat on a hill which is now called Shchekavitsa, and Khoriv on a third, which was after him called Khorevitsa. And they founded a city and called it by the name of Kiev in the name of their eldest brother, Kiy. They were brave people who called themselves Polyanians. Their descendants still live in Kiev."

Actually, the Polyanians (which means "dwellers of forest clearings"), as well as the Drevlianians ("forest dwellers") whom Nestor forgot to mention, were not the first occupants of the ancient city. Its history, archaeologists say, goes back to the fifth century AD. Kiy wasn't a Slav, either — as some Chronicles attest, he was probably Rurik's son or nephew.

In 882, Prince Oleg of Novgorod and his warriors were making their way down the Dnieper "from the Varangians to the Greeks". As Kiev appeared before Oleg's astonished eyes, he was so taken in by its majesty that he exclaimed, "This shall be the mother of Russian towns!" Which was, admittedly, not bad as prophecies go. A half-century later, Kiev was firmly established as the capital of Kievan Rus, the powerful Slav realm stretching from the Black Sea to Lake Ladoga in the north, and from the Volga in the east to the Western Bug in the west. It was compared to Constantinople and Rome.

Kiev owes much to Prince Vladimir "the Red Sun" (whose name you have already come across on these pages). The place where he baptized his subjects was a small stream in 988; today, it flows below one of the city's streets.

Kiev flourished and soon became one of the largest capitals in the known world. It easily equaled Novgorod as a center of arts and crafts: in eleventh-century Kiev, they tanned leather, made shoes, weapons and jewelry; they manufactured clothes and painted icons. Military expeditions sailed down the Dnieper into the Black Sea in the south. Kievan merchants developed extensive trade ties and diplomatic relations with their mighty neighbor to the south.

Word of the wondrous Slav capital traveled far and wide. Unfortunately, fame, as many other things in Russian history, proved to be a double-edged thing: as soon as the Mongols got a whiff of Kiev's new-found prosperity and wealth, they attacked.

Wrote Plano Carpini, the Pope's Emissary: "This city... is nearly razed to the ground. You can hardly find two hundred houses here." This was six years after the Mongol invasion of 1240.

Approximately at this time, the Slav tribes which had started to acquire the makings of a nation owing to centralized rule and Christianity, first started to drift apart because of feudal fragmentation and constant pressure from the Horde. Three hundred years later, their dialects and cultures were different enough to warrant mention in Czar Ivan the Terrible's title "Grand Prince and Czar of *the Great, the Little, and the White, Russia*". Today, in the twentieth century, these names are still understandable, but almost never used with the exception of Byelorussians (*byely* means "white"): "Great" Russians are

Exquisite dome of the cathedral in Pechersk Monastery.

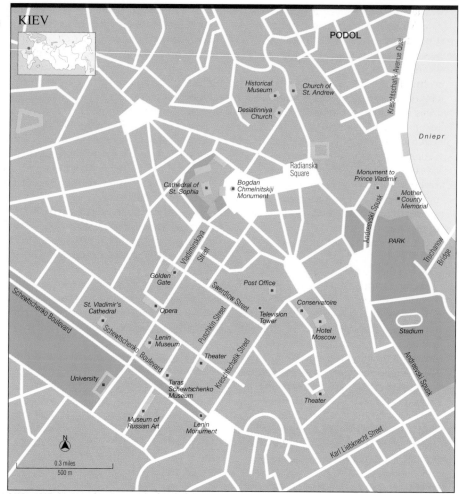

KIEV

PODOL

Krasctschatik Avenue Quai

Historical Museum

Church of St. Andrew

Desiatinniya Church

Dniepr

Radianska Square

Cathedral of St. Sophia

Bogdan Chmelnitskiji Monument

Monument to Prince Vladimir

Mother County Memorial

Andrejewski Spusk

PARK

Truchanow Bridge

Vladimirskaya Street

Golden Gate

Swerdlow Street

Post Office

Conservatoire

St. Vladimir's Cathedral

Opera

Television Tower

Hotel Moscow

Stadium

Schewtschenko Boulevard

Lenin Museum

Puschkin Street

Theater

Kreschtschatik Street

University

Taras Schewtschenko Museum

Theater

Andrejewski Spusk

Museum of Russian Art

Lenin Monument

Karl Liebknecht Street

N

0.3 miles
500 m

called Russians, and "Little" Russians are called Ukrainians.

Kiev was on its way to becoming the capital of the Ukraine, meaning "the Edge". In the next two centuries, it was occupied by the Lithuanians, the Mongols, and the Lithuanians again. In the fifteenth century, the town was granted the Magdeburg Right, which envisaged public administration of the city. Trade picked up again. There were communities of Muscovite, Polish, Turkish, Greek, Armenian, and even Genovese, merchants.

The Liublin Union Treaty of 1569 gave most of the Ukraine, Kiev included, to the Poles. The population was catholicized, at times forcibly. Yet the Slav culture was too deep-seated to go without a fight. In 1648, a revolt of the Zaporozhye Cossacks

sparked off a six-year war for national liberation, which ended with the *Pereyaslav Rada* (Russian — Ukrainian council).

The Rada was coaxed by Bogdan Khmelnitsky, the military leader of the Ukrainian forces, into a reunion with Russia. The decision was to go down in history as one of the greatest cases of political shortsightedness. While the Poles cried "Stop, thief!" and branded Khmelnitsky (who was a Pole himself) a traitor, there was nothing they could do against Russia. Yet who could have thought that the Ukrainian nationalists (the third — and weakest — party to that conflict) would keep it smoldering for nearly 340 years? The Ukrainians, as it turned out in 1991 when they were finally asked about it in a referendum, did not want to be part of any empire — Polish, Lithuanian,

Russian, or Soviet. As a presidential candidate, Mr.Kravchuk promised his voters independence — and won by an Ukrainian version of a landslide.

The second half of the seventeenth century ushered in the golden age of architecture. Made into a near-impenetrable fortress by Peter the Great, Kiev became the birthplace of the Ukrainian baroque, an architectural style that only peace and security could produce. First came the heavy monumental souvenirs of patriotic euphoria, such as the Klov Palace. By the middle of the eighteenth century, Pechersk became a huge *lavra* ("foremost monastery" in the Orthodox tradition), and St. Sophia was fully restored. Then came Bartholomeo Rastrelli's time. He did not build much in Kiev, but the Church of St. Andrew is quite in keeping with his style, familiar if you've been to Petersburg. The city continued to grow, especially after the Contract Fair was moved there from Dubno. After the disintegration of Poland and the division of its territories between its European neighbors, Kiev — together with what was described as "right-bank Ukraine" — became a part of Russia once again.

The twentieth century has not been kind to Kiy's city. First came the "class struggles" of 1905 and 1912, followed by a Bolshevik coup in October, 1917 (abortive), and another coup in January, 1918 (successful this time because of Red Army support).

Then came the Civil War of 1918–1920, and the war with Hitler. Kiev was bombed on the very first day of the war, June 22, 1941. Not two months after the blitzkrieg started, Kiev became the site of one of the greatest battles in history, which ended, alas, with a stunning defeat of Red Army forces. The damage caused in the years of German occupation made the Mongols look like upstart amateurs; suffice it to mention that 800 of the 1176 industrial enterprises within the city limits were razed to the ground. The Germans also blew up the Assumption Cathedral in Pechersk and set the university on fire for good measure.

But that was not all the twentieth century held in store. The Chernobyl disaster came in May, 1987. Amid the panic that ensued (it was made worse by the clumsy attempt to hush things up), people couldn't help wondering if there remained any kind of future for Kiev at all. Which was understandable: even the most destructive invaders come and go, but the effects of radiation remain for hundreds of years.

But it seems that St. Andrew the First-Called, whose church proudly graces the Kiev skyline, intervened. Kiev did not become a ghost town in the middle of a nuclear desert. Independent experts say that the city is quite safe for tourists, at any rate.

Terrible as the subject of Chernobyl is, it is characteristic of the Ukrainians to laugh through the worst moments (and with a history such as theirs, who can blame them?). One of the first Chernobyl jokes to get around had to do with the rather touchy subject of irregular sexual practices. "There are *three* kinds of homosexuals in Kiev now," it ran, "passive, active and radioactive."

GENERAL INFORMATION

You can find the Intourist/Inturburo representative at 5 Druzhby Narodiv Boulevard. (268 34 06; 268 90 96. Other Intourist offices are at Borispol Airport and all major hotels.

SPECIFIC TRAVEL INQUIRIES:

Aeroflot Peremogy Square (274 51 52.
International telephone (071 072 (074 from hotels).
Taxi Bookings in Ukrainian (058; 082.
Railways General information (223 30 53, Vokzalnaya Square.
Boat Terminal Pochtovaya Square (416 12 68.
Borispol Airport (295 67 01 (information)
City terminal, 4 Karl Marx Street (229 3841.

EMERGENCIES

Fire (01.
Police (02.
Ambulance (03.

MONEY

The Ukraine has recently introduced a national currency of its own, the *grivna*. Until the currency is released into circulation, however, there is a system whereby the republic makes use of the old Soviet rouble and the new *kuponi* (coupons). You can get both in exchange for hard currency. Coupons are valid for all types of transactions; roubles are good only for restaurants, cafes and the like. Be sure to consult your Intourist bureau at the hotel before you exchange money.

PASSPORT

I again remind you to keep your passport with you at all times.

WHAT TO SEE

To make it easier for you to find your way across Kiev's nearly 800 sq km (288 sq miles) of territory, I suggest that you travel across time rather than space.

UPPER TOWN

The year was 1037. Prince Yaroslav, called the Wise by his subjects largely for his acumen in handling the unruly bands of war-mongering Pecheneg nomads, who attacked Kiev with metronomic regularity (and whom his troops defeated the year before), decided that it was time to found what he somewhat immodestly referred to as "a great city". Yaroslav, whose lifelong ambition was to attain parity with his arch-rival, Byzantium, did not want to start small.

Nor did he: the **Cathedral of St. Sophia** cannot be called small even by twentieth-century standards. Its cross-domed nineteen-cupola construction covers an impressive 55 by 42 m (178 by 138 ft) rectangle of what has proved to be arguably the most significant piece of land in Russian history.

I won't bore you with the details of its rather intricate architecture. If you've been to Novgorod, I'm sure you'll agree with me

that the St. Sophia there compares to the one in Kiev as a merchant's daughter would to a princess. St. Sophia dazzles with integrity of light, color and form; its effect on anyone living in the eleventh century must have been on the fine side of traumatic.

Yaroslav chose to build a cathedral instead of a palace, and for a century or two St. Sophia was a kind of medieval public relations center: it had a library (the first ever in Russia, and the librarians wrote chronicles); a seminary and, of course, the Metropolitan's residence. It is, however, strange

for the Orthodox See to double as a reception grounds for foreign ambassadors, most of whom were not Christians, and as a coronation hall for Kievan princes — an example of propriety bowing before necessity. Ironically, the last addition to its many functions had been that of its creator's tomb: you can see Yaroslav's sarcophagus of carved marble in a side altar, and a portrait of Yaroslav and his family in the central nave.

The other buildings and the walls date to the eighteenth century. On the grounds, you'll see architectural models of old Russian towns; there's also an archaeological section. The cathedral grounds is now a **museum**, open 10 am to 5 pm except on Thursdays. To get there from Bogdan

Khmelnitsky Square (where the equestrian statue of the famed Ukrainian liberator-turned-traitor, Polish turncoat, and Russia's friend points in the direction of Moscow), walk through the gate at the foot of the tiered 80-m (262 ft) tall **bell-tower** nearby (it's so tall you can't miss it).

Near the entrance to the museum in Vladimirskaya Street is what's left of the tenth-century **Desiatinnaya Church**, destroyed by the Mongols in 1240. If you look closely, you'll see its outline on the ground marked in quartzite.

As you leave the St. Sophia, walk along **Streletsky Street**, and then up **Polupanov Street** to **Yaroslav Val** (rampart) and the **Golden Gate**.

Ever wary of the Pechenegs, Yaroslav surrounded his Upper Town by earthen ramparts, which gave him a fortress without an entrance.

Hence the Golden Gate, which was also founded in 1037 and served the dual purpose of frightening the foe and impressing the friend. Even though the Golden Gate failed as a deterrent (the Mongols apparently did not find it sufficiently awe-inspiring), it certainly kept friendly minds impressed enough to become, over the years, the stuff of chronicles, songs, and even legends. The folk tales described Yaroslav's second creation as "the gate to heaven", through which the sun would pass every morning to enter "the city in the sky": Kiev's guarantee against darkness and doom. (The Golden Gate was fully restored in 1982 and enclosed in the pavilion which also displays a collection of weapons.)

Rastrelli's **Church of St. Andrew** stands on Old Kiev Hill. Built in five years (construction started in 1749), the church is vintage Rastrelli: airy, graceful and surprisingly light for its bulk (it is 60 m, or 200 ft, high). The interior is Rococo (garish in my opinion, but tastes differ). The terrace of the church is a good spot for picture taking — you can see the parks along the Dnieper from there.

It is from the St. Andrew's that **Andreevski Spusk** (descent) starts. A cross between Moscow's Arbat and Paris's Montmartre, the street is a pedestrian-only zone usually overflowing with tourists, street vendors, and artists. Mikhail Bulgakov, one of the foremost writers of our time, spent a good part of his life living on this street (N°13). At the spot where Andreevski begins, there is a **park**. It can be crossed by cable-car to Podol in several minutes. The main feature of the nineteenth-century park is the monument to Prince Vladimir by Demut-Malinovsky and Klodt. Above the monument, there's the Refectory of the Mikhailovsky Monastery (1712). At the foot of the hill is a monument celebrating the baptism of Russia.

Once, the street which starts from the bottom of the hill had been the central street of Kiev. The street, called **Vladimirskaya,** was chosen as the site for the **university.** The heavy building with the portico was built by Vikenty Beretti between 1837 and 1843. Kiev University has over 20,000 students in its 17 departments. It bears the name of Taras Shevchenko, the wonderful Ukrainian poet. A statue of him (by Manitser) stands in front of the main facade. On the other side of the building, you'll find the **Botanical Garden** and the **Universitet Subway Station.**

OPPOSITE: Relaxing in the sun on the Dnieper.
ABOVE: The church of St.Andrew is vintage Rastrelli: so light you could hold it in the palm of your hand.

Not far from the university, there are two museums: the **Museum of Russian Art** (N°2 Repin Street) and the **Museum of Western and Oriental Art** (N°16). The expositions include the icon of Boris and Gleb, and works by Russian masters Kiprensky, Repin, Ivanov; the western exposition boasts Donatello, Tiepolo, Velasquez, and Rubens.

There is another famous building in Vladimirskaya Street — the **Opera Theater**. Here, the great reformer and statesman Piotr Stolypin was assassinated in 1911.

Some of his ideas are being given serious consideration by the reformers of today. Be sure to visit **St. Vladimir's Cathedral** on Shevchenko Boulevard. Inside, you'll find a pleasant surprise: frescoes by Vasnetsov, Nesterov and Vrubel. Don't forget to light a candle.

PECHERSK

Three years before his death, Yaroslav founded the Pechersk Monastery. "Founded" may be a misleading term in this case; rather, the Prince of Kiev had again lived up to his nickname by giving his official blessing to that rather strange breed of true Christians who'd obviously found

Kievan Rus seventy years after Vladimir baptized it pagan (and dangerous) enough to take to… the catacombs. The monks, Anthony and Feodosiy, lived in two labyrinths known as the **Near Caves** and the **Far Caves**. The very name Pechersk is probably derived from the Russian *peschera* — cave. The Near Caves are some 1,500 m (4,900 ft) long; there are monastic cells, three churches, and crypts with 73 tombs (of which the most famous is that of Nestor the Chronicler). The inscriptions you see on the walls are in Russian, Polish and Armenian. The Far Caves have only one-fifth the length of the Near Caves, but what they lacked in size they made up for with a secret passage to the surface, which was the only way out for the monks if the enemy broke down the "front door". The only way to go between these caves is through a covered gallery.

The stone **Assumption Cathedral** was built in the monastery between 1073 and 1078, a quarter century after Yaroslav's death. After the cathedral was finished, the monastery became a kind of a test grounds for architects. The distinction between clerical and secular architecture was first made in Pechersk. Vladimir, Rostov the Great and Suzdal each built replicas of the Assumption Cathedral. (Unlike the one in Kiev, they survived the German invasion of 1941). Another highlight of the lavra is the **Church of the Saviour of Berestovo**, built early in the twelfth century just outside the walls as a burial place for Kievan princes. Yury the Long-Armed, the founder of Moscow, lies here. Two other famous personages, the Cossack leaders Kochubei and Iskra, immortalized in Pushkin's Poltava, lie buried near the refectory (according to Pushkin, they were executed by the evil Ivan Mazepa because they stood in his way towards supreme power and the hand of Kochubei's daughter).

To me, the *piece de resistance* of Pechersk is the **belfry.** It is almost 100 m (330 ft) tall. The amount of work that had gone into building what is still the highest bell tower in the Orthodox world must have been staggering (the Pyramids invariably come to mind). A friend in the construction business insists that for all the advanced materials, equipment and high-rise cranes that our construction workers rely on today, there isn't a contractor in the land capable of building a replica of the Pechersk belfry. How they did it in the eighteenth century (1731) is, frankly, beyond me. (If you take the guided tour of the monastery, they'll probably tell you the legend about how the belfry was built through divine intervention: it sank deeper into the ground as more and more of it came up. Unabashed, the builders went on with their work — and the tower, once completed, rose from the earth overnight).

area, which is Kiev's administrative district, was developed in the eighteenth century. The central street of Pechersk — **Kirova** — is where the **Mariinsky Palace** is. The palace was designed by Rastrelli and built in five years by a team of Russian architects (construction was started in 1750). The building burnt down but was restored in 1819 in time for the visit by Alexander I and Empress Maria (hence the name). The next building with the flag is the **council of ministers.**

If you walk up from the palace towards **Kreschatik,** you'll come to a monument to

Most of the buildings around the ruins of the Assumption Cathedral date to the eighteenth century, as well. They are the work of Stepan Kovnir, a serf.

When the Millennium of Orthodoxy was celebrated in 1988, most of the monastery was turned back over to the Church. The monastery was promptly reopened, to the believers' joy.

There's a **seminary** (clerical school), as well.

The exit from the Far Caves is through the Moscow Gate. From there, you can see the giant statue of the Motherland in the distance.

Once you're through with the monastery, take a stroll around Pechersk. Most of the

the football players of Kiev Dynamo who got shot for playing too well against the Luftwaffe team during the German occupation of Kiev in 1942. **Grushevsky** (formerly Kirova) **Street** leads up to **Askold's grave.** Kievan Prince Askold was assassinated by the Novgorod Prince Oleg, who'd later conquered Constantinople and imposed a tribute on the mighty city in a poetic enough way — he nailed his sword to its gates.

OPPOSITE: The Cathedral of Pechersk Monastery is the burial site of Prince Yury the Long-Armed, believed to be the founder of Moscow. ABOVE: Orthodox mass can be very elaborate — and physically exhausting (believers are expected to stand through all three hours of it).

There's a nice **rotunda church** for you to feast you eyes upon, too.

If you are game to see another old church after all that walking, head south towards the **Vydubitsky Monastery**. The eleventh-century church there has frescoes dating almost as far back; some of them have already been restored (they were only found in the 1960s).

KRESCHATIK

Kreschatik is the Broadway of Kiev. The

find the store amusing, try the **market** at the end of the street — it is the biggest in the Ukraine. The art nouveau structure dates to the 1910s.

PODOL AND THE LEFT BANK

Podol starts at the foot of Vladimir Hill. It was once an artisan suburb of Upper Town. After Upper Town was destroyed by the Mongols, Podol became the center of Kiev. Early in the eighteenth century, Podol was chosen as the site for the **Kiev Academy**, the

name probably comes from *krest*, which means "cross": it is believed that Vladimir's much-publicized baptism took place in one of the streams which used to run here in the old days.

Kreschatik is a nice place for a walk. The street isn't long. It starts near the park where you can see one of the most bizarre monuments to be found in this country; in fact, if I were not told what the monument signifies in advance, I would never have guessed. The metal rainbow with two figures underneath symbolizes, of all things, Ukrainian-Russian friendship.

The architecture of the street is one hundred percent Soviet. Stroll down to the **Central Department Store**. If you don't

educational institution attended, among others, by Grigory Skovoroda, a prominent philosopher and poet. Today the building belongs to the Academy of Sciences. Another side of the square is formed by the **House of Contracts**, which used to host the Kiev Fairs since 1817 (the first fair was held in 1798). Nearby is the classical building of the **Gostiny Dvor** (guesthouse for merchants). After you're through inspecting the **Samson Fountain** and the **Church of the Intercession** (N°5 Pokrovskaya Street), both of which are the creations of Ivan Grigorovich-Barsky, you can take a stroll on the beautiful embankment.

To the west, in Korotchenko Street, is the **Babi Yar Memorial** to the 100,000 victims of the Nazi regime who were shot right in the middle of the park.

To dispel the sadness of Babi Yar, let us head to the left bank of the Dnieper. To get there, you'll have to cross the river, which is almost a mile wide. The most impressive bridge across the Dnieper is **Paton Bridge**, named after the scientist who designed it and, among other things, invented electric welding. In his memoirs, Nikita Khrushchev recalled how his underlings (he was the party boss of the Ukraine at the time) had wanted to name the bridge after him. But Khrushchev directed otherwise.

One of the attractions of the left bank is **Hotel Slavutich**, which rises quite near the Paton Bridge. The hotel has a restaurant which is above average. There are wonderful parks on the left bank, particularly enjoyable when the chestnuts are in bloom. The chestnut, by the way, is part of the Kiev coat of arms.

WHERE TO STAY

All the better hotels are controlled by Intourist, or used to be, at any rate. Now that the Ukraine is independent, the futures of the tourist industry are hazy. At any rate, the hotels are still there. Here's a list, starting from the most expensive:

Rus 4 Gospitalnaya Street. (220 42 25; 220 51 22; 220 52 33. The twenty-two storey hotel is one of the newest in Kiev. A good choice — if they let you choose.

Dnipro 1/2 Kreschatik. (229 82 87. A typical Intourist establishment with a better-than-average bar and a good restaurant which is, for some strange reason, closed on Monday.

Lybed Peremogy Square. (274 00 63. Surprisingly good service for an Intourist hotel.

Moskva 4 October Revolution Street. (228 28 04. A towering mediocrity.

Slavutich 1 Entuziastiv Street. (555 79 26; 555 79 11. A wonderful location, worth the 20-minute trip downtown.

Bratislava Andrii Malyshko Street. (559 69 20. Medium-range prices. Passable restaurant and bar.

Druzhba 5 Druzhby Narodiv Boulevard. (268 34 06. The hotel with the Intourist/Intourburo offices. Convenient location, fairly decent service.

Ukraina 5 Shevchenko Boulevard. (221 75 84. Large, with a stab (unsuccessful) at sophistication a la modern. The restaurant is okay, though.

Leningradskaya-1 4 Shevchenko Boulevard. (225 71 01.

Leningradskaya-2 3 Lenin Street. (221 70 80.

Leningradskaya-3 36 Volodimirskaya Street. (224 42 26. Cheap and generally available on short notice plus three different locations to choose from.

Mir 70 Fortieth October Anniversary Avenue. (268 56 00. The cheapest they come. This hotel, managed by Sputnik Youth Travel, is the back-packer's dream. Try not to eat there.

Prolisok Motel Fifth Proseka Sviatoshina. (444 00 93. There is also a camping area near this Intourist motel. Good idea for family travel.

Darnitsa Campsite Follow the signs on the Kharkov Highway to Chernigovskoye Highway on the far side of the Dnieper. An

OPPOSITE: Kreschatik is one of the few main streets in the world short enough to walk through. ABOVE: The sunshine can be very enjoyable after a trip through the caves in Pechersk.

ideal place in summer — there's a cafe, kitchen facilities, showers and a laundromat. The mosquitoes are something else, though.

WHERE TO EAT

Welcome to the home of Chicken Kiev!

Of all the Slav nations, the Ukrainians have come closest to developing a full-fledged cuisine of their own. You should read up your Nikolai Gogol on the wonders

varieties, the most famous being pepper gorilka — *Gorilka z pertsem*. Approach with caution! They make excellent beer in Kiev, and the locals rank among the world's greatest beer drinkers. To go with the beer, they have a variety of salted/smoked freshwater fish. A note of warning: do not try to keep up with the Ukrainians if they enter a drinking contest (a favorite national pastime).

Restaurant reservations essential!

All the hotels have restaurants, some of which are not bad.

of Ukrainian cuisine, but if you don't have the time, here's a brief list of what you must try. First and foremost, hearty Ukrainian *borscht* (which has several important distinctions from Russian borscht) — and don't forget the sour cream! Then there's *vareniki*, a kind of ravioli bigger than the Russian *pelimeni,* which come floating in generous amounts of sour cream either as dumplings — *galushki* — or stuffed with cottage cheese, fresh cherries or potatoes. There's also a selection of meat and fish dishes which should be discussed with the waiter if you are wary of spicy foods.

Gorilka ("flammable vodka") is the drink of the Ukrainians. It comes in dozens of

In addition, try:

Dynamo 3 Grushevsky Street. (229 40 38. Located at Dynamo Stadium, the restaurant offers a wide selection of national dishes. You would do well to bring your own liquor.

Maxim 21 Lenin Street. (224 12 72. Kiev's first co-op featuring while-you-wait cooking, something almost unheard-of anywhere in the former Soviet Union. Beer for hard currency. Bring your own liquor.

Dubki 1 Stetsenko Street. (440 51 88. National cuisine, nice location. Waiters do not speak English.

Stolichny 5 Kreschatik Street. (229 81 88. Russian and Ukrainian cuisine. Try the fish — the sturgeon is excellent. Conveniently located next-door to the Hotel Dnipro.

Krakiv 23 Peremogy Avenue. (274 19 08.
Hearty Ukrainian meat dishes and salads.
Kureni 19 Parkova Doroga. (293 40 62.
Excellent with private rooms and a wonderful location. Dancing in the open air, when the weather is right.
Zoloti Vorota 8 Lvivska Square. (212 55 04.
National cuisine.
Mlyn Gidropark. (517 08 33. A summer-only place on an island. Converted Ukrainian-mill setting, park location. The speciality is *bitki*, meatballs served in a pot. Good wine list.

with reservations to East European trains!
Make sure that your ticket states the number of your sleeping berth, carriage number, etc.

One of the fun ways to arrive is by water (ask your agent for Dnieper cruise information). There are cruises to Kiev from Odessa May through September. Intourist offers a package of air tickets from London to Kiev with return tickets from Moscow in two weeks. There is a shuttle taxi service from the River Terminal and downtown Kiev.

Beer Pubs
5 Igorevska Street; 10 Rusanivska Quay; 11/11 Vasilkivska Street; 49 Voloshska Street.

HOW TO GET THERE

The usual way is by air to Borispol International Airport (buses and taxis from the terminal). Borispol is approximately 20 minutes from downtown Kiev.

If you go from Moscow, you'll probably be booked for the railway (the station is in downtown Kiev). You can also arrive by train from Czechoslovakia or Hungary through Uzhgorod. Be careful

If you go by car, you can enter at Uzhgorod and reach Kiev via Rovno and Zhitomir. You can also get to Kiev from Moscow via Kharkov or directly via the Kievskoye Highway.

To get around, use the subway. The fare is 50 kopecks for all kinds of municipal transport. Kiev is also famous for its trams. In fact, it is a much livelier way of getting to know the city than the average bus tour.

OPPOSITE: *Mlyn* Restaurant in Kiev's Gidropark: casual entertainment in an easygoing atmosphere (plus a Ukrainian dish or two).
ABOVE: "Once upon a time, there lived an old man and his wife".

Cruising the Volga and the Don

THEY SAY that you haven't seen Russia if you haven't seen the Volga. From what I hear, as well as from personal experience, however, most Volga towns are not exactly the international tourist's dream. The only way for the tourist to be reasonably comfortable *and* to enjoy this part of Russia is to take a boat cruise. The best time to go is in summer, although Intourist and several independent companies offer cruises May through late September. There are cruises of different length; you can spend two or three days or see the whole thing in two weeks. The new boats can be surprisingly comfortable, with single/double cabins with showers or deluxe suites (although you'll have to book that well in advance) for as little as $50 and $100 a day, respectively. This also includes board. However, this does not mean that you have to be ready for it in advance. Just approach the cruise as you would the Transsib journey (see the Siberia chapter for detailed instructions).

Ancient Greeks called it the *ra* ("generous"); the Arabs — *itil* "river of rivers". The Slavs thought it "light" and "glistening", the two meanings conveyed by the word *volga* in ancient Slavonic.

It starts as a small stream lost in the the Valdai Hills. As it flows downwards and to the south, the waters of some 151,000 rivers and rivulets contribute to make it Europe's longest river (3,530 km or 1,900 miles). The Volga makes its way into the Caspian Sea through several climatic belts. It flows through the dense forests and the rocky ranges of the near Urals, the meadows and steppes further down south, and finally, the desert sands. When spring comes to its lower reaches near the Caspian coastline, it's still winter in the Volga's upper basin.

The left bank of the Volga is flat, covered with fields and meadows. The right bank is mostly cliffy. The most beautiful part of the river basin is the **Akhtubinsk Delta** with its ancient oaks, willows, and tall black poplars. The delta is home for hundreds of bird species, pheasants, snow-white swans, flamingoes, pelicans among them. There are some 70 kinds of fish: freshwater herring, pike, sturgeon, beluga,

catfish, and so on. The fauna is made up of huge populations of beaver, raccoon, wild boar, and assorted water-rat species known for their fur.

The Volga has four main "professions". It gives fish, electric power, water for irrigation and, of course, shipping.

BACKGROUND

People have lived here for ages. The Bulgars moved to the Volga from the steppes between the Caspian and the Azov Seas in the sixth century. In the tenth century, they had all the makings of a proper kingdom. The Bulgars were adept at agriculture and animal husbandry, various if somewhat lackluster arts and crafts, and international relations — they had extensive trade ties with their neighbors.

The mighty Khasar Khanate appeared between the Volga and the Don in the seventh century. Arab and Persian merchants came to Itil, the capital of the Khanate, to trade their famous wares — weapons and fabrics — for furs, skins and wax brought by the Slavs.

Yet the steppes of the south were destined to act, time and again, as a gateway for the assorted nomad peoples making their way from Asia into Europe. In the tenth century, a nomad tribe called Polovtsians came to the lower reaches of the Volga. This spelled trouble for all the inhabitants of the region, but, as Prince Yaroslav the Wise had so convincingly demonstrated by defeating the Polovtsians in Kiev, nothing the Slavs couldn't handle.

In the thirteenth century, that precarious balance of forces was forever upset by the Mongol invasion.

The Mongols conquered the Bulgar Kingdom in the 1230s and annexed the lands in the middle and lower reaches of the Volga into their Golden Horde. The capital city of the Horde, Sarai, was situated in its lower reaches, on the left bank. For three hundred years, things remained unchanged, until the Horde broke up into

Palekh illustration to the Russian fairy tale *Firebird*.

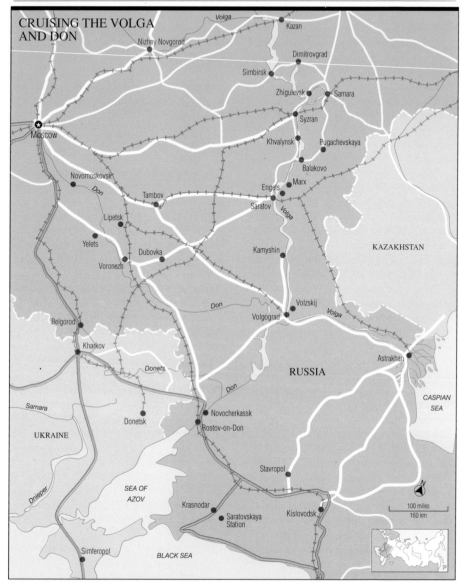

CRUISING THE VOLGA AND DON

four parts—the khanates of Kazan, Crimea, Astrakhan and the Nogai Horde. Of these, the Kazan Khanate was the strongest. Nevertheless, Ivan the Terrible managed to defeat the Mongols, taking Kazan in 1552 and Astrakhan in 1556. The Volga became Russian property.

At the end of the sixteenth century, the Russians built several forts on the Volga to protect their presence there: Samara in 1586, Tsaritsyn in 1589, Saratov in 1590.

Russia was a land of serfs, who were not free to move to the newly won lands.

Stymied by this problem, yet unwilling to abolish serfdom, the czars found what they thought was an ideal way out: they offered a number of privileges and benefits to potential foreign settlers. The foreigners who came were German and Dutch for the most part. Other settlers included runaway serfs and assorted Orthodox sects such as the Old Believers. And, of course, there were the Cossacks.

During the nineteenth century, the fertile Volga basin became the breadbasket of Europe. The twentieth century hit off with

VOLGA FISH

The Volga is full of fish. From April to August, huge sevriuga sturgeons travel upstream alone and in small schools. Sturgeon comes in July, and the largest fish of them all, the 800 kg (1700 lbs) beluga — in October. These migration patterns are "programmed" into the genetic code of the species. There aren't that many migrating fish: of the 25,000 or so known species, only slightly over a hundred migrate. All of them belong to seven families: salmons, sturgeons, herrings, smelts, carps, eels and lampreys.

The sturgeon family is widespread: the Baltic, Lake Baikal, Siberian rivers, the Black Sea, Sakhalin rivers, and the Amur. But it is in the Caspian that the sturgeons seem to really feel at home.

The sturgeon spends the first 10 to 13 years of its life growing and prowling around looking for underwater pastures. Then, after the fish matures, it is driven by instinct into the mouth of the river and upstream to the spot where it itself was born. These spots may be anywhere between 100 and 1,000 km from the river estuary.

Once it enters fresh waters, the fish stops feeding, existing only on its internal reserves of energy. The sturgeon does not appear to hurry, making not more than 25 to 35 km (15 to 20 miles) a day, moving quicker in the morning and at night, slower during the day, with frequent stops for rest.

Sturgeons spawn in deep water where the bottom is hard and rocky. Spawned caviar sticks to the pebbles, and three to five days after that, the larvae appear.

Immediately after spawning, the sturgeon's digestive organs are "switched on". The fish has enough vitality to make it back to the sea. Some sturgeons hibernate. Schools of them spend the winter in deep holes, "clothed" in several layers of slime. As soon as spring comes, they head for their spawning site.

The sturgeons (together with the sharks) are the oldest species of fish in the world. They may soon become obsolete.

As the villages along the Volga turned to towns and cities, as more and more fields went under the plow and new factories were built, man's impact on nature reached critical proportions. Shipping, industrial sewage, oil-tanker spills pollute the water. The huge pumps used in irrigation dump entire schools of newborn fish on the fields. Fishing techniques and equipment have developed to the point where all the fish in the sea can be caught in a matter of weeks. Poachers kill thousands of sturgeons just for the caviar.

But it is the dams that are the greatest danger. Fish cannot get to their eternal spawning sites as they have done for ages.

The situation can be remedied with "fish elevators", which lift schools of fish over dams and into reservoirs, man-made spawning sites, and fish-breeding factories. Nearly every beluga fish caught in the Caspian nowadays comes from an incubator (there are six in the Astrakhan region, producing some 50 million fish every year).

one of the most terrible famines in human history (cannibalism was widely practised), continued with fratricidal civil war, and topped things off with World War II. Stalingrad (formerly Tsaritsyn and now Volgograd) was the town where the fortunes of, some say, the entire war were turned around after the Red Army routed Gen. Paulus' group of armies, taking over 100 thousand prisoners after months of bitter fighting.

The twentieth century also brought ecological problems for "the mother of all Russians". It is comforting to know, however, that these problems are now being addressed by the people who live there — something the communist regime would never have tolerated.

TOWNS EN ROUTE

KAZAN

Kazan is the capital of the Tartar Republic. It is a medium-sized city with a population of just over a million and deep-rooted cultural traditions. In 1758, Kazan became the only provincial town to get a *ghimnasia* (secondary school) of its own. In 1804, a university was opened here, Russia's second after Moscow.

in the village of Kokushkino (now Lenino-Kokushkino). The university, by the way, is not named after Lobachevsky — it is named after Lenin.

Today, Kazan is trying to shed "the Russian yoke". The government of the republic wants out of the Russian Federation. They way things are right now, Tartaria may well become independent. In 1552, Ivan the Terrible was so overjoyed with the taking of Kazan by his troops that he commissioned the construction of St. Basil's. Now, it would seem, no one wants the town

The university largely owes its fortunes to Nikolai Lobachevsky, the renowned mathematician. He headed the university for 19 years. It was here that Lobachevsky created his non-Euclidean geometry.

By the 1870s, Kazan had a veterinarian school, a teachers' college, and one of the best drama theaters in the country. Gavriil Derzhavin, Sergei Aksakov and Leo Tolstoy are but a few literary lights who worked here. Gorky spent a part of his life in Kazan, and today you can visit the museum of "the father of socialist realism".

Kazan was where Lenin went to school. In 1887 he was arrested for taking part in a student's rally and exiled for almost a year

anymore — except the native Tartars. It is a shame, because for all its pressing problems (including the highest rate of juvenile delinquency in the nation), Kazan is a beautiful town with a sprinkling of world-class architectural monuments and museums. The white walls and towers of the Kazan Kremlin, for example, were built under the guidance of Pskov's Ivan Shirai and Postnik Yakovlev (of St. Basil fame), who also built the Annunciation Cathedral there. Before the Kremlin, there is a monument to Musa Dzhalil, the poet who'd perished in a Nazi concentration camp during the war.

Enjoy every minute of your tour — it'll be brief.

FROM KAZAN TO ULIANOVSK

Back on board, relax and take in the view of the Volga as it sharply curves to the south immediately below Kazan. You'll be passing several old villages and small towns on your way to Simbirsk, the town where Lenin spent his childhood (and which was subsequently renamed, but after his real name, Ulianov, and not his party pseudonym). The first interesting place is the village of Antonovka, where the special

ULIANOVSK (SIMBIRSK)

You are really deep in the heart of Russia now. Founded in 1648 as a fort to keep out the nomads, the city was probably named after a Bulgar Prince by the name of Sinbir. The town he founded in the fourteenth century was situated 18 km (11 miles) downstream from the contemporary city, where some 600,000 people live today.

The singular most important thing about this town is that it is the birthplace of

kind of huge yellowish-green sour-sweet apples was first bred. You won't find apples like these anywhere else in the world.

Thirty kilometers (19 miles) downstream you'll see the **Volga-Kama Preserve**. Somewhere in that dense forest the local "scientists" are trying to turn the moose into a domestic animal (I swear it's true — I read about it in a newspaper).

Further downstream, the Volga meets the Kama. The river is 40 km (25 miles) wide here. The hill you see on the right as you move downstream is the spot where Ilya Repin painted one of his more famous works, *Volga Boaters*, in 1870. You may have seen it in the Tretiakov Gallery or a copy of it in the Russian museum in Petersburg.

Vladimir Ulianov, the man who is better known throughout the world under his *nom de guerre* — Lenin. Aren't you glad to be near the house where "humanity's foremost revolutionary and thinker, the founder of the Communist Party of the Soviet Union and the world's first socialist state" spent his youth? Personally, I envy you the opportunity.

FROM ULIANOVSK TO SAMARA

Leaving Simbirsk/Ulianovsk behind, you'll see an oak grove on the right bank. The

OPPOSITE: Street vendors get tired, too.
ABOVE: Volga dwellers take their festivals seriously: girl in folk costume during Ulianovsk City Festival celebrations.

rotunda you see there was installed in 1912 to commemorate the centennial anniversary of the birth of one of our best nineteenth-century writers Ivan Goncharov. The site, knowledgeable sources say, was described by the author in one of his novels *The Cliff*.

You'll pass several villages and a small town or two before you get to the ancient village of **Usolye**. The village appeared near the mouth of the Usa River early in the sixteenth century. Here, they produced salt, one of the most expensive consumer goods of the Middle Ages.

were discovered nearby late in the nineteenth century. The next town on the map is **Zhigulevsk**, where the oil people live and, I'm sure, do more than enough to pollute that unique environment.

The huge dam up ahead is **Volzhskaya Hydroelectric Power Station**.

As you dock, look around. The power station was something of a feat for its time (1958). It produces some 11 billion kilowatt-hours of electricity annually.

The next city you'll see was founded in 1737 as Stavropol. After the completion of

Usolie is the gateway to the Zhiguli Mountain Range. The mountains are not high (the highest rock is just over 375 m or 1,230 ft), but very beautiful. This is the place where the assorted romantic bandits of Russian history, such as Stepan Razin and Kondraty Bulavin, hid from the authorities when their luck ran out.

Further downstream where the Usa falls into the Volga, you'll see several *kurgans*, or burial mounds, on the right bank. Beyond these is the **Zhiguli Preserve**, where some 700 species of vegetation, including trees that predate the ice age, grow. The fauna is typical of central Russia: deer, badgers, rabbits, foxes, black storks, etc. Unfortunately for the national park, deposits of oil

the power station, it started to grow and was renamed after Palmiro Togliatti (the Italian communist), of all people. It is here that FIAT built the first Russian auto factory in 1969. Today, the auto factory churns out 720,000 little Ladas every year.

Downstream, in the Morkvashinskaya Valley, lies the ancient Bulgar village of **Morkvashi**. It dates to the thirteenth century.

SAMARA

Samara (previously Kuibyshev originally Samara) is the largest town on the Volga so far. The population is 1.5 million.

The town was founded as a frontier outpost for the protection of the Volga trade route. When the nomad threat dwindled, Samara quickly spread outwards; in 1851 it became the capital of the region.

The two most interesting contributions of Soviet power to the venerable town (besides the name change) are one of Russia's largest chocolate factories and a subway, which was opened in 1987.

FROM SAMARA TO VOLGOGRAD (TSARITSYN)

A couple of hours or so downstream from Samara lies the village of **Yermakovo**, named after Yermak the Conqueror of Siberia. The place, with its forests, secret caves and sharp bends of the river, must have been an ideal spot for Yermak's river pirates to ambush the slow, overloaded merchantmen. Come to think of it, it must have been tough being a merchant in those savage days. If you made it past Yermak, you'd find his right-hand man Ivan Koltso and his merry men waiting near Vasilievsky Island. The brigands probably stashed their loot in the cave which can be entered not far from the river. They say that Razin (who was drawn and quartered in Moscow's Red Square) planned to make a passage all the way between the entrance to that cave and the Zhiguli Range. I have a feeling that there's a lot more to learn about that place, which makes one think of treasure, Mark Twain style.

Further downstream you'll be passing the town of **Syzran**, where a railway was built in 1872 (featuring the first-ever bridge across the Volga) to transport shipped freight. Then, behind the low Khvalynskiye Hills, you'll see the town of **Khvalynsk** (the Caspian was also known as the Khvalynskoye Sea). It was founded by serf fishermen who made sure that the Father Superior of Moscow's Chudov Monastery, their seigneur, always had fresh fish on his table.

The next town on your way, **Balakovo**, was founded in 1762 by a sect of emigre Old Believers who had been allowed to return to their home country. It was here that the world's first tractor allegedly appeared. I wouldn't believe this information too much (the communists claimed that

Russia gave the world everything, and evil tongues asserted that Russia was the birthplace of elephants), but it is said that an engineer by the name of Blinov designed his tractor with two steam engines in 1888. Another thing about Balakovo is that it is the birthplace of Vasily Chapayev, a minor Civil War military leader who was made famous by the film *Chapayev*. The film appeared during World War II and was probably wonderful for its time (when it was shown near the front, soldiers shot at the screen where the white guards were killing poor, wounded, drowning Chapayev). In the seventies, however, it became the target of numerous jokes and anecdotes because of the stubbornness with which it was shown on Soviet TV in Brezhnev's heyday (Brezhnev must have liked it). Come to think of it, the reason why he must have liked it was because Chapayev became the butt of more jokes than Brezhnev; I recall seeing a collection of Chapayev jokes that had been published in Paris.

There is another power station coming your way. The Saratovskaya Station produces some 5.4 billion kilowatt-hours of electricity annually. Beyond the dam, on the right bank stands the town of Volsk. In the old days, it was known for the particularly nasty *zmei* ("serpent" or "dragon") that lived in the nearby Zmeinye Hills. The dragon was lecherous, bloodthirsty, and had a terrible temper, which was, in the end, his undoing: a mighty Russian warrior slashed him to pieces with his trusty kladenets (sword). The pieces turned to rocks, which you can still see today.

The next two towns on your way make me think of a joke a doctor friend of mine once told me.

At the graduation exam in medical college, a student is shown two skeletons, one of a man, the other of a woman. "What are they?" he is asked. He thinks and thinks, but does not know.

"Think!" He thinks some more, but still does not know. "What's got into you?" the professor rages, "most of the seven years you've spent here were dedicated to these...

OPPOSITE: "Forever from afar it flows without boundary, without end."

"Oh, I get it," the student answers, "they're Marx and Engels!"

That's what the next two towns on your way are — Marx and Engels.

The town of **Marx**, founded in 1767 as Yekaterinstadt by German and Austrian settlers, became a large machine-building town in the Soviet time. As you pass under the huge bridge, look to the left. What you see is the town of **Engels**, formerly Pokrovskaya Sloboda. When the state monopoly was imposed over the salt trade in 1747, a road was built between the

salt Lake Elton and the village. In 1931 the town was renamed (see cameo on page 137).

The town on the opposite bank is **Saratov**. It lies in a rather picturesque hollow formed by three hills. The town, a regional center, is fairly large (900,000 people). Some of the country's best wheat is grown in the region. There's also meat and dairy farming.

Founded as a frontier fort in 1590, Saratov was simply too far from Moscow for the czars to exercise firm control over its inhabitants, who seemed to be on the wrong side of every peasant revolt that chanced to come their way, including the

ABOVE: Orthodox belief centers around the Virgin, whom Russians call "Mother of God".

Razin and Pugachev wars. These noble traditions were continued when the Bolsheviks founded an organization here in 1898. In 1912, the female wing of the Ulianov family took part in provoking unrest here, as the result of which Lenin's sister Maria was exiled.

Downstream from Saratov, near the village of Privolzhsky, is the spot where Yury Gagarin landed after making his memorable orbit around the Earth. Further downstream, near the village of Durman, you'll see a flat-topped rock with steep sides. Legend has it that behind this rock was "Stenka's prison", where Razin kept his hostages while he waited for ransom (that was in his early days, when he didn't meddle in politics and contented himself with river piracy). There is a rather famous folk song about this rock.

You are about to enter the steppe zone, the land of wheat and watermelons.

The town of **Kamyshin** is associated with watermelons and Peter the Great. The czar attached great strategic importance to the nearby Kamyshinka River, which comes quite close in its upper reaches to a tributary of the Don. Merchants who dragged their boats over the patch of land separating the two rivers dreamed of building a canal there some day. Peter set out to dig the canal, but the war with the Swedes thwarted his plans. The canal was dug to only half the planned depth. You can still see what remains of it today.

Enjoy your watermelon.

The town of **Dubovka** was founded in 1734 by the Don Cossacks. In 1742 Dubovka became their capital. The ataman's residence was here. The Cossacks were granted great privileges, such as tax-free winemaking and fishing.

After the local Cossacks supported Yemelian Pugachev's peasant war, Catherine the Great exiled some of them to a settlement on the River Terek, and some to Astrakhan.

We are now in the middle of the **Volgograd Reservoir**. The reservoir stretches for 560 km (347 miles) from Volgograd to Balakovo. Up ahead is the town of **Volzhsky** (250,000 inhabitants) and the **Volzhskaya Power Station**. The station produces roughly 11 billion kilowatts of some of the world's cheapest electricity. It was built in the early 60s.

VOLGOGRAD (TSARITSYN)

The old town was founded in 1589 as a river fort. Floods were a great problem, and the fort was moved to the right bank, near the estuary of the Tsaritsa River. As several other outposts on the Volga, Tsaritsyn had a loyalty problem. In 1670, the city opened its gates before Stepan Razin's rebels and continued to resist the regular army even after Razin was captured and executed. A century after that, Pugachev tried to take the city to no avail. Where Pugachev failed, the Bolsheviks succeeded: Soviet power was proclaimed in Tsaritsyn on November 17, 1917. In 1918, Tsaritsyn became the site of a major battle between the White guards of General Krasnov and General Denikin and the Red guards of Comrades Voroshilov and Stalin. The white generals failed to capture the city.

The next battle fought near its walls was to bring Tsaritsyn (renamed Stalingrad by that time) world fame. The battle of Stalingrad was one of the greatest and bloodiest in history. Over two million troops, 2,000 tanks, and 26,000 pieces of artillery (on both sides) were thrown into the 200-day battle. Houses and streets passed from one side to another. Mamayev Kurgan (Hill) was defended for 140 days against incredible odds. The thousands of tons of metal with which the Germans showered the hill did not help their advance.

Today, the huge statue of the Motherland, sword in hand, reminds us of those bloody yet glorious days and nights.

Modern Volgograd is not a nice place to live in. It is, in fact, one of the most polluted urban areas in Russia.

FROM THE VOLGA TO THE DON

The time has come for us to say goodbye to the mighty Volga. We shall go up the Volga–Don Channel into the Tsimlianskoye Reservoir, which was formed by the Tsimlianskaya Dam across the River Don.

There are 13 shipping locks in the Volga–Don. As the White Sea–Baltic Channel, the Volga—Don is a monument to Stalin's victims, the twentieth-century slaves who built the channel mostly with picks, shovels and wheelbarrows. The channel was built in two-and-a-half years. It is 10 km (6 miles) long. Unlike the White Sea–Baltic, which is not used today at all, the Volga–Don is important for the national economy. It acts as the link between five seas.

Leaving the channel, you enter Tsimlianskoye Reservoir. It is approximately 200 km (120 miles) long. On your way, you'll pass several places where you'll see monuments to the soldiers of the Civil war and World War II. On November 23, 1942, the troops of two Soviet fronts rendezvoused here, encircling 22 Wehzmacht divisions.

On the left bank, there's the Cossack village of **Pugachevskaya**. The village has a troubled history. It was first razed to the ground in 1774 after Pugachev was drawn and quartered in Moscow's Red Square. Both Pugachev and Razin hailed from this village, and Catherine the Great evidently decided that she wasn't going to wait for the village to churn up a third bandit of such devastating magnitude. The second time, the village was flooded by the waters of the reservoir.

Up ahead on the starboard side is the town of Volgodonsk. They make very good wine there. After you lock through, you'll get a breathtaking vista of meadows, fields and vineyards. You are in Cossack country now.

THE DON RIVER

The Don isn't large as Russian rivers go. It is 1,870 km (1,159 miles) long. The river originates near the town of Novomoskovsk and flows into the Sea of Azov. The river is an important economic asset. Its waters are replenished mainly with snow.

The Don has a distinct character. It is invariably calm and peaceful. The Cossacks could not have chosen a better one to soothe their savage spirit. In fact, the Don crops up

THE COSSACKS OF THE DON

In the days of yore, the boundless expanses of southern Russia, the Don basin, the northern shores of the Azov and Black Seas were known as "the Wild Field". As far back as the seventh century BC, the Greeks founded a town here. The town, Tanis, quickly became a center of trade and was granted substantial privileges by the Bosporian Kingdom.

The word itself is Turcic, meaning (just as the Slav word Brodnik) "a free, unattached person". The Cossacks were great horse lovers, which is not surprising: in pitched battle, their very lives depended on their mounts. This is illustrated in the lore with such proverbs as "A Cossack will go hungry to feed his horse."

Contrary to Western thinking, the Cossacks are not a tribe or a nation. Theirs is not a national distinction but

In the era of the great migration from Central Asia, this region was flooded with the Hun hordes. The nomads had it all to themselves for the following three centuries. Slavs first came here in the seventh century.

The Cossacks started out as stray bands of runaway serfs who settled on the Dnieper, the Don and in the Urals. As the fortunes of Muscovy picked up, more and more peasants, loath to stay in Central Russia as serfs, ran away and drifted to these parts. The Wild Field welcomed these freedom-loving people, who were first known as Brodniks, and subsequently — Cossacks.

an economic and military one. After they ran away and settled in small villages, they found themselves pushed into a life by the sword for two reasons: they had to resist the czar's soldiers who came in search of the runaways, and they had to survive. And since there was nothing they knew better than fighting, they used their weapons for gain. The only thing that distinguished them from run-of-the-mill highway robbers was that the latter did not care who it was they robbed, whereas the Cossacks never attacked their own (meaning Orthodox Slavs), preferring to organize expeditions into nearby Persia, Turkey, Poland, Lithuania, and the khanates. As their numeric strength and murderous "skills" improved, they ceased to be a mere nuisance to their neighbors. They became a problem. In fact, the populations of neighboring countries feared them like the plague. This set the wheels of politics rolling. The issue of the Cossacks, who were, after all, operating out of Russian territory, was brought before the czars. It happened at one of

those rare times in our history when the czars, doubtless because they were out of money or fighting men, vied for peace. The Cossack atamans (leaders) were summoned to Moscow and told to put a stop to their devastating "expeditions". Czar Ivan the Terrible recognized their right to keep the runaways, and offered them to enter his service as his official frontier guards. They were allowed to keep their landholdings in exchange for presenting themselves, with weapons and mounts, whenever Moscow needed them, "to do battle for the crown". They were also paid a salary. Another thing they got was a

semblance of political autonomy (the czars promised not to interfere in their "internal affairs"). The way the Cossacks solved their domestic problems was by convening a "circle" on a one man — one vote basis. It was this way that they elected their leaders and treasurers for each campaign.

Once robbery as a modus vivendi had been ruled out, the Cossacks gradually grew into the image that brought them world-wide fame, that of free landholders (similar to American farmers) who could, in a matter of hours, assemble themselves into fully armed and equipped cavalry units and be off to fight the enemy of the czar's choosing, foreign or domestic — the best mercenaries the world had ever seen.

Actually, the Cossacks at first believed that landholding would hamper their military efficiency. They preferred hunting, fishing and raising cattle.

In 1721, Peter the Great incorporated the Army of the Don into the authority of his War College. The Cossacks took part in Peter's campaigns against the Turks, in the Seven-Year War (1756–1763), in Suvorov's famed Italian and Swedish campaigns, in the war against Napoleon and, come to think of it, in just about every major campaign of the nineteenth century. They also took part in World War II. Today, when the Cossack tradition is undergoing large-scale revival, the Cossacks are fighting on the "home fronts". Last heard, they were "helping out" to solve the Moldova territorial dispute.

OPPOSITE: Riverbank panorama.
ABOVE: An archaeological find from a Volga *kurgan*, or burial mound.

in nearly every Cossack folk song. In the West, it was made famous after a writer named Mikhail Sholokhov received the Nobel Prize for Literature for a novel entitled *And Quiet Flows the Don*.

The first stop on your way is a Cossack village.

Your next stop is the surprisingly green town of **Novocherkassk**, which was founded as a Cossack capital by Matvei Platov, the dashing hero of the Napoleonic wars. The town had a pronounced military profile. There was a cadet corps school, a

Junkers College, a military medical college, and several similar institutions.

Novocherkassk is full of monuments. You've seen old and very old churches during your tour of Russia. Well, go look at one of Russia's youngest churches for a change, the Byzantine-style church that was built early in this century.

There's also the **Cossack Museum**. Be sure to drop in and see at least some of its more than 40,000 items.

ABOVE: Seeing a beard like this one, it is easy to understand how difficult it must have been for Peter the Great to make his subjects shave their most treasured possession.
OPPOSITE: Nomads have lived on the Volga for thousands of years.

The town is not large, and everything is within walking distance.

ROSTOV-ON-DON

The city is one of the largest regional centers in Russia. It has a population of over one million.

Rostov is often called "the gateway to the Caucasus", because many of the water, air, rail and auto routes converge here. The city owes its origins to the customs post which was founded here in 1749. A fortress named after Dmitry of Rostov was built nearby to keep out the Turks. The peculiar name comes from the need to distinguish the town from Rostov the Great in northern Russia.

Rostov is known for its industry, unusually good drama theater, and an incredible crime rate. Hold on to your pockets and purses: our criminals were so impressed with the action going on in the city on the Don that they gave it the loving nickname "Rostov-papa" (it became the second town to merit such distinction after Odessa-mama).

CRUISE INFORMATION

Overall distance: 1,891 km (1,172 miles)
Distances between stopovers:
KAZAN to ULIANOVSK: 223 km (138 miles); ULIANOVSK to "ZHIGULI:" 150 km (93 miles); "ZHIGULI" to "MAIDEN'S ISLE:" 351 km (217 miles); "MAIDEN'S ISLE" to VOLGOGRAD: 544 km (337 miles); VOLGOGRAD to "COSSACK VILLAGE:" 483 km (299 miles); "COSSACK VILLAGE" to ROSTOV: 140 km (87 miles).

LOCK INFORMATION

Between Kazan and Rostov-on-Don, your boat will lock through two locks of the Lenin Power Station to minus 28 m (92 ft); one lock of the Leninsky Komsomol Power Station to minus 10 m (33 ft); two locks of the 22nd CPSU Congress Power Station to minus 27 m (88 ft); nine locks of the Volga–Don Channel to 88 m (288 ft); four locks of the Volga–Don Channel to minus 44 m (144 ft); two locks at the exit from the Tsimlianskoye Reservoir to minus 20.4 m (67 ft).

Have fun!

European
North

BACKGROUND

The first thing that strikes you about the Russian North is its size. Stretching well beyond the Arctic Circle in the north, it borders on the watershed of the Western Dvina and the Volga in the south, on Finland in the west, and on the Northern Urals in the east, forming a rectangle 1,600 by 2,000 km (1,000 by 1,300 miles).

The north is grim, to be sure, but never bleak. The Alpine peaks of the Polar Urals and the Pai-Khoi Mountains, the fjords of the White Sea coast, the blue-gray lichen-covered tundra, the thousand lakes of Karelia, and the century-old forests — the trademark of the place — never fail to impress even the most impassive explorer.

The Russian North is in many ways the birthplace and the cradle of our culture. Much of the credit for this goes to Novgorod, the town which our ancestors reverently called "Our Lord," and probably the only place in medieval Russia that resisted every foreign invader.

The eighteenth century saw the foundation and meteoric rise of St. Petersburg, the biggest military port and, eventually, the capital of the nation.

If Russia may still be said to possess an economy, then this is the region with the greatest economic potential. The two things going for it are Petersburg's machine-building factories and probably the world's foremost timber industry.

The North doesn't offer much in terms of creature comforts. In fact, if you stray from the beaten track (Novgorod — St.Petersburg), you can forget about the comforts and safety of orthodox "sightseeing" tourism. It is only the so-called "survival tourists" who are a match for the myriad problems and, very often, perils, of travel in these uninhabited and, to me, unforgettable parts.

NOVGOROD

Both are old. Starting from the ninth century, the fortunes of Novgorod (which means "New Town") were tied to the famed "way from the Varangians to the Greeks." In fact, it could have been the Varangian princes who founded the place.

At the height of its power in the fourteenth century, Novgorod was easily one of the largest towns in the known world. It had well-established relations with most of Western Europe, and served as a beachhead for the settlement of the North.

Russia's first scribes and chroniclers appeared in Novgorod sometime in the eleventh century. Beresta (birch-bark scrolls) was used for paper.

Novgorod was the place where you went to buy a pair of shoes in the fifteenth century. The town's small army (5,500 strong) of tanners, shoemakers, silversmiths and carpenters was its pride and, for the foreign merchants of the German Hanseatic League, the best insurance policy for doing business with the Russian city. Novgorod had an impressive import/export turnover: hammered iron, leather, firs, honey and such exotic items as walrus fangs were traded for spices, silks and precious metals.

Until Ivan III submitted the city to his will in 1478, Novgorod was a rudimentary republic, governed by the veche — the assembly of free citizens. The veche was called together with a special bell, which Ivan III took away to Moscow and installed on a belfry in the Kremlin to show who was the boss. For Novgorod, the days of independence were over.

WHAT TO SEE

Situated some 620 km (380 miles) north of Moscow, the town stands on the banks of the ill-tempered Volkhov River. On the west bank, there's the *Detinets* (**Kremlin**) with the eleventh-century **Cathedral of St. Sophia**. Notice the helmet-like cupolas — they signify that the church dates to the earliest architectural period. Pay a visit to the **Faceted Chamber** — the collection of silver-plate there is worth seeing. The last time I was there, they also exhibited Russia's first state decree, written on parchment. The St. Sophia and the Kremlin are open 10 am

Ice cream works! ...even in Arctic Murmansk.

to 6 pm except for Wednesdays and the last Monday of the month.

There are two things you are bound to like about the Kremlin. The first is that unlike its sister citadel in Moscow, it is very "unofficial." If you go in summer, you are bound to notice the hilarious sign "No sun-tanning in Kremlin!" — a futile attempt of the now-defunct Communist authorities to cling to their puffed-up prestige. If you have a swimsuit along, don't hesitate — strike a blow for democracy and take a dip yourself.

The second is a small plaque on the gates facing the former town Party Committee building. "Here lies," it says, "a message from the Komsomols [members of the Young Communist League] of the 30s to the Komsomols of the twenty-first century." I don't know about you, but I personally would love to be around when the message is extracted from the ancient wall — if they find a Komsomol in the twenty-first century to do it.

Across the river is the site chosen by Yaroslav the Wise for his estate. The square

RURIK AND THE RUSSES

Says the first Chronicle (852–862): "The tributaries of the Varangians drove them back beyond the sea and, refusing them further tribute, set out to govern themselves. There was no law among them, but tribe rose against tribe... and they began to war one against another. They said to themselves, 'Let us seek a prince who may rule over us, and judge us according to the law.' And so they went overseas to the Varangian Russes: these particular Varangians were known as Russes, just as some were called Swedes, and others Normans, Angles and Goths... They said to the people of Rus, 'Our land is great and rich, and there is no order in it. Come rule and reign over us.' They thus selected three brothers, with their kinsfolk, who took with them all the Russes and migrated. The oldest, Rurik, located himself in Novgorod... On account of these Varangians, the district of Novgorod became known as the land of Rus. The present inhabitants of Novgorod are descended from the Varangian race, but aforetime they were Slavs..."

is surrounded by churches; one of them was built in the twelfth century by the merchants who traded with Germany and Sweden. Nearby, there's a two-story building with a tent-roofed turret — the orphaned home of the veche bell.

There's plenty of architecture for you to see. While you're at it, look at the people around you — they are the closest thing to ethnic Russians (fair-haired and blue-eyed) you'll see in all of Russia, the explanation being, of course, that the Mongols never made it to Novgorod.

WHERE TO STAY

Tourists usually come to Novgorod on a one-day trip from Petersburg, but if you find the place enticing enough to merit a longer stay, try the **Sadko Hotel** (16 Gagarin Prospekt, (9 51 70) — it is definitely the best in town, probably because it is not controlled by Intourist. There's also the **Volkhov Hotel** (24 Nekrasova Street, (9 24 98), and the **Novgorod Intourist** (16 Dmitrievskaya Street, (7 50 89; 9 42 90). Then there's a **motel** with a cafe ten kilometers or so (six to seven miles) to the south (7 24 48). It is open only in summer. There is parking and camping facilities.

WHERE TO EAT

Each of the hotels has a restaurant, offering a selection of what they call "European" dishes. As usual, don't expect much. There is a hard-currency bar at the Intourist.

Try the small **Detinets Restaurant** in midtown — it offers the best Russian cuisine in town.

PSKOV

Situated on the western frontier of ancient Russia, Pskov was initially a part of the Novgorod Republic (it was called "Novgorod's junior brother"). In the twelfth century, Pskov became a key military stronghold of fledgling Russia; in the fourteenth, it gained independence from Novgorod. Even though the town lived in what can only be described as a perpetual

state of war — it was taken and looted several times by the Teutons, Lithuanians, Poles and, yes, Ivan the Terrible's "brother" Russians in the course of three hundred years — it nevertheless prospered owing to its fortunate location and trademark entrepreneurship.

A visit to Pskov is usually included into the Novgorod tour. The moment you see the churches of Pskov, you will realize

OPPOSITE: You'll find the grounds of the Novgorod Kremlin quite relaxing.

that they belong to an architectural vision with enough differences from traditional Russian church-building to be termed a school. **Vasily-on-the-Hill** (1413) is a case in point. Laconic, purposely underdecorated, monumentally compact yet noble in line and shape, the church offers a glimpse into the mentality of its fifteenth-century creators. In fact, such people could only have come from a culture with an astonishingly high literacy rate, widespread knowledge of foreign languages and an explorer's itch that drove Novgorod and Pskov merchants

cially the fifteenth-century Church of Assumption.

For poetry buffs, there's the side trip **Svyatogorsky Monastery**, where Alex der Pushkin was buried not far from familial estate of Mikhailovskoye (th is a museum there now). The trip ta 10 hours.

The twentieth century has not b kind to Pskov. There was vicious fight here in 1918 (the Red Army scored its victory here on February 23, which since been celebrated as Red Army D

to such distant places as Spain, Siberia, India, China, and even Africa.

There is a number of things for you to see besides the Kremlin. You could start with the architectural **museum-preserve** (7 Nekrasova Street, ℓ 2 25 18). The museum is open 11 am to 6 pm except for Mondays and the last Tuesday of the month.

You could also visit the nearby towns of **Izborsk** and **Pechory** (about an hour away). Izborsk, which dates to 862, is known for its fortress and the beautiful early fourteenth-century Church of St. Nicholas. Pechory was the site chosen by Hieromonk Jonah for the Pechorsky Monastery, which is still functional. I'm sure you'll like the four churches in the monastery, espe-

During the last war, the town was stroyed by the Germans. Today, it faces numerous, and largely insurmounta problems of any small town (it has a po lation of 190 thousand) in the provinces

WHERE TO STAY

It isn't a good idea to stay in Pskov for m than a night. In fact, groups of fore tourists are usually shown around place as a one-day tour out of Novgo or Petersburg. If you are interested eno to spend more time here, you could try **Rizhskaya Hotel** (25 Rizhskoye Sho ℓ 3 32 43; 9 16 37). A single room there c $65. The only other hotel in town is n like a students' hostel (in other words, you're not going to like it). But just in case, the name of the hotel is **Oktiabrskaya** (36 Oktiabrsky Prospekt, (9 94 00; 2 55 93).

WHERE TO EAT

Both hotels have restaurants. In addition, there are small cafeterias on the first, third, fifth and seventh floors of the Rizhskaya. There are two other restaurants near Pskov: **Rus** in the town of **Pechory**, and **Lukomorye** in the village of **Pushkinskiye Gory** (in

Everywhere you look, there are hills. Some are quite large, with flat crests; others are smaller and usually come in strings of several miles; finally, there are sand hills covered with dry pine groves. The troughs in between are usually long and narrow, and almost invariably stretch from the northeast to the southwest. These are the tracks left by the ice cap as it moved across the continent eons ago.

The capital of Karelia is **Petrozavodsk**. The town stands on the banks of **Lake Onega**, in a location that's conveniently

the Druzhba Hotel). Please do not go there for dinner, because you may not like the way people entertain themselves there (at times these places have Western-style saloon brawls). Lunch is all right, though.

OFF THE BEATEN TRACK

KARELIA

It lies to the north of Petersburg, flanked by the Gulf of Finland in the west and Lake Ladoga in the east. A land of stone-strewn forest and ten thousand lakes: without question, one of the most beautiful places in the world.

European North

close to several places of interest. One such place is Russia's first spa, **Martial Waters**, which is 60 km (37 miles) away. The museum there is open between 11 am and 2 pm (5 pm in summer). The attractions include a lovely wooden church and several mineral-water springs.

Another trip you can take out of Petrozavodsk is to the **Kivach Falls** (the largest in European Russia), 86 km (53 miles) away.

OPPOSITE: The walls of the Kremlin in Pskov were last used to hold back an invader in 1941. Hopefully, it was the last time.
ABOVE: When you live in the Yamal Peninsula, you go in style.

The star attraction of Karelia, however, is the island of **Kizhi**. The museum there offers a unique glimpse into Russian wooden architecture, from the tiniest izba's (peasant dwellings) to huge multidome churches. Everything in the collection, which was gathered from the whole of Northern Russia during the last few decades, was built without nails and with one tool only — the axe.

The trip from Petrozavodsk takes 70 minutes by hydrofoil (the excursion itself takes around six hours). Unfortunately, it is only

possible when the lake is navigable (May through November).

Where to Stay

There isn't much of a choice. The best you could do, I suppose, is opt for the **Karelia Tourist Complex** (2 Gulling Quay. (5 88 97). There is also the **Severnaya Hotel** (21 Lenin Prospekt. (7 63 54).

ABOVE: Wild berries are the national craze. When they ripen in the forests, the cities virtually empty. The wild strawberries you see here are going to last, as jam, throughout the winter. OPPOSITE: It's a thousand hues and shades... but they call this sea White.

Be warned that neither hotel has a service bureau, so chances are that they will only speak Russian.

Where to Eat

Both hotels have restaurants. There are two bars in the Karelia, as well.

MURMANSK

If you feel adventurous enough to go even further north, you could try Murmansk. It lies well beyond the Arctic circle on the 69th parallel, on the Kola Peninsula.

The climate is unusually warm. The sea along the coast is warmed by the Gulf Stream and is free of ice year-round. Another peculiarity of the place is the polar day, when the sun never goes beyond the horizon. In fact, it is an eerie picture when you arrive there in the small hours of the morning (if you are taking the Moscow flight), and see the sun shining on totally empty streets.

The time to go there, by the way, is summer — unless you want to see what polar night is like. The only place worth visiting in the area is the salmon waterway, a canal built to make sure that fishes of the valuable salmon family would get past the Nizhne-Tulomskaya Hydroelectric Power Station into the reservoir for spawning.

Where to Stay

There is only one place, an old five-storey hotel called the **Severnaya** (sorry, no elevator). The address is 20 Ulitsa Profsoyuzov, Murmansk-29, 183029. (5 50 40.

Where to Eat

There is a restaurant in the hotel, offering a selection of European dishes. Another two places you could try is a restaurant called **Polarnye zori** (21 Ulitsa Knipovicha), and also **Vstrecha** (28 Ulitsa Askoldovtsev). Both have European cuisine. If there are fish dishes on the menu, try them. Murmansk is famous for its salted halibut, smoked haddock and, of course, cod.

Siberia

WITH an area of 9.7 million square kilometers (3.8 million square miles), the chunk of Asia between the Arctic Ocean in the north and the dry steppes of Kazakhstan in the south which is known as Siberia, occupies roughly half of Russia.

Most of Western Siberia is one huge plain, which is, unfortunately, open to the masses of Arctic air coming from the north yet partitioned from the hot breath of Central Asian deserts by the Tien Shan and the Pamirs in the south. The result is a peculiarly dry and cold continental climate. As for Eastern Siberia, it is the coldest place in Russia.

For most people who have never been there, Siberia associates with the taiga, the dense forest which is the home of the brown bear, the lynx, and the famed Siberian sable. "It's not the giant trees, nor the deathly stillness that constitutes its power and enchantment," Anton Chekov reported from his travels there a century ago, "rather, it's in that only the migrating birds know where it ends. You don't pay attention to it on the first day of travel; on the second and third, you are surprised; the fourth and fifth day give you a feeling that you'll never get out of that monster of the Earth." The description is accurate (it's a bit on the gloomy side because the only means of transportation across Siberia at the time was a horse-drawn cart or sled).

The other attraction of Siberia is **Lake Baikal**, the legendary "sea" (as it is still referred to to this day), whose exceptionally clear waters run extraordinarily deep.

Even though Siberia is associated with endless winters, impenetrable forests and GULAG camps in the Western mind's eye, for Russians it is, more than anything else, a land of hope.

For one thing, the people who live there are respected throughout the land, although whether this respect is founded on their legendary ability to consume near-lethal amounts of alcohol or to build gigantic power projects is unclear. At any rate, it is

Khanty tribesmen discussing oil futures in Tiumen, the oil/gas region that Western investors find particularly attractive.

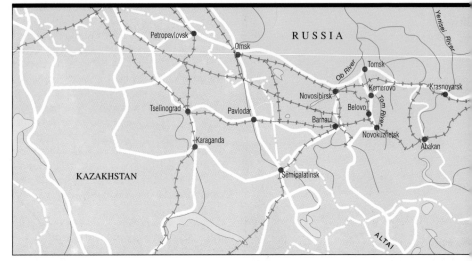

the highest praise to call someone a real *Sibiryak* (Siberian).

The other thing going for Siberia is its huge deposits of mineral resources. Siberia's reserves of oil, gas, precious metals and stones, timber and fur remain largely untapped owing to numerous political and technological complications; once these are resolved, everyone in Russia is certain to benefit from these immense riches.

Finally, the power of such great rivers as the Yenisei, the Angara, and the Lena can, if properly harnessed, supply all of Russia with cheap hydroelectricity.

Added up, these three factors could help transform today's half-starved, weary Russia into a livable country.

BACKGROUND

Man first came to the Altai Mountains twenty thousand years ago, when the forebears of the Scythians and, very probably of the modern Hungarians, Finns and Khanty's, settled the area to the north of the range. By the time they got to the Bronze Age some five thousand years ago, the Altai tribes knew animal husbandry and the rudiments of agriculture. They knew copper, bronze and gold. They made jewelry of stone, earthenware, animal horn and wood. They created striking paintings and sculptures. The reason why we know so much about their

accomplishments is because the Scythians believed in life after death, and tried to provide their deceased with everything they might want to use in the other world. As a result, their burial mounds contained everything from tiny gold earrings to huge wagons.

In the seventh century, the forebears of modern-day Turkic Altaians united into a large feudal empire, the Turkic Kahanate. The tribes of the empire attained impressive results in agriculture (they even used artificial irrigation).

All this came to an end, however, when nearly the entire territory of the Altais fell under the control of Genghis Khan's hordes, who plunged south Siberia back into the stone age. In the fifteenth century, Siberian Tartars formed several Khanates (with Tiumen and Sibir among them), which were finally united under the Siberian Khan in the early sixteenth century.

In 1563, Khan Kuchum came to power, and started a small war against the Russian merchants who had, by that time, established trade relations with his subjects. The Khan banned the fur trade and would not let the Russians sail the mighty rivers Pechora, Ob and Taz, which he considered to be his personal property (see cameo opposite).

In the following three hundred years of largely unplanned development, Siberia was gradually transformed into Russia's industrial back yard. In the political sense, it

What Kuchum did not anticipate, however, was that his hostile actions against his neighbors to the west jeopardized the interests of the Stroganoffs, one of the wealthiest families in Ivan the Terrible's Russia. The Stroganoffs were the owners of what we would today refer to as "an exclusive license" to operate factories in the Urals and beyond. Since these territories were considered a kind of no man's land between Russia and Kuchum's domain, the Stroganoffs maintained a military force to protect their not inconsiderable interests there. So, when salt stopped coming in from the mines, and furs from the forests, this small army was sent across the Urals. It was headed by Yermak, a Cossack soldier of fortune (and very probably highway robber). Yermak's merry men made short work of Khan Kuchum's nomads, who were still armed with bows and arrows at the time. In as little as two years (1581–1583), Yermak conquered nearly the entire khanate, and was hailed by the Czar of Moscow as a "noble hero." He later returned to Siberia where he was killed in an ambush. Yet there was no stopping the Russians; by 1605 they already controlled the basin of the Ob River from the newly founded fort of Tomsk.

The newcomers soon depleted the population of fur animals in Western Siberia. Driven by greed and the adventurer's thirst for danger, they grouped into small armed bands and proceeded further east. In 1631, a small Cossack unit reached Lake Baikal; by 1650, Russia was in complete control over most of Siberia. This proved to be a crucial development for the Russian Empire, since Siberian furs amounted to 10 percent of the czar's revenues throughout the seventeenth century. All in all, it took a little over fifty years for the Russians to conquer Siberia.

was regarded by the powers that be as our version of Australia, the waste basket for the dregs of society — criminals and opponents of the regime.

The first political prisoners were Radischev, the freethinker who dared cross Catherine the Great with his anti-serfdom pamphlet, Journey From Petersburg to Moscow, and the hapless Decembrists. A hundred years later, they were followed by GULAG prisoners.

In recent years, Siberia has undergone a change of image. It is no longer regarded as one big corrective-labor prison with a few showcase power stations and railroad projects thrown in. If you ask a teenager from Petersburg or Vologda to name the two most famous things about Siberia, you're likely to hear "pelimeni and frosts" (ten years ago, it would have been BAM, the Baikal-Amur Railway, and troubles on the Chinese border).

NOVOSIBIRSK

The city on the banks of the Ob was founded as Novonikolayevsk in 1893 by the builders of a bridge for the future Trans-Siberian Railway. The designer of the bridge, by the way, was an engineer by the name of Garin-Mikhailovsky, who is better known for his literary accomplishments.

Today, Novosibirsk is the fifth largest city in Russia. One of the notable things

about this town is that most of its 1.5 million inhabitants are scientists in the employ of the Siberian HQ of the Academy of Sciences.

GENERAL INFORMATION

The Intourist office is in the Novosibirsk Hotel. (22 02 50.

WHAT TO SEE

After you've taken your picture on the banks of one of the largest rivers in Siberia, be sure to visit the **Akademgorodok** (Town of Academics) on the banks of the **Obskoye Sea** (Reservoir). The main attraction of this trip is the **museum of ethnography**, where ancient Siberian statues are exhibited.

To get an overall picture of local flora and fauna, you don't have to go into the *taiga* — just drop in the **Museum of Local History** (11 Vokzalnaya magistral. (21 42 92). The museum is open between 11 am and 7 pm, and closed Mondays.

Novosibirsk has Russia's largest collection of paintings by Nicholas Roerich. The address of the art gallery is 13 Sverdlov Street. It is open between 11 am and 7 pm, and closed Tuesdays.

WHERE TO STAY

The choice isn't large. Chances are you'll be put into the **Novosibirsk Hotel** (3 Lenina Street, (22 03 13), a six-storey shabby building with all the usual problems of Intourist hotels. Single rooms start at $60.

WHERE TO EAT

Although you may not like the hotel, the fact is that it has a decent **restaurant.** Siberian cuisine is what you should be after, so call 22 72 44 and reserve a table.

HOW TO GET THERE

Refer to the chapter on the Far East on the Trans-Siberian Railway. A faster way into

PRECEEDING PAGES: Fishing weekend on the southern coast of the Kara Sea.

Novosibirsk is, of course, by plane, although I doubt that you'll be taking that route: Intourist usually includes this town on your program as a stopover for those who come on the Trans-Siberian Express.

IRKUTSK

The city sprawls on the banks of the Angara, the only river which flows out of Lake Baikal, not far from where the Angara joins up with its first tributary, the Irkut.

Founded in 1661 by explorer Ivan Pokhabov, the small fort received the status and coat of arms of a township in 1684. Soon afterwards, it became the residence of the Governor General for the entire territory of Eastern Siberia.

Irkutsk became a beachhead for further explorations. For example, the first Russians to make it to Alaska were sent there by Bichevin, an Irkutsk merchant, in 1761. In 1784, Grigory Shelekhov, "the Russian Columbus," founded the first settlement on the American Pacific coast.

Starting in the forties of the last century, Irkutsk became the center of international trade (primarily with China and Mongolia). As the gold started flowing in, the local merchants donated some of it to build a theater, museums, schools, and residential quarters in downtown Irkutsk. Unfortunately, most of the town was destroyed by the great fire of 1879.

GENERAL INFORMATION

The Intourist offices are in the Intourist Hotel (44 Bulvar Gagrina. (91 354).

WHAT TO SEE

Lake Baikal, first and foremost. "Baikal fascinates," Chekov wrote, "it's not for nothing that the Siberians call it a sea, and not a lake. The water is transparent beyond belief, to an extent that you can see through it as you would through air; it's tender turquoise color soothes the eye."

Over 1,600 m (almost a mile) deep, Baikal is a unique habitat for life forms of eons past (three-quarters of them are endemic to the lake). It takes the 300 or so rivers which flow into Lake Baikal 332 years to completely replace its water volume.

The excursion usually takes between seven and eight hours (from Irkutsk). In summer, you can go up the Angara by hydrofoil. After you get an eyeful of Baikal, you'll be taken to the local museum of wooden architecture.

Another place you should probably visit is the **Museum of Decembrists** (64 Dzerzginskogo Street, (45 245). The museum is open 10 am to 6 pm, and closed

three-storied building is situated practically on shore. Be sure to ask for a first-category room, however.

WHERE TO EAT

There is a restaurant with European cuisine at the Intourist Hotel, and a restaurant with a bar at Hotel Baikal. Aside from these, I would not recommend anything because the other two restaurants in town looked extremely suspicious to me when I was there (for instance, the "beef steak" I ordered

Mondays. The exposition, which takes up most of the house of Prince Sergei Trubet-skoi, the would-be dictator of the ill-starred coup, shows how several thousand Decembrists coped with life in Siberia after being exiled or imprisoned there in the 1820s.

WHERE TO STAY

In Irkutsk, your best bet is the **Intourist Hotel** (44 Bulvar Gagarina, (91 353). The hotel is fairly new (it was built in 1978), and conveniently located in the downtown area.

If you want to spend more than an afternoon on Lake Baikal, try the **Baikal Hotel**, which is also run by Intourist. The small

turned out to be a piece of contraband moose which the poachers stock the restaurant with).

HOW TO GET THERE

Your options are pretty much the same as with Novosibirsk or Khabarovsk. You can fly, or you can take a train on the Trans-Siberian Railway. The advantages (and disadvantages) of both types of travel are discussed in the Far East chapter.

ABOVE: Fishing is an important source of income for the local tribesmen; here, boats in cold storage.

The Far East

IT IS the last place God made. There's proof.

Remember trying to draw your first circle as a child, and how difficult it was to keep it reasonably round and get the beginning and the end to match at the same time? Well, when He started with the Kuril Hollow (9,754 m or 32,000 ft deep) off the Pacific coast, He must have had the same kind of trouble after coming full circle to Kliuchevskaya Sopka (at 4,269 m or 14,000 ft, one of the world's highest volcanos). The mismatch amounts to more than 15 kilometers or nine-and-a-half miles.

The Far East is big, spanning five time belts and covering a full one-sixth of the country's territory.

Between the frozen tundra of the Chukotka Peninsula and the rice fields of Primorye lies a geological wonder known as the Pacific Ore Belt — a zone of huge deposits of gold, tin, tungsten, lead, mercury and, in fact, nearly every metal in the periodic table.

During the Ice Age, when most of Siberia lay enshrouded by the glacier, the ocean's warmth kept the ice cap at bay, and the luxuriant subtropical vegetation survived. It did get sufficiently cold, however, for such dwellers of the north as giant taiga firs to have "settled" the coastal area.

Something of the kind happened with the fauna, too: the Far East is the only place in the world where the Ussuri tiger stalks the reindeer.

The climate is unusual (if, indeed, there is such a thing as "usual" climate). Every summer, the monsoons blowing from the sea relocate huge masses of humid warm air, making Vladivostok, the locals will proudly tell you, "just like the Crimea." They prefer to keep quiet about their strictly Siberian winters, which are so cold that at night, you can hear what the guidebooks refer to as "the whisper of stars" (although it must have been some half-frozen Chukchi poet who coined the term): as you exhale, the vapor crystallizes and bursts with a barely audible tinkle.

Industrially, the Far East is in just as sad a shape as the rest of Russia. On the one hand, it's potential is enormous: besides mining and fishing (every third fish sold on the domestic market is caught here), there's timber and pushnina (furs). Soy beans can be grown in the south. Then, of course, there are the huge rivers, ocean tides up to 13 m (40 ft) high, and geyser springs — a power engineer's dream.

On the other hand, the Far East really is far away from the European center of a country which has used the far-from-eye, far-from-heart principle during the last eight decades of economic construction (whereby the showcase center took what it wanted while the provinces invariably got the short end of the stick). Secondly, despite the half-hearted, albeit well-publicized, resettlement campaigns of the sixties and the seventies, the place is hopelessly underpopulated (just under six million inhabitants). Finally, the Far East is still hostage to the dog-on-hay ideology typical of totalitarian regimes everywhere. Here's an example. When the great hydroelectric power stations were built in the Asian part of Russia during the last few decades, huge territories were flooded by the dammed rivers. Since this mainly took place in the taiga, millions of dollars' worth of timber went to waste. Yet when a consortium of Japanese companies offered financial aid in exchange for the right to evacuate that timber, they were rebuffed. What, after all, is a few million dollars compared to ideological purity?

If the Far East is to have any kind of future at all, our more logically-minded economists say, it has to attract capital and knowhow from resource-poor Japan, and labor from overpopulated China. Yet attempts to lure Japanese business into the area come up against what the Japanese call "the issue of Northern territories" — a piece of Sakhalin and several Kuril islands which Stalin took away from Japan after World War II; meanwhile, cooperation with China develops at a snail's pace, because the Chinese want nothing to do with the "Russian revisionists."

Chukchi tribesmen rank among some of the best hunters in the world.

THE GREAT EXPLORERS

When the weather-beaten captains from Britain, Spain and Portugal opened the Age of Discoveries in the warm seas of the Atlantic and the South Pacific, their Russian counterparts set out for equally savage—and decidedly less pleasant—parts of the world: the Arctic Ocean, Siberia, and the northern part of the Far East.

After the foundation of Yakutsk in 1632, the search for new and better lands in the East began in earnest. The agents of this search, motivated by the mixture of devil-may-care curiosity, greed, and an itch for travel that is collectively interpreted as "adventurism" by contemporary historians, made what can only be called incredible progress. In 1639, Ivan Moskvitin became the first Russian to see the Pacific Ocean. In 1646, Vasily Poyarkov returned to Yakutsk after three years of travels in the upper reaches of the Amur River. In 1648, Semyon Dezhnev sailed around the Chukotka through the strait between Asia and America. In 1650, Yerofei Khabarov reported to the governor of Yakutsk that the lands along the Amur had "meadows large, and forests with every kind of beast, sable particularly; a good place for oats, millet, peas, buckwheat, and even hemp" (this last was to transform the Far East into a Russian Colombia in our time). It was Khabarov, in fact, who had blazed the trail for the wave of settlers who came in the eighteenth century and founded the town of Petropavlovsk on the "Peninsula of Volcanos" — Kamchatka. By the middle of the nineteenth century, the Far East was full of Russians. Three new towns — Blagoveshchensk, Khabarovsk and Vladivostok — appeared in the course of two years (1858–1860).

BACKGROUND

Archaeologists say that as far back as in the third millennium BC, the forebears of today's northern Chukchi, Koryak and Nanai tribes fished in the lakes and hunted in the forests in the center of the Chukotka Peninsula. In ancient Primorye, the domain of the Mohe, there was agriculture, animal husbandry, and rudimentary crafts.

The new age brought intermittent wars with assorted Chinese dynasties and the Mongol invasion. Genghis Khan's hordes left behind a trail of blood and destruction which was to become so familiar to the Slavs fifty or so years later. The Mohe never recovered. When the Russian explorers came to the Far East in the seventeenth century, the entire population of its southern part was on the short side of twenty thousand.

The twentieth century brought civil disorder, the 1904–1905 war against Japan, which ended in humiliating defeat for Russia, more civil disorder (the Bolsheviks knew their business well), the revolution of 1917, foreign intervention, guerilla warfare, and, ultimately, the Sovietization of the Far East by Gen. Bliukher's troops in 1922.

After a 15-year respite, there was more fighting with the Japanese at Lake Hasan. The Soviet Union entered World War II in the Far East on August 8, 1945, when Stalin declared war on Japan. In a way, this war is still going on, because the USSR never signed a peace treaty with Japan after its surrender on September 2, 1945.

GENERAL INFORMATION

There is an Intourist representative office in Vladivostok ((25 88 39). Don't hesitate to call them if you have any questions or problems; the director, Alexander Rogolev, is very helpful.

In Khabarovsk, which until recently has been the only "open city" in the Far East, there's a service bureau at the Intourist Hotel (2 Amursky bulvar. (34 43 47).

WHAT TO SEE

The **Amur River,** first and foremost. There is something about it which stubbornly defies description. "Don't look at me for an account of such beauties as the Amur's banks: here I'm totally at a loss, a self-confessed pauper," wrote a perplexed Anton Chekov sometime at the turn of this century. "How does one go about describing them, anyway? Imagine a huge mountain range which was forced to become a river bank: that's the Amur for you. Rocks, cliffs, forests, ducks, herons and other assorted beaked rascals by the thousands." I'm sure you won't expect this humble author to do better than the immortal creator of The Sea Gull, but it seems worth a try.

Known as Hara Muren to the Mongols and Heilungkiang to the Chinese, the Amur starts in the confluence of two minor rivers and empties into the Sea of Okhotsk 4,440 km, or 2,730 miles, to the northeast. The river, which is fed mostly by monsoon rains, is notoriously ill-tempered; in the high-water season every autumn, the current, which moves forty or so thousand cubic meters of water over a river bed between 200 m and 40 km (650 ft and 25 miles) wide every second, habitually runs out of control, flooding large parts of the river basin.

The strangest place on the Amur is known as Burning Mountains, situated in its upper reaches where the river runs past the high jagged edge of the Amur-Zeia Plain. The sandy cliff face incorporates streaks of brown coal and highly flammable lignite. Every night for several centuries now, Mother Nature has staged her own fire show as burning pieces of lignite slide down the cliff face, tracing vertical lines of flame over a mile-wide stretch of river bank. Few are there to see this incredible spectacle: save for a handful of villagers from the nearby one-horse Yermakovo, the only people brave enough to venture this far into the wilderness are stray hunters, deerherds and survival tourists.

In the northern part of the region, where harsh winters last from mid-October to early April, one can sometimes see an air avalanche: masses of supercold air slide down steep mountain slopes into the ravines, where sunlight does not penetrate. The lowest temperature recorded here in January was minus 58℃ (minus 35°F). Birches and larches, seemingly the only trees capable of surviving such cold, cover

the sharply sloping banks of the still-narrow Amur, whose roars echo from the canyon-like banks as the river, enshrouded in hazelike mist, makes its eternal way over the rapids. The only other form of vegetation here is the dwarf cedar, whose small cones contain oily nuts in thin shells. Come harvest time, the dwarf cedar groves fill with man (drawn by the medicinal properties of cedar oil) and beast (the brown bear and the sable are great fans of this exotic fare).

Speaking of beasts, the land in the northern reaches of the Amur is one of those rare places still left on the planet where hundreds of animal species are free of the Damoclean sword of human civilization. In the Zeisky National Preserve, for example, south meets north as the comparatively warmth-loving boar, the badger and the raccoon mingle with the famed Siberian sable, the wild reindeer, and the local black grouse, a melancholy bird known (and appreciated) among hunters for its weariness of life: flying away from what any other bird would regard as a suspicious creature with a rope is too much of a bother for this feathered denizen of the taiga; in fact, it can be caught with bare hands or snatched from a tree branch with a noose.

The Amur is the home of over a hundred species of fish. Summer and fall is the time for "red fish" as Russians call the assorted representatives of the salmon family which nature has "programmed" to spawn in fresh water. There's also lamper eel, herring, flounder, halibut, smelt, and dozens of exclusively freshwater species (including the amur, a beautiful — and very tasty — member of the carp family which draws its origins from the Far East — hence the name).

Mainstream Amur runs mostly through the territory of Khabarovsk Region, a huge expanse of steppe-like plain separated from the Pacific coast by several mountain ranges. The river is calmer here, and most of its 1540 km (970 miles) in the territory of the region are navigable. The last port on the Amur is **Nikolaevsk**. On a good day, you can see a piece of Sakhalin coast from the quay. You are also bound to notice (weather permitting), the color difference at the interface of fresh water from the Amur and salt water of the Sea of Okhotsk.

The largest port on the Amur is **Khabarovsk**. It is also the tourist center of the Far East, the only city which has never been placed off-limits to foreign tourists in a region obsessed with secrecy. It is funny how Vladivostok, for example, which has been open to foreign visitors for almost two years now, was still closed to Russians late in 1991.

Khabarovsk was founded in 1858 and named after Yerofei Khabarov. With a population of over 500,000, it ranks among the largest cities in the Russian Far East.

Make a point of visiting the **museum of ethnography** (21 Ulitsa Shevchenko). Established in 1894 as a subsidiary of the Russian Geographic Society, the museum offers a fascinating insight into what I described earlier as unused opportunities. A sizeable portion of the exposition extolls, and with reason, the natural wealth of the region; yet the only thing the assorted natural gifts of the land seemed to inspire in homo sapiens was a desire to kill and plunder. Suffice it to say that out of a 52,000-strong population, 22,000 died during the Japanese intervention and ensuing guerilla war (1918–1922).

There's also an interesting section on the assorted tribes of aborigines (known as

"small nations" in bureaucratic lingo) inhabiting the region. The museum is open 10 am to 5 pm. It is closed Tuesdays.

Another place you could try is the **Museum of Art** (45 Ulitsa Frunze). The icons aren't bad, and there's always an interesting exposition of Oriental art. The museum is open 9:30 am to 6:30 pm, and closed Mondays.

The largest city in the Far East is **Vladivostok**, the center of the coastal territory known as Primorye. It is perhaps best known as the starting point of the Trans-Siberian Railway and a port. Vladivostok was founded in 1860 by the crew of the S.S. Manchur as a rudimentary naval base. In the spot where the crewmen disembarked from the sailship, there stands one of the strangest

monuments I have ever seen. It has the shape of a rostral column topped by a model of The Manchur, which makes sense; what does not, however, is the quote from Lenin (who was born ten years after the town was founded): "Vladivistok may be far away," it says, "but it is ours, for all that."

In a way, Vladivostok is an illustration of what could have happened to San Francisco if the Bolsheviks ever got there. Fortunately for San Francisco, the only similarity today is the way the trams roller-coaster over hilly cityscape. Still, it is a nice place for a walk on a good day. Golden Horn Harbor is certainly pretty in any weather. To enjoy the view, just stop at any of the numerous observation platforms along the embank-

ment; in summer, you can try the beaches with the medicinal muds (Vladivostok is a famous resort area) or venture to the town of Sanatornoye for a tour of the Botanical Garden.

WHERE TO STAY

In **Khabarovsk**, there's the **Intourist Hotel** (2 Amursky bulvar. (34 43 47). Be sure to ask for the best rooms (there are only 14, so they have to be booked well in advance). There's also the decidedly less fancy **Tsentralnaya Hotel** (52 Ulitsa Pushkina. (33 47 59).

Vladivostok Harbor by night.

In **Vladivostok**, there's **Hotel Vladivistok** (10 Naberezhnaya Ulitsa. (22 22 08), **Hotel Equator** (20 Naberezhnaya ulitsa. (21 28 64), and **Amursky Zaliv** (9 Naberezhnaya Ulitsa. (22 55 20). All are located on the same street, and all aren't exactly what you'd term Sheraton class, but the only alternative is sleeping in a tent by the sea — or flying to Tokyo, where the hotels are good from what I hear.

WHERE TO EAT

In **Khabarovsk**, both of the hotels have restaurants; the Intourist also has a hard-currency bar. Then there are the assorted co-ops, ice cream places, and the like.

In **Vladivostok**, you'd best leave it to Intourist to keep you fed (probably at the restaurant of the hotel you'll be staying at), since the service industry in a town which had been a hush-hush strategic naval base for almost eight decades is, unfortunately, even worse than could be expected under the circumstances.

HOW TO GET THERE

For people who like trains, this may well be the best part, since Khabarovsk, Vladivostok, and Nakhodka (on the Sea of Okhotsk) are all stops along the **Trans-Siberian Railway**, the much-publicized communications artery which some say transformed Siberia and the Far East beyond recognition.

The Trans-Siberian was finished in 1916. It linked the town of **Cheliabinsk** in the Urals with **Vladivostok** on the Pacific coast. The railway project was regarded as a national priority: it was the future Emperor Nicholas II who laid the first stone into the foundation of the Vladivostok Station in 1891.

The distance from Moscow to Nakhodka is 9,500 km (5,930 miles); this journey across seven time zones takes eight days (although trains at times arrive a day or even two behind schedule).

A word of warning: go first class (meaning a two-berth compartment for two

with a sink); take plenty of books, food and drink (more than you would need just for yourselves, because you will almost certainly be invited to several train parties), and remember that there are no showers on the train.

If you want a ride on our version of Reading Railroad nevertheless, contact your agent or Intourist well in advance (say two or three months before you plan to go), particularly if you want to stop over along the way, or if you want to go part of the way by air. As it is, apart from the usual starting points such as Leningrad, Moscow or, in fact, any East European city, you can get on the Trans-Siberian either in Japan, or China, or even California (there is now air service to Khabarovsk).

Speaking of flying, it is possible to get to the Far East that way. I advise against it, however, since air travel has become a nightmare in Russia in the last two years, when such traditional problems as Russian weather and what we somewhat sarcastically refer to as "non-obtrusive" service were further aggravated by severance of economic ties between the assorted territories vying for independence (in plain language, no fuel), skyrocketing airfares (and airport taxi fares, too), and civil war in Transcaucasia (which affects Siberia and the Far East, as well, since the flight schedule is composed for the entire territory of the former Soviet Union).

Perhaps the best way to discover Siberia and the Far East is to take a package combination tour (including tickets from a European or American destination and back, a ride on the Trans-Siberian from, say, Irkutsk to Khabarovsk, and then a plane to Moscow), which should cost under $1,000 if you go from Europe.

In any event, whatever the advantages (or disadvantages) one or another form of transportation may hold in store, you always have the consolation that travel to and about the Far East is nowadays much easier than in Yerofei Khabarov's time.

OPPOSITE: "All in the Family", Yakut style.

Traveler's Tips

GETTING THERE

It's fairly easy, provided you plan your trip well in advance. Consult your travel agent (if you're coming as a tourist, that is). If you are visiting friends or going on a business trip, you are required by Russian law to present the relevant invitation from the host (person or organization) to the Russian embassy (consulate) in your country. If you do not have an invitation, you'll be expected to submit an official application form plus confirmation of hotel reservations, together with your passport, which should be valid for at least 30 days from the date of your arrival in Russia. If you plan to visit more than one city in Russia, please include a detailed itinerary, because you'll still need internal visas to move about the country in 1992.

BY AIR

If you go by air, you can arrive in Moscow, St. Petersburg, Kiev (in the Ukraine, which is a foreign country for us Russians now, but still just a night's train ride away from Moscow) and Simferopol (in the center of the Crimean Peninsula).

All major international airlines (thirty-four, to be exact) have regular flights to Moscow's Sheremetievo Airport. A non-stop flight from New York takes about nine hours (while an Aeroflot flight with stopovers in Shannon and Gander may take as many as twelve). European cities are two or at the most three hours away, India, six, and China, eight.

Built in the blissful epoch when foreign travel was a luxury attainable only for the high-placed, Sheremetievo is on the verge of being swept away by the tide of Armenian refugees, Jewish immigrants, black market-eers, Vietnamese "guest laborers" (whose real business, as the beleaguered customs officials will tell you, is smuggling everything they can get their hands on — from needles and pins to automobile engines — out of the country), tourists, and those lucky devils who have relatives they can visit in faraway lands. Combined, all these people are more than the overworked airport staff

can handle, yet, aside from vague plans to build a superfast monorail connection to downtown Moscow in the coming few years, little is being done to remedy the situation.

As it is, you should prepare yourself to spend at least thirty minutes waiting in line for passport control, another thirty or forty minutes for your battered suitcase to appear (be sure to pack all breakables in something soft, and to lock all your luggage), and God knows how much longer for customs, depending on what mood the inspector happens to be in on that particular day. Theoretically, you can use a "green corridor" to get through customs, but if you carry foreign currency in cash, you have to fill out a customs declaration, which means the "red corridor," and a longer line. Sorry.

For all this, arriving at Sheremetievo is much simpler than leaving. On certain days, when several Aeroflot jumbo jets leave in the course of an hour-and-a-half, waiting in line for customs can take forever, and I know a few people who actually missed their flights because they couldn't get to the customs gate in time (you are allowed to register for the flight only after clearing customs). Be warned, and arrive at least an hour before your flight is called, which usually happens one hour and forty minutes before the departure time stamped in your ticket.

As a rule, it takes around 50 minutes to get to midtown Moscow from the airport. If no one is there to meet you, and if you are not part of a group, remember that the taxi fare is around $20 now; make sure the taxi you get into is a regular one (yellow with the checkered symbol on top).

BY TRAIN

Don't go unless you are a dedicated train buff. If you are, or if you have no choice, then remember that the quickest way into Russia is from **Helsinki** (eight hours to Petersburg, sixteen hours to Moscow). From Western Europe, the trip to Moscow will take about three days, of which you'll spend at least a day traveling over Russian territory (bring

Passengers getting ready to board an Il-86, Aeroflot's answer to the Western Jumbo Jet.

food). Don't forget about the transit visas that you will be expected to present en route. And one more thing — trains actually tend to be more expensive than airplanes, so consult your travel agent.

BY BUS

There are no regular bus lines to Russia, but there are special bus tours which can be booked in Britain, Germany and Finland. Consult your travel agent for more detailed information and prices.

ing a look at this beautiful town on the spur of the moment, officer" will not pass muster with the traffic cop who is bound to stop you at the next checkpoint.

Should you decide to take the plunge, you can enter from Finland at **Brusnichnoye** and **Torfianovka**; from Poland — via **Brest** and **Shegini**; From Czechoslavakia and Hungary — via **Chop**. If you come from Finland, Intourist will most probably chart your route through **Torfianovka** to **Vyborg** to **St. Petersburg** to **Moscow**. From Western Europe, you can get to Moscow

BY CAR

The advantages, which include greater mobility once you get to wherever it is you are going, the chance to see a lot of Russian countryside, and the relatively low cost of motor travel in Russia, are, in my opinion at least, far outweighed by the inconveniences and even dangers of going by car, especially if you go on your first trip: inferior or non-existent auto service, scarcity of gasoline, dingy on-the-road accommodation and, worst of all, the infamous Russian roads. In addition, once you've cleared your route with Intourist, you are not allowed to stray from the highway, since "I just felt like tak-

via **Brest** and **Minsk** (in Belarus), and **Smolensk** (in Russia).

Don't be taken aback if you see a line of cars stretching beyond the horizon at the border — being a foreign national, you are exempt from this ordeal, and should proceed straight to the top of the line, in which the less fortunate Russians sometimes spend several days.

If you are driving a non-Soviet make, or a Soviet model manufactured for export, be sure to check if it's equipped with a catalytic converter, since that paragon of environmental safety has one minor drawback: it is totally incompatible with Russian gasoline.

Intourist will expect you to sign a statement to the effect that you pledge to take your car out of the country, even if it is damaged.

BY SEA

If you are coming from London, Helsinki, Giteborg or Oslo, all of which are connected to St. Petersburg (see the ST.PETERSBURG section), chances are that you'll enjoy your trip — if the weather gods of the Baltic smile at you, that is. An infinitely more enjoyable way into Russia lies through the Ukrainian port of **Odessa** on the Black Sea, which has direct links with Alexandria, Varna, Piraeus, Istanbul, Barcelona and Marseilles.

You could also come in from Vienna or Budapest up the Danube River to **Ismail**.

In the Far East, the port of **Nakhodka** on the Sea of Japan has connections to Hong Kong, Singapore, and even Sydney.

Prices and schedules vary depending on season. Please consult your travel agent, or go directly to Intourist or Morflot, the Russian company specializing in sea travel.

USEFUL ADDRESSES

For general information contact one of the Intourist offices.
USA NEW YORK: 630 Fifth Avenue, Suite 868. (757 38 84.
Canada MONTREAL: 101 McGill College Avenue, Suite 630, Quebec H3A 2N4. ((514) 849 63 94.
Britain LONDON: 219 Marsh Wall, Isle of Dogs, E14 9 FJ. ((1) 538 32 02.

CHARTER FLIGHTS AND TOUR OPERATORS

For information about air travel on scheduled carriers contact your travel agent or the local offices of the international airlines. For information about charter flights get in touch with one of the tour operators.

IN THE UNITED STATES

Anniversary Tours 330 7th Avenue, Suite 1700, New York, N.Y. 10001. ((212) 465 12 00, outside New York ((1-800) 336 13 36.

Five Star Touring 60 East 42nd Street, New York, N.Y. 10165. ((212) 818 91 40, outside New York toll free ((800) 792 78 27.
General Tours 770 Broadway, New York, N.Y. 10003. ((212) 598 18 00, outside New York ((800) 221 22 16.
Russian Travel Bureau 225 East 44th Street, New York, N.Y. 10017. ((212) 986 15 00, outside New York toll free ((800) 847 18 00.

Besides these four, there are hundreds more, so consult your travel agent for the best deal.

IN BRITAIN

The Barry Martin Group Suite 343 Linen Hall 162 Regent Street, London W1X 1 RA. ((1) 439 12 71.
American Express Co. Inc. 6 Haymarket, London SW1.
P&O Holidays 77 New Oxford Street, London WC1.

SPECIALIST TOURS OF RUSSIA

For information about specialist tours of Russia you should contact one of the following.

In America
American Travel Abroad 250 West 57th Street, New York, N.Y. 10107. ((212) 586 52 30, outside New York ((800) 228 08 77.

OPPOSITE: "Baikal tour for a bottle of rum? Yo-ho-ho!". ABOVE: Sometimes the helicopter is the only solution... besides reindeer, that is.

Adventure Center 1311 63rd Street, Suite 200, Emeryville, CA 94608. ((415) 654 18 79, outside Emeryville ((800) 227 87 47.

Trek Holidays 17 Hyden Street, Toronto, Ontario M4Y 2P2 Canada. ((416) 922 75 84.

Four Winds Travel 175 Fifth Avenue, New York, N.Y. 10010. ((212) 777 02 60.

Innerasia 2627 Lombard Street, San Francisco, CA 94123. ((415) 922 04 48, outside San Francisco ((800) 551 17 69.

International Bicycle Tours 12 Mid Plaza, Chappaqua, N.Y. 10514. ((914) 238 45 76.

World Travel Quests 690 Market Street,

Coventry Street, London W1V 8 HT. ((1) 930 24 52.

You can also try getting hold of a copy of *The Motorists' Guide to the Soviet Union* by Progress Publishers (Moscow, 1980). You'll find the book informative if slightly outdated.

TRAVEL DOCUMENTS

Aside from the passport and visa (the latter may take some time to get — please

Suite 810, San Francisco, CA 94104. ((415) 397 62 00, outside San Francisco ((1-800) 345 62 00.

In Britain

Explore Worldwide 1 Frederick Street, Aldershot, Hants, GU11 1LQ. ((252) 319 448.

London Walkabout Club 20-22 Craven Terrace, Lancester Gate, London W2.

MOTORING INFORMATION

In USA, contact the **American Automobile Association**, 1000 AAA Drive, Heathrow FL. (32746-5063, and in BRITAIN the Automobile Association, Fanum House, 5 New

refer to the beginning of this chapter), it would be a good idea to bring a driver's license and, if you are a student, an International Student Identity Card (which makes you eligible for discounts on plane and train tickets, accommodation, and museum tickets).

CUSTOMS

Please remember that the customs officers who stamp your declaration as you enter the country take their job seriously. Don't lose the stamped declaration — it may cost you a lot in terms of time and nervous anxiety when you pass customs on your way out.

And, yes, you'll be expected to fill in another declaration as you leave.

Russian customs policy, which has followed a jerky pattern betraying the absence of basic orientation in the last three years, is now firmly targeted against that part of our population who make their living by hoarding all types of scarce Russian goods and smuggling them for resale into Eastern European countries (Poland is the most popular choice). In a sense, it's good news for the Western tourist: aside from the usual no-nos such as firearms, drugs, and so on, you are free to bring anything you want, in any quantity within reason, into Russia. This does not mean, however, that you will be able to take all of it out again. On my last trip to the United States at the end of 1991, when the new regulations were already in force, all the video cassettes I was taking over for a friend of mine were confiscated. When I pointed out to the customs official that Russia has yet to produce a video cassette of its own, that the tapes in my bag had, in fact, been manufactured in the United States, and why couldn't they go back home, so to speak, he shrugged and showed me a copy of some document or other saying that under no circumstances are video tapes to be taken out of the country. This is why I recommend that you hang on to your declaration: be sure to list your more expensive personal items, such as video cameras, jewelry, laptop computers and so on, on the reverse side of the form; this will give you bargaining power when you are told that under no circumstances is the wedding ring your grandfather gave to your grandmother to cross the Russian border on your finger. Please take this advice seriously, and remember the formula: everything in, nothing out unless you have the appropriate papers for it (proof of purchase for antique-looking souvenirs, permissions from the Ministry of Culture for paintings bought for something other than convertible currency, and so on). And two more things: (*a*) some high-placed customs lunatic has recently declared antique samovars a "strategic resource," so if you have one with you, make sure it's sufficiently shiny and new

to pass muster, and (b) make sure that when you leave, you have less money than when you arrived. The latter piece of advice is for those adventurers who are not pleased with the official rate of exchange, and prefer to try their luck on the black market. The only disadvantage of this approach (besides the obvious fact that it is not safe) is that you do not get a receipt from the waiter, cabbie or whoever you buy your roubles from, and without a receipt, you cannot change your roubles back into dollars as you leave, at least not officially.

WHEN TO GO

The answer to that question would depend on your favorite time of year. The Northern Causasus and points south are best in spring; Siberia is strictly for the summer tourist, unless you want to freeze to death, and so on. Of the larger cities, St. Petersburg is never more delightful than in summer, the season of white nights,

ABOVE: Having a fashion pageant is one way to break the monotony of Artic night.
OPPOSITE: Despite a shortage of materials, fabrics and just about everything else a fashion designer needs, the fashion industry manages to come up with collections for every new season.

and Moscow, to me at any rate, is always prettier when most of the dust and dirt is covered by several inches of snow. Think well, and remember that in a continental climate (which is what most of Russia has), it is always wise to bring another sweater along, just in case.

The following table will give you an idea of the average temperatures (Centigrade) you can expect from January to October in five cities across Russia. To convert to Fahrenheit double the figure given and add 32.

CITY	JANUARY	APRIL	JULY	OCTOBER
Irkutsk	-10	0	15	0
Khabarovsk	-14	4	17	8
Moscow	-8	10	16	4
Petersburg	-10	2	15	5
Volgograd	9	0	13	3

WHAT TO TAKE

The way I see it, this section should contain instructions similar to those I would give someone planning to survive for several weeks on a desert island.

Start with everything you need to function normally: a set of spare glasses, contact lenses (with a cleaning kit), hygienic tampons, and warm clothes if you go in winter.

Then add everything you are used to at home. This includes things which are supposed to be there but never are, such as facial tissue, napkins, toilet paper, books in English, soap, shampoo, toothpaste (you wouldn't believe how terrible Russian toothpaste is), batteries for your radio, corkscrew/bottle opener, Barbie doll, spare razors, shaving cream, camera film, and all the clothes you think you might need — you're certainly not going to buy any in Russia, not in the coming year or two, that is.

Finally, bring some cigarettes, chewing gum, cheap cosmetics, etc. for the little bribes which make life so much easier in Russia.

Food does not present such a problem anymore: hard currency supermarkets are being opened almost every week in major cities. Prices are slightly higher than in Europe, but I'm sure you'll agree with me that expensive food is much better than no food at all. Most of these stores accept US dollars, Deutsche marks, French francs, Finnish marks, and pounds sterling; all of them accept major credit cards. Thanks to them, going to Russia no longer means going without 7-UP or Gordon's.

As far as the rouble market is concerned, the best approach would be to advise you what NOT to bring, since you can be reasonably sure that you'll find most of the following imported items at the new *kommer-cheskiye* ("commercial") stores: cigarettes (Marlboro, Winston, Salem, Camel and Rothmans being the most popular brands), cheap cigarette lighters, soft drinks in large plastic bottles; mineral water; Scotch, vodka, Russian champagne, brand-name liqueurs and other alcoholic beverages; canned and bottled beer from Belgium, Germany, Czechia, Sweden and Britain; chewing gum; caviar, chocolates and, last but not least, prophylactics made, of all places, in China. All this is of passable quality (although it is always prudent to check the expiry date), and very cheap, considering the exchange rate of the dollar (as a matter of fact, you can get a pack of Marlboros cheaper in Moscow than just outside the fence of the cigarette factory in Richmond, Virginia).

GETTING AROUND

BY AIR

If you plan to visit more than one region, you'll find flying the best way. It is also an unforgettable experience for anyone who does it for the first time. Foreign Aeroflot clients as a rule experience all the pleasures of airborne apartheid, a segregation system dating to the good old days when our government went out of its way to preclude its subjects from having undue contacts with foreign nationals. At overcrowded and dirty Vnukovo Airport, for instance, there is an excellent cafeteria, a souvenir shop and a comfortable waiting lounge for foreign passengers, all of which are, of course, strictly off-limits to "ordinary" Russians. After your flight is called, you are whisked off to your plane in a huge, near-empty bus shuttle, while we Russians are either squeezed together into one bus as so many sardines in a can, or told to walk to wherever the plane is parked, which is usually too far. The tightness of airport security depends on the proximity of the state border. Generally, it's not anywhere near as strict as one could expect from such a controlled society as ours. The rules you have to observe are very similar to those in the rest of the world, although once in a great while you may run into some over-zealous megalomaniac in a police sergeant's uniform who'll warn you that no cameras are allowed (or something of the kind. I recall being told on one occasion that I had to remove the batteries from my Walkman because "spy instruments" were prohibited).

Once you are in the air, remember that smoking is prohibited on all national flights, and that drinking is not (be sure to bring your own liquor, though, because Aeroflot never stocks any). Try not to eat the food, which will be served only if it's a long flight.

Being, until recently, a company owned by the defense ministry, Aeroflot, which now consists of several purportedly independent airlines, is surprisingly reliable in terms of air safety. Aeroflot planes, especially the new Iliushin 86's, are very safe, a fact which never ceases to amaze me bearing in mind that the whole country seems to be going to the dogs these days.

When you plan your trip, you'll want to make all reservations well in advance (60 days should be enough). Remember that you have to pay in convertible currency for seats on national flights. Following is a list of Aeroflot offices.

Moscow 4 Frunzenskaya Naberezhnaya. (245 00 02.

St. Petersburg 7/9 Nevsky Prospekt. (211 79 80.

Khabarovsk 5 Amursky Bulvar. (332-071.

BY TRAIN

Russia has one of the world's longest railway systems. Nearly four billion passengers use its services every year. In all likelihood, you will become one of them at some point of your stay in this country.

Train journeys fall into two distinct categories. The perfect example of the first is the inexpensive, comfortable and relatively short trip on the busiest line in European Russia between Moscow and St. Petersburg. The second category is strictly for that rare animal, the rail buff. Taking a train from Moscow to anywhere in Siberia or the Black Sea coast, say, requires infinite patience and special survival skills.

If you want to transform what could very possibly become a tedious ordeal into an interesting experience, you should become an adept of the train philosophy most Russians seem to follow. The first thing you have to learn to live with is sharing the cramped confines of a two (or even four) berth compartment with perfect strangers. You'll find that the natives are quite nonchalant about it, as you should be. There is no segregation of the sexes, and passengers usually take turns changing into their pyjamas (most Russians prefer track suits) before bedtime, while the opposite sex waits in the corridor. On a train, friends are easily made, and sharing your food (and maybe even a drink or two) with your fellow travelers is a perfect way to break the ice. As far as food is concerned, the more you take the better, because there's usually little to choose from on the menu in the restaurant car.

The other thing you'll have to learn to live with is toilet conditions, which range from very clean to arguably the most disgusting you've ever seen (there are two toilets at either end of the car). This, of course, depends on your *provodnitsa* (carriage attendant), the lady whose other responsibilities include providing you with tea and bedclothes. If the bathroom is too impossible, you could try complaining, I suppose, but it's been my experience that it rarely amounts to anything.

The third problem is boredom. Bring reading matter, games, tape players — anything that may help you pass the time.

Be sure to book your tickets well in advance (a week should suffice). Ask for *SV* (pronounced "es-veh") tickets, which are the closest thing we have to first class. The place to do it in Moscow is the **Intourtrans** office (15 Petrovka Street), or call the **Intourist** information office, (921 45 13.

BY BUS

To get on a long-distance bus, you should go to the *avtovokzal* (bus station), where tickets are sold in advance. This form of travel is not recommended for the independent tourist, however, since buses have been known to break down in the middle of nowhere, which isn't exactly the place for a person unable to understand Russian. Besides, you can always hop on a train, which will take you wherever it is you want to go faster and cheaper than a bus.

BY TAXI

Five years ago, we had one of the world's cheapest and most reliable taxi services. Today, it's a nightmare. A friend of mine who'd recently visited New York for the first time in his life, started his account of the virtues of capitalism by saying, "I know you won't believe me, but I swear the taxis always stop!" This is how bad things are.

Because (and this first and foremost concerns major cities such as Moscow and Petersburg) our taxis don't stop. On those rare occasions that they do, the cabbie won't let you in until after a discussion of destination and fare. (The meter which you'll see in his cab if you're lucky enough to be asked in has long since lost its original function and is now merely a relic of the good old days of "developed socialism.")

The good news for foreigners is that for five dollars, you can get to practically anywhere in whatever city you may be at the time, except possibly airports. To minimize you taxi bill, however I suggest that you try the following.

Assuming that you know how to pronounce the name of your destination, you should open the door and let the cabbie have it, together with your proposed fare, in one volley. It would be in your best interest, mind, that the driver not realize you are not a native. For this reason, you should use the briefest possible descriptions. If, for instance, you want to go to the Bolshoi, look mean and bark: "Balshoi teatr za polshtukee!" If the driver nods, you've pulled it off (" polshtukee" means 500 roubles in the peculiar vernacular used by veteran taxi passengers). If the driver says, "Mala!," say: "shestsot!" (600 roubles, which is more than enough for any destination in Moscow). If he agrees, you'll have saved between 200 and 500 roubles. Sometimes, it pays to know a foreign language.

BY THUMB

In Russia, it's not the thumb, it's the entire outstretched palm. In the city, the gesture will stop private cars (usually the older models whose owners need extra money to keep them going), who'll be glad to take you anywhere you want, provided you use the method described in the previous chapter (they actually charge slightly less than state-operated taxis). Again, the fare must be settled in advance.

Hitch-hiking in its pure form exists only on the highways. Be warned that no one will stop after nightfall, unless you are a woman alone (but in that case, you should not be there at all). Near the end of your trip, it would be only polite to offer to pay; in nine cases out of ten, your offer will be turned down.

BY CAR

Car rentals are expensive (refer to the MOSCOW and ST. PETERSBURG sections). The roads are terrible. So are the traffic cops and, worst of all, the other drivers on the road (driving is perceived by the Russian male as a kind of masculinity contest with no mercy for the vanquished). Don't expect people to give you the right of way, slow down to make it easier for you to pass, and so on — it just isn't done here, and we have our terrified pedestrians — along with an accident statistics that reads like a report from a local war theater — to prove it. There is no auto service to speak of. There are no emergency telephones on the highways. Finally, gasoline is always a headache.

If that did not scare you, try it. It does, after all, save time, and lets you see that much more of Russia. But seriously — watch out for the pot holes: the deeper ones may damage your vehicle.

To drive in Russia, you need a valid driving license and an International Driving Permit, which you can get from your automobile club or through Intourist.

The rules of the road are just about the same as everywhere else. In fact, the only difference between Russian and American regulations I am aware of is yielding the right of way in a circle: in Russia, the car to your right always gets the right of way, even if you happen to be in the circle already, whereas in America it's the other way around.

Gas stations (the Russian word for gas is benzin) are few and far between. The low-grade A76, which you must never use if you can help it, costs 20 cents per liter, and the higher octane Au93 and Au95 — 25 cents per liter. At Russian gas stations, you pay first and fill up second, so it's always a little gamble whether you'll come short of a full tank, or get too much (in which case it is a point of principle to let the next person in line — and not the gas station attendant — have those two or three remaining liters with a conspiratorial wink).

Traffic cops are stationed at cross-roads (in little booths commonly referred to as "vodka glasses"). You'd have to think hard to come up with places where they would have less control over traffic violations such as passing on the right, swerving from lane to lane, tailgating, crossing solid lines, making illegal U-turns, and every other imaginable violation committed by almost every driver several times every day in major cities (be warned). In Russia, you do not have to break a rule to be pulled over by traffic police; this circumstance, which would have been possible only under an emergency powers act in a European country, is widely capitalized upon by Moscow's finest, whose only source of income besides their skimpy salaries is bribes wheedled out of motorists. (I have never seen a traffic cop who refused to take a bribe in my ten years behind the wheel.) This is especially true on weekends, when traffic is light and the police are bored.

If you are stopped, and know that you are guilty of something (be it an unwashed car or a faulty headlight), the key word in your conversation with the traffic cop is *pro-*

tokol. When you hear it spoken, take your cue and come up with a pack of cigarettes or a fifty-rouble bill, or both. In most cases, you'll get a salute with a cheerful "Good luck!" thrown in for good measure. Fifty roubles is one-half of the minimum official fine (so everyone is happy, except the state which will get nothing because no receipt is filled out). Be extra careful on Friday and Saturday nights, when nearly every other driver on the road is usually anywhere between slightly intoxicated and roaring drunk. If a traffic cop suspects you of having had a drink or two (which is strictly prohibited under Russian law and may be regarded as a criminal offense under certain circumstances), he will invite you to sit inside his car, with the windows rolled up to get a better chance to smell the alcohol in your breath (breathalyzers are in extremely short supply and rarely resorted to). The fine for drunken driving is five thousand roubles (if you are lucky, because usually they just take your license away for two or three years). So please don't drink and drive, but if you do, remember that you are risking a fine of 5,000 roubles, or a bribe of least 2,500 (half the official rate).

The rules that you should really observe for your own safety are as follows:
— don't stop in a no-stopping zone, especially on highways after nightfall;
— observe the speed limits: 60 kph (35 mph) city, 90 kph (55 mph) highway;
— buckle up.

One last thing: if, God forbid, you have an accident, you must report it to the police at once.

GENERAL INFORMATION

Your best source of information in Russia is Intourist (which is now not one, but several companies). Here is a list of Intourist offices in Russia.

Moscow   16 Teatralny Proyezd. (203 69 62.
St. Petersburg   11 Isaakievskaya Ploschad. (214 64 20.
Irkutsk   44 Gagarinsky Bulvar. (446 86.
Ivanovo   6 Naberezhnaya Ulitsa. (785 58.
Kazan   9/10 Baumanskaya Ulitsa, Suite 212. (32 01 45.

Khabarovsk 2 Amursky Bulvar. (33 76 34.
Kislovodsk 24 Dzerzhinsky Prospekt. (534 97.
Krasnodar 109 Krasnaya Ulitsa. (588 97.
Kursk 72 Ulitsa Lenina. (29 98 40.
Murmansk 20 Ulitsa Profsoyuzov. (543 72.
Nakhodka 11 Nakhodkinsky Prospekt. (573 44.
Novgorod 16 Dmitriyevskaya Ulitsa. (742 35.
Novosibirsk 3 Ulitsa Lenina. (22 52 81.
Orel 37 Ulitsa Maksima Gorkogo. (674 63.
Petrozavodsk 21 Prospekt Lenina. (763 06.
Pskov 25 Rizhskoye Shosse. (332 43.
Rostov-on-Don 115 Ulitsa Engelsa. (65 90 00.
Smolensk Motel Feniks. (214 88.
Stavropol 2 Ulitsa Bulkina. (391 72.
Togliatti 24 Ulitsa Zhilina. (22 20 97.
Tver 130 Peterburgskoye Shosse. (556 92.
Ulianovsk 15 Sovietskaya Ulitsa. (948 16.
Vladimir 74 Ulitsa Tretiego Internatsionala. (242 62.
Volgograd 14 Ulitsa Mira. (36 45 52.
Vyborg 5 Zheleznodorozhnaya Ulitsa. (212 58.

EMBASSIES AND CONSULATES

A WORD OF WARNING: hold on to your passport! Keep it with you at all times!

"If you keep yourself, God will keep you, too," as the proverb goes; but if you do run into trouble, here are the phone numbers of several embassies in Moscow:

US Embassy (252 24 51; (252 24 59 (open 9:30 am to 5 pm with a break between 1 and 2:30 pm Monday through Friday). 19/23 Tchaikovsky Street (Ulitsa Chaikovskogo).
American Consulate St. Petersburg: 15 Ulitsa Petra Lavrova. (274 82 35.
British Embassy (231 85 11; (231 85 12 (open 9 am to 5 pm with a break between 12 noon and 2:30 pm Monday through Friday). 14 Naberezhnaya Maurisa Toreza .
Canadian Embassy (241 90 34 (open 8:30 am to 5 pm with a break between 1 and 2 pm Monday through Friday). 23 Starokoniushenny Pereulok.

Australian Embassy (246 50 17 (open 9 am to 4:15 pm with a break between 12:30 and 1 pm Monday through Friday). 13 Kropotkinsky Pereulok.
German Embassy (252 55 21 (open 8:30 am to 5:30 pm with a break between 12 noon and 1 pm Monday through Friday). 17 Bolshaya Gruzinskaya Street.
Austrian Embassy (201 73 17 (open 9 am to 6 pm with a break between 1:30 and 2:30 pm Monday through Friday). 1 Starokoniushenny Pereulok.
French Embassy (236 00 03 (open 9 am to 6 pm with a break between 1 and 3 pm Monday through Friday). 10 Kazansky Pereulok.
Irish Embassy (288 41 01 (open 9 am to 5:30 pm with a break between 1 and 2:30 pm Monday through Friday). 5 Grokholsky Pereulok.

HEALTH

You need no health certificate if you come from America or Europe. If you go to Central Asia via Russia, it might be a good idea to have a cholera vaccination and a hepatitis shot. If your stay in Russia is going to be a long one, you may have to submit to an AIDS test. In any case, you would probably do best to consult your physician.

As for health insurance, remember to make sure (as with car insurance) that it covers both European and Asian Russia.

For minor health problems, use the medicines you've brought along. If you haven't any, try getting some at the nearest hard currency department store.

As for prescription drugs, it's a good idea to bring an ample supply, and to take precautions against losing the lot. This eggs-in-one-basket advice also applies to eyeglasses, contact lenses, respirators, and so on.

Be sensible, and never drink or eat what you should not, even if it looks good. Never drink tap water. Mineral water (in bottles) is not difficult to come by.

In an emergency, Intourist will help. You'll get a doctor free of charge, but you'll have to pay for medicines and a hospital (if needed). On the whole, it's best to keep out of Russian hospitals. Remember to

The two-headed eagle is the symbol of the Romanovs.

bring several disposable syringes, just in case. (See EMERGENCIES on page 197).

MONEY

Russia's currency is the rouble. The coins are called *kopecks*, 100 to the rouble. At the moment of writing, the Central Bank of Russia was issuing one, three, five, ten, twenty-five, fifty, one-, two-, and five hundred rouble notes, as well as one thousand and five thousand banknotes.

This may be bad news for the rouble, but not for the tourist. For anyone with so-called "convertible currency" (US dollars, British pounds sterling, French francs, Deutsche marks, etc.), the pirouettes of our national currency are as important as last year's snow, since the rate of inflation seems to follow the fall of the rouble. In plain language, a pack of cigarettes always costs one dollar on the street, even though its rouble price may come up from 70 to 110 in the course of a few days.

There's little point in trying to give currency equivalents for the rouble. At the time of writing in June 1992, it was 150 roubles to the dollar (black market rate). Today, you can freely — and legally — convert your money in a number of conveniently located banks. If you plan to change a lot of it, remember to bring a shopping bag, because if they give you denominations smaller than 200 or 500, you'll need something to carry all that cash in. Then again, there's little need for the average tourist to buy a lot of roubles, because there's little you can buy with them, and whatever there is to buy can be usually paid for in dollars (this does not apply to state-run stores).

Credit cards are accepted in all tourist haunts, and you can get cash on your American Express or Visa card in major cities (see the relevant chapters). To get roubles in exchange for traveler's checks or Eurocheques or a credit card charge you will need your passport. In fact, now that credit card theft has become fashionable, you may be asked to present your passport every time you use a credit card. This is, of course, done in your interests.

To change whatever roubles you haven't spent in Russia before you leave, you must present the relevant currency exchange slip at the bank (there's one in every international airport).

ACCOMMODATION

Tourist accommodation is regulated by Intourist, the monopolist state-operated international travel agency. As I have already mentioned, Intourist does not deign to bother with such trifles as clients' interests. You may therefore rest assured that if your pig-in-a-poke tour is booked through that particular agency, you will have no choice of accommodations in a given price range. You simply take what is offered, and that is that. You may, however, choose between "deluxe" (suite with bath) and "first class" (single/double room with bath) accommodations. Remember that when you book as an individual, the rates are astronomical.

When you check in, your passport will be taken for registration and returned the next day. You will be issued a hotel card, which you are to present to the doorman every time you come in. Some hotels take this card away in exchange for your room key. A word of warning: try not to leave valuables in your room.

The new joint venture hotels offer a better deal, but their services don't come cheap. For additional information, refer to the Moscow and St. Petersburg chapters.

A "hotel day" usually starts (and ends) at noon; to avoid paying for an extra day if you need to stay two or three hours longer, talk to the receptionist.

ETIQUETTE

There is a cult of the foreigner in Russia. People love an American (German, Spaniard); they shower you with questions, give you directions in peculiar Russian-accented English (almost everyone knows at least a few words), invite you to dinner, offer all kinds of advice on every imaginable aspect of daily life from shortcuts on the subway to marital problems, and generally pamper and spoil you beyond all measure.

There are some things that you are supposed to know, because, after all, as Russians say, "you do not barge into a neighbor's monastery with your own rules."

Men must take off their hats before entering a church. For women, it's a good idea to wear a headscarf. Shoes are usually taken off before entering a home (you should ask). If you are invited to someone's home, it's always a good idea to come with a small gift (a bottle of wine, flowers for the hostess,

home with half-empty bottles in the bar: once a bottle is opened, it is usually finished. This part is easier for women, though, because drinking isn't really regarded as a feminine thing to do. To ease yourself out of this situation, you may follow the advice of a British correspondent who'd spent two years in Moscow. "To avoid getting drunk," he wrote, "you must sit close to a potted plant, into which you should empty the contents of your glass when no one is looking; failing that try drinking half of your glass with every toast, and sniffing a piece of

candy for children — anything will do). If you are invited to something other than dinner, but your hosts nevertheless offer you something to eat, you must decline as politely as possible (which does not mean a thing, of course — you are still getting food whether you want it or not). If you really aren't hungry at the time, follow my example and ask for tea or coffee to throw 'em off: Russians take their tradition of hospitality seriously.

If there's drinking to be done, remember that Russians drink their liquor neat, that they always eat when they drink, and that they like to drink together ("clinking" glasses is obligatory). They also drink too much, and I, for one, have never seen a Russian

black Russian bread immediately afterwards." And don't, I might add, chase down your vodkas with beer. Please.

On the subway (or in a bus) it is *de rigueur* for men and younger people to offer their seat to women and older people. It isn't your choice, really, and on several occasions I have witnessed verbal lynchings of culprits who failed to observe this unwritten rule, in which the entire bus would gleefully take part. In fact, it is a good idea not to sit down at all.

Russians have a keen sense of propriety (or what they regard as propriety), which

"From dust you come, to dust you go": funeral mass at an Orthodox Church.

they readily share with perfect strangers. Such readiness, which would qualify as rudeness in a European country, stems from a desire to help. I remember walking with a rather hot-tempered Latin American friend of mine in a subway corridor. As soon as we stepped off the train to make the transfer we wanted, my friend was accosted by a pudgy old lady. "Young man," she informed him, "you shoe lace is untied." He paid no heed, however, and pressed on. Several steps later a girl separated from a bunch of her giggling friends, who were

obviously waiting for someone in a corner, very politely excused herself and told him that his shoe lace was undone. He growled his thanks but refused to yield and walked on. As we reached the escalator which was to take us to our station, another old lady bellowed that he would certainly fall and break his neck if he didn't tie his shoe lace NOW! At that point, however, it had become a matter of principle for the poor guy, and he pretended not to hear, although the woman's charming baritone turned every head on the escalator. Finally, as we reached the boarding platform, a balding elderly man ran up to him and said, panting, that... but you know what he said. The man clearly expected thanks for his troubles, and was therefore taken aback when my friend calmly took off the shoe with the untied lace and tossed it under the approaching train, anger and defeat on his face. It took us a good thirty minutes, I should say, to retrieve the hapless shoe which had fallen victim to its owner's poor knowledge of local habits.

PUBLIC HOLIDAYS AND FESTIVALS

HOLIDAYS

January 1 New Year's Day
January 7 Orthodox Christmas
March 8 Women's Day
May 1 "Spring" Day
May 9 Victory Day
August 21 Anniversary of the Coup

FESTIVALS

JANUARY
"Russian Winter" Festival of Music and Dance in Moscow.
MARCH
"Festival of the North" in Murmansk (skiing, skating, reindeer racing — anyone may take part).
MAY
"Moscow Stars" (art and music).
JUNE
"White Nights" (music and ballet in Petersburg).
AUGUST
"Crimean Dawns" (art and music in Yalta).
DECEMBER
"Russian Winter" Festival of Music and Dance in Moscow.

RELIGIOUS FESTIVALS

Orthodox Christmas is both a religious and a national holiday, fast on becoming the most popular festive occasion of the year now that the tanks and ICBM's are no longer displayed in Red Square on November 7, formerly celebrated as the anniversary of the Great October Socialist Revolution.

Easter, to be celebrated on April 18 in 1993, is arguably the second most important religious festival. Don't forget to bring painted eggs.

Ivana Kupala is celebrated on the night of July 7, which is considered perfect for fortune-telling.

They say that it is the only night of the year when the fern blooms; if you find this blossom, you'll see all your dreams come true.

MAIL

If Russian watches are believed to be the fastest in the world, Russian mail is certainly the slowest. It takes a letter between three and five weeks to reach the United States (send Christmas cards in the first week of November), if, indeed, it gets there at all. Incoming correspondence is habitually opened and resealed (with a lack of finesse, I might add, that is a trademark of our state security).

lin. There are a million limitations, and every item you want to send is examined in great detail. Parcel service is cheap but slow. In a word, FedEx it! (In Moscow, ℂ 253 16 41).

TELEPHONES

Our minister of the automobile industry once remarked that the level of economic development of any society is best reflected by the cars in the streets. He was wrong. It's not cars, it's telephones.

There are two ways you can get your mail in Russia. The first is to have it addressed to Intourist in the city where you are staying. The second is to address it to the central (international) post office of that city (Poste Restante); you will then need your passport to collect your correspondence.

Incoming parcels have to be collected, too. It isn't really a good idea to send a parcel from abroad to a Russian citizen, because it is usually pilfered by either customs or post office people, and there is a duty to be paid on what's left of it in hard currency, which is usually too much for a Russian.

If you are sending a parcel abroad, bear in mind that as far as our postal service is concerned, Joseph Stalin is still in the Krem-

In December, 1992, we still had the world's cheapest telephone service. The price of a single call was fifteen kopecks (0.1 cents).

To use a public pay phone, deposit a fifteen-kopeck coin in the slot on top of the phone, wait for the station signal (continuous tone), and dial the number.

To call long distance within Russia from a pay phone, first you must find one (every hotel usually has several). If you

OPPOSITE: Morning mass at a church in Yaroslavl: men were afraid to go to church under the communists for fear of losing their party cards, jobs, or even freedom; thank God for the old ladies who kept the fire burning.
ABOVE: Yamal Peninsula: Letters from Santa?

know the city code and have a handful of 15 kopeck pieces, you're in business. If you don't know the city code, chances are you'll find it in the diagram on the wall. From your hotel room, dial 8 (you must first check if the hotel has a direct line to the city telephone system), wait for the continuous tone, and then dial the city code and the number. The cost of the call will then be placed on your hotel bill.

Calling long distance abroad is another story. Theoretically, there is a direct-dial connection with Europe and several Latin American countries. In practice, you need to keep trying for an hour to get through, and the fact that Russia still has rotary-dial phones doesn't help much, as you'll soon see. If you are willing to try, dial 8 (after whatever digit that gets you the city telephone system from your hotel, usually 8 or 9), wait for the continuous tone, and then dial 10, the country code (see below), city code and number; cross your fingers and wait.

To call the United States, you need to do the same, but only between 12 midnight and 9 am Moscow time, and only from Moscow or Petersburg.

To save time (and your index finger), call the Moscow international telephone exchange (℡ 8-190, 8-194; 8-196). Tell the operator at what time the call should be placed. The operator, in turn, will tell you the time the call *can* be placed (there's a waiting period between 8 and 72 hours for the United States), and you'll eventually come to an agreement. If the operator gives you any trouble, call her *nachalstvo* (chief): 339 84 22. You should be in your hotel room at the appointed time; if nothing happens for an hour, call the operator and find out why (they are supposed to connect you within 60 minutes).

Just as local calls are absurdly cheap, long-distance calls are absurdly expensive. A minute with the United States cost 108 roubles at the time of writing.

EMERGENCIES

The emergency two-digit phone numbers (identical in all cities):
Fire Department ℡ 01

Police Department ℡ 02
Ambulance ℡ 03
Gas leaks ℡ 04
General emergency ℡ 05
Phone information ℡ 09
Emergency numbers of Moscow's better hospitals:
HCI at US Embassy ℡ 252 24 51-9
IHC ℡ 253 07 03
Sana Medical Center ℡ 464 12 54
Botkin Hospital ℡ 255 00 15. Western-level medical service and medicines to all foreigners.
Credit card loss or theft ℡ 203 80 79 (Intourservice) ℡ 254 17 95 (American Express).

OTHER HELPFUL NUMBERS

Information — ℡ 09
Long-distance information (operator) — ℡ 8-dial tone-13
International information (operator) — ℡ 8-dial tone-190 (or 194 or 196)

COUNTRY CODES

USA and Canada   1
United Kingdom   44
Ireland   353
Australia   61
New Zealand   64
Austria   43
Belgium   32
Denmark   45
France   33
Greece   30
Holland   31
Italy   39
Norway   47
Sweden   46
Switzerland   41
West Germany   49

RUSSIAN CITY CODES

Moscow   095
Arkhangelsk   37422
Irkutsk   3952
Ivanovo   0932
Kaliningrad   01122
Krasnodar   0422
Murmansk   815

Nizhny Novgorod 8312
Novgorod 816
Novosibirsk 3832
Perm 3422
Petersburg 812
Pskov 81122
Rostov-on-Don 8632
Smolensk 081
Stavropol 86522
Tver 08222
Ulianovsk 84222
Vyborg 278

BASICS

TIME

Russian time is two hours ahead of Green-wich Mean Time, except in the summer when clocks are put forward one hour. However, as most of Europe and America also switches to summer time, Russia remains one hour ahead of Western Europe, two hours ahead of the British Isles, seven hours ahead of New York, ten hours ahead of Los Angeles, and so forth.

ELECTRICITY

Russian current is 220 volts, although it is not always up to full strength. The outlets take European-style plugs with two round prongs.

WATER

It's safe to drink, except perhaps in St.Petersburg. I advise against drinking tap water anywhere, for two reasons: the mineral composition may be "unfamiliar" to your stomach, which will react accordingly; and tap water is heavily chlorinated.

Mineral water in bottles can be obtained locally, and Vichy is sold at hard currency stores.

WEIGHTS AND MEASURES

Russia uses the metric system. Following is a conversion chart you might find helpful.
LENGTH kilometer: 0.62 miles; meter: 39 inches; millimeter: 0.04 inches.

AREA square kilometer 0.37 square miles; hectare 2.5 acres
CAPACITY liter: 1 quart.
MASS AND WEIGHT kilogram: 2.2 pounds; gram 0.04 ounces; milligram 0.015 grains.

CRIME

There's none to speak of, particularly if we compare our larger cities to places like New York City or Marseilles. As far as tourism is concerned, there's little you need to be afraid of if you behave sensibly. It is never a good idea to leave valuables in your room, buy roubles on the street, get into private cars if you are alone, or take midnight walks in the park. Our streets are still safe, and what the public worries about most is the emergence of organized crime and the growing drug traffic (both being upstarts by Western standards, of course).

Law and order is maintained by the "militsia" (militia or police), recognizable by their blue uniforms. Traffic police usually wear white belts and, in wintertime, heavy boots to cope with the frost. You'll find them helpful, ready to give you a smart salute and all the directions you may need. If you run into real trouble, however, it would be best for you to contact your embassy.

RADIO AND TELEVISION

Five years ago, our radio broadcasts were close to the ideal soporific. Old patriotic songs, "ideologically correct" love songs ("Why did you come to our *kolkhoz*? Why did you interrupt my peace?"), classical music ad nauseam, and constantly repeated propaganda.

The first ray of hope shone through about two years ago, when we got our first Franco-Soviet radio station, Yevropa plus. The station, modeled after the Western stereotype, excels in its selection of rock music, and broadcasts nothing but rock music and advertising. Today, there are several of them. The only problem you may have is that our FM band starts *after* 108, making imported radios quite useless. To fill the gap, one station now broadcasts in the 101 frequency; hopefully, there will be more.

The only news station in English is **Radio Moscow**, the dinosaur which hasn't changed in the last thirty years and probably never will. So unless you are interested in the virtues of Marxism, tune into the **BBC World Service** (the reception, as Gorbachev attested in August 1991, is quite good): 9410 Hz in the 19 meter band, and 12095 kHz in the 25 meter band.

Russian television is still struggling to shed the vestiges of bureaucratic control. For every good program such as Leonid Parfyonov's *Portret na Fone* or Petersburg Television's *600 Seconds*, there are a dozen boring,

shows. There is nothing in English except for video clips broadcast by 2x2 Station. There are some old American TV series such as *I Spy* and *The Lone Ranger*, a few game shows (in Russian), plus several very interesting news programs which, I'm afraid, you'll miss because they are in Russian too. The only news in English is broadcast by the BBC at around eleven pm every night (there is a simultaneous Russian translation, but you can usually hear enough of the English text). There is a fair amount of sports programs, including recorded NBA games every Sunday at six pm.

Most hotels have one or several cable channels with anything from old movies to latest Hollywood films to CNN News to outrageous pornography — democracy comes in strange ways.

NEWSPAPERS AND MAGAZINES

English-language newspapers are usually sold at newsstands in hotel lobbies. The problem is that they are at least a week old, and very expensive. If you don't mind reading rather stilted English, try a copy of Moscow News, arguably the best Russian newspaper in terms of objectivity and straightforwardness. Moscow News is published in several languages.

On the whole, you must prepare yourself for an information diet while in Russia, unless, of course, you are willing to visit one of several libraries in the foreign embassies merely to read today's newspaper.

Time, Newsweek, and most major European magazines are available in the hard currency supermarkets.

TOILETS

Public toilets are the testimony that socialism does not work. A few years ago, when it was decided after several months of parliamentary debate to allow private persons to own and run paid public toilets, the nation witnessed a miracle. Overnight, the smelly, dimly lit and dirty places where only someone in desperate need would venture, turned into spic-and-span oases of perfumed air, bright light, glittering mirrors, and miles of toilet paper. A WC in a hotel I stayed at on the Black Sea coast boasted potted palms; it was much more pleasant than my room.

As time passed, prices went up and standards went down, but not enough to justify the horror stories you hear on occasion.

Scarcity is another problem. I remember calling a friend in St. Petersburg once to ask him how things were with sausage over there. "With sausage," he replied, "things are just dandy. It's without sausage that life is miserable." The same, I admit, applies to paid toilets.

STEAM BATHS

There are two kinds. What the Russians call "Finnish baths" have a hot room with a stone-laden stove. The temperature in a Finnish bath, or sauna, can go up to 110°C (250°F), but the air is dry there, which is, of course, the reason why such intense heat is bearable. Then there are the "Russian baths", where the stove in the hot room has a special opening into which small amounts of water (beer, herb mixtures, or whatever) are thrown at regular intervals to produce superheated steam, which the experienced bath-house goer takes out of the air with a pair of birch or oak besoms and spreads over the body of whoever happens to be the victim on the receiving end (it is always better when someone does it for you). The sensations produced by this procedure (which, I admit, looks very much like a flogging to the layman's eye) range from delicious to heavenly, depending on the skill of your "steamer" (another Russian term. In fact, Russians never say, "Let's go to the bath-house to wash." They say, "Let's go to the bath-house to steam.").

Saunas, which for some reason are considered "upper class," are to be found at practically every Intourist hotel in the major cities. One of the beauties of dry heat is the temperature contrast you get by plunging into a small pool filled with icy water immediately after emerging from the hot room. Make sure to ask whether they have such a pool when you book the sauna. You should also ask about massage, which is still unbelievably cheap in this country, and invariably a pleasure. To me, the best thing about steam baths is that delicious first breath of fresh air I get when I go out in the street, a sensation no doubt experienced by the newborn babe fresh out of the womb.

Although a visit to a Russian bath-house is as important — and enlightening — a part of your tour as going to the Bolshoi ballet, please remember that it isn't recommended during pregnancy. People with a heart condition should stay away, too.

WOMEN ALONE

… are welcome, that's all there is to it. If you behave in a sensible way, and remember that the pair of jeans you're wearing is worth two or three months' work for the average citizen — and is therefore a considerable attraction for the street mugger — you'll be perfectly safe. So stay out of dark corners, and never sit in a private car that appears instead of a regular taxi.

As for the other thing every guidebook is supposed to warn women traveling alone about, you'll find that a damsel in distress — or in a restaurant — attracts the chivalrous attentions of Russian men. And no, you don't have to sleep with the fat little Georgian even if you do accept the bottle of wine

he sends over to your table. In fact, friends are easily made that way; at any rate, you are the one who decides how far a relationship should go.

If things do get out of hand, however, feel free to call on the nearest militiaman for help — you'll find him firmly on your side (the militia are chivalrous too).

TIPPING

Tipping is common practice. In fact, even if a service charge is included into your restaurant bill, you should still give between five and seven percent to the waiter. It does not necessarily have to be cash, either: your guides, waiters, maids, and cab drivers will gladly accept cigarettes, chewing gum, cosmetics and the like for "tea money" as a tip is called among Russians.

Sometimes it is a good idea to give a tip in advance, because some of the people you'll deal with find it difficult to understand that to extract a tip from their customer, the customer has to be pleased first. Of course, you don't have to tip anyone for rude or slow service, but since you deserve neither, try tipping beforehand, and the result will be much better, I assure you.

SURPRISES

There will be many, most of them pleasant. We Russians are great believers in soul power, and perhaps the greatest surprise Russia has in store for you is to find your soul transformed by the beauty of our land, the hospitality of the people, the small joys of seeing new faces and places.

You are bound to feel something of the kind when you visit the great churches and monasteries, such as Sergiyev Posad, for example. You will feel more of the same if you are lucky enough to make friends and be invited to their home. To me, and to a great many of my compatriots, the greatest attraction of life in general and travel in particular is the opportunity to monitor, so to speak, the reactions of one's inner self to different environments. In short, going to Russia is always a notch above common-or-garden tourism; it is closer to a pilgrimage.

As for the unpleasant surprises, I hope this book allows you to avoid most of them. I hope that the things beyond your control (such as absence of hot water, no electricity, no toilet paper, no gasoline, etc.) will not smear your overall impression, which I'm certain will be a favorable one.

Another thing that may surprise you is that even if you do get more than your share of nasty little surprises during your stay in Russia, you'll find your thoughts returning to the place two or three weeks after you come back home.

STAYING ON

Should you decide to stay on in Russia, you can make arrangements to extend the length of your stay. If you come on an invitation visa, your host person (or organization) should contact the Ministry of Internal Affairs at least a week before your visa is due to expire. If you are in Russia on a tourist visa, you'll need to buy Intourist services for the period of extension (they will tell you how at the service bureau at your hotel).

If you want to buy an apartment in one of the major cities or a house in the suburbs, you'd need to contact one of the numerous real estate brokers who sell for convertible currency. Other companies offer exchanges (apartment in New York for an apartment in Moscow, for example). Paperwork is still a problem, but you'll find that there are several legal firms who will be willing to help for a nominal fee.

RUSSIAN FOR TRAVELERS

The bad news is that Russian is arguably the most difficult language in the world after Chinese and Hungarian; the good news is that you don't have to know a lot to communicate with the locals who are usually patient and willing to help you out of your linguistic predicaments, particularly because they probably speak at least some English themselves.

I have therefore decided to stick to the basics. If you want to learn Russian, try getting hold of a copy of Russian for Beginners (Russky Yazuk Publishers, Moscow, 1984), which comes with a set of tapes. If you cannot get that, consult the nearest university with a Russian-language course, or write to ELIS School of Russian, 46 Piatnitskaya Ulitsa, 109017 Moscow, Russia.

PRONUNCIATION

There are several things to remember about Russian pronunciation. First of all, the "r" sounds are hard (not drawled), which is a problem for the English speaker (unless you come from Liverpool). Secondly, many consonants are "soft," a phonetics category which simply does not exist in the English language. Thirdly, all vowels in each word are "reduced" (pronounced like the "er" in waiter) save for the vowel in the stressed syllable (cf: the word "moloko" is pronounced "malako" — remember that when you ask for a glass of milk). The problem with stress is that you never know which syllable it falls on (there are rules, but in the Russian language, there are usually so many exceptions that rules are almost useless). Finally, once you learn how to pronounce the unfamiliar Cyrillic letters, you may rest assured that if a letter is there, it is almost always pronounced, which makes things decidedly easier.

Following is a description of the letters you may find difficult to pronounce:

Б — [b]
В — [v]
Г — [g]
Д — [d]
Ж — [zh]
З — [z]
И — somewhere between [i] and [I:], "it" and "eel"
Л — [l]
Н — [n]
П — [p]
Р — [r]
С — [s]
У — [u]
Ф — [f]
Х — [kh]
Ш — [sh]

Ⅲ — [shch]
э — [e]
Ю — [ju]
Я — [ja]

VOCABULARY

NUMBERS

0 *nol*
1 *odin*
2 *dva*
3 *tri*
4 *chetyre*
5 *piat*
6 *shest*
7 *sem*
8 *vosem*
9 *deviat*
10 *desiat*
11 *odinnatsat*
12 *dvenatsat*
13 *trinatsat*
14 *chetyrnatsat*
15 *piatnatsat*
16 *shestnatsat*
17 *semnatsat*
18 *vosemnatsat*
19 *deviatnatsat*
20 *dvatsat*
21 *dvatsat odin*
30 *tritsat*
40 *sorok*
50 *piatdesiat*
60 *shestdesiat*
70 *semdesiat*
80 *vosemdesiat*
90 *devianosto*
100 *sto*
200 *dvesti*
300 *trista*
400 *chetyresta*
500 *piatsot*
600 *shestsot*
1,000 *tysiacha*
2,000 *dve tysiachi*
3,000 *tri tysiachi*
4,000 *chetyre tysiachi*
5,000 *piat tysiach*
6,000 *shest tysiach*
10,000 *desiat tysiach*
100,000 *sto tysiach*

1,000,000 *milion*
1,000,000,000 *miliard*
One half is polovina or, in colloquial usage, simply pol. Thus, one-half kilo is polkilo.

CALENDAR

Sunday *voskresenie*
Monday *ponedelnik*
Tuesday *vtornik*
Wednesday *sreda*
Thursday *chetverg*
Friday *piatnitsa*
Saturday *subbota*
January *yanvar*
February *fevral*
March *mart*
April *aprel*
May *mai*
June *iun*
July *iul*
August *avgust*
September *sentiabr*
October *oktiabr*
November *noiabr*
December *dekabr*
spring *vesna*
summer *leto*
autumn *osien*
winter *zima*
day *den*
week *nedelia*
month *mesiats*
season *sezon*
year *got*

CLOCK

hour *chas (pl.chasof); after number, it means "o'clock"; thus "nine o'clock' is deviat chasof*
time *vremia*
now *seichas*
later *pozhe*
morning *utro*
noon *polden*
evening *vecher*
night *noch*
today *segodnia*
yesterday *vchera*
tomorrow *zavtra*
what time is it? *skolko vremeni?* or *kotory chas?*

KEY WORDS AND PHRASES

yes *da*
no *niet*
much *mnogo*
please *pzhalsta*
thank you *spasiba*
…very much *bolshoye spasiba*
you're welcome *pzhalsta*
hello *zdrastvuite*
good morning *dobroye utra*
good evening *dobryi vecher*

good night *spokoinai nochi*
goodbye *do svidania*
bye *poka*
welcome *dobro pozhalovat* (the reply is *spasiba*)
excuse me *prosteete*
good *khoroshii*
lovely, beautiful *prekrasny*
very lovely *zamechatelno*
how lovely *kak kraseevo*
there is *yest*
is there…? …*a yest?*
how? *kak?*
how are you? *kak dela?*
how many? *skolko?*
what? *shto?*
what is this? *shto eto?*

what is your name? *kak tebia zovut?* (the plural or polite form is *kak vas zovut?*)
when? *kogda?*
who? *kto?*
why? *pochemu?*
which one? *kotory?*
where is…? …*gde?*
how much is it? *pochem eto?*
I want *ya khochu*
I understand *ya ponimaiu*
I don't understand *ya ne ponimaiu*
I know *ya znaiu*
I don't know *ya ne znaiu*
I don't speak Russian *ya ne govoriu po russki*
this *etot*
that *tot*
here *zdes*
there *tam*
this one *vot etot*
that one *vot tot*
near *okolo*
far *daleko*
left *levy*
go left *nalevo*
right *pravy*
go right *napravo*
hot *goriachi*
cold *kholodny*
big *bolshoi*
small *malenky*
open *otkryto*
closed *zakryto*
new *novy*
old *stary*
cheap *deshevy*
expensive *dorogoi*
money *dengi*

PLACES AND THINGS

airport *aeroport*
bakery *bulochnaya*
bank *bahnk*
barber's *parikmakherskaya*
bay *zaliv*
beach *pliazh*
boarding house *gostinitsa*
bookshop *knizhny magazin*
bus station *avtovokzal*
butcher's *miaso*
cake shop *konditerskaya*
cathedral *sobor*
church *tserkov*

cigarettes *sigarety*
cigars *sigary*
city *gorot*
dry cleaner's *khimchistka*
fish shop *rybny magazin*
florist *tsvetochny magazin*
fountain *fontan*
grocery *produkty*
hotel *otel*
island *ostrov*
jewelry shop *juvelirny magazin*
lake *ozero*
market *rynok*
mountain *gora*
museum *muzei*
palace *dvorets*
pharmacy *apteka*
photographic shop *foto magazin*
police station *otdelenie militsii*
post office *pochta*
restaurant *restoran*
school *shkola*
sea *more*
small street *ulochka, pereulok*
square *ploschad*
steam bath *bania*
street *ulitsa*
theater *teatr*
toilet *tualet*
town center *tsentr goroda*
train station *vokzal*
village *derevnia*

ON THE ROAD

highway *shosse*
map *karta*
car *mashina*
bus *avtoboos*
gasoline *benzin*
regular *devianosto tretii* (meaning 93 octane)
super *devianosto piaty* (meaning 95 octane)
oil *maslo*
service station *avtoservis*
engine *motor*
tire *sheena*
battery *akumuliator*
headlisght *fara*
brakes *tormoza*
spark plugs *svechi*
speed *skorost*
accident *avaria*
CAUTION *VNIMANIE*

IN THE HOTEL

room *nomer*
single room *odnomestny nomer*
double room *dvukhmestny nomer*
double bed *bolshaya krovat*
bath *vannaya*
room with bath *nomer s vannoi*
shower *dush*
room with shower *nomer s dushem*
hot water *goriachaya voda*
no hot water *nyet goriachei vody*

soap *mylo*
towel *polotentse*
toilet paper *tualetnaya bumaga*
laundry *prachechnaya*
key *kliuch*

IN THE POST OFFICE

stamp *marka*
letter *pismo*
envelope *konvert*
postcard *otkrytka*
parcel *posylka*
air mail *aviapochta*
special delivery *srochno*
money order *pochtovy perevod*
telephone *telefon*

IN EMERGENCIES

hospital *bolnitsa*
doctor *vrach*

OPPOSITE: Evenki mother in Siberia.
ABOVE: The Russian word for honey is *myot*.

nurse *sestra*
dentist *zubnoi vrach*
sick, ill *bolnoi*
pain, ache *bol*
fever *temperatura*
allergic to *allerghia na*
toothache *zubnaya bol*
help *pomosh*
first aid *pervaya pomosh*

IN RESTAURANTS

breakfast *zavtrak*
lunch *obed*
dinner *obed, uzhin*
menu *meniu*
waiter *ofitsiant*
bill, check *schiot*
plate *tarelka*
glass *stakan*
knife *nozh*
fork *vilka*
spoon *lozhka*
napkin *salfetka*
salt *sol*
pepper *perets*
sugar *sakhar*
bread *khlep*
butter *masla*
water *vada*
mineral water *mineralnaya vada*
lemonade *leemonat*
fruit juice *sok*
milk *malako*
ice *liot*
coffee *kofe*
instant coffee *rastvorimy kofe*
unsweetened *bes sakhara*
slightly sweetened *chiut-chiut sakhara*
sweet *sladky*
tea *chai*
beer *peeva*
wine *vino*
red wine *krasnoye vino*
white wine *beloye vino*
gin *dzhin*
vodka *votka*
whisky *viske*
cheers *vashe zdorovie*
bon appetit *priatnava apetita*
appetizers *zakuski*
cheese *syr*
olives *olivki*

pickles *solenia*
soup *soop*
broth *bulion*
fish soup *ukha*
salad *salat*
Russian salad *stolichny salat*
mixed vegetable salad *salat iz avashei*
green salad *salat iz zeleni*
meat *miasa*
beef *gaviadina*
lamd *barashek*
mutton *baranina*
veal *teliatina*
pork *svineena*
chicken *kuritsa*
roast chicken *tsypliata tabaka*
turkey *indeika*
liver *pechen*
kidney *pochki*
beef steak *beefshteks*
rare s *kroviu*
well done *prozharenny*
lamb cutlet *barania katleta*
fish *ryba*
anchovy *kilka*
sardine *sardeena*
trout *farel*
tuna *tunets*
halibut *paltus*
cod *treska*
sturgeon *osetrina*
caviar *ikra*
crab *kraby*
crayfish *raki*
squid *kalmary*
vegetables *ovashi*
eggplant *baklazhan*
beans *fasol*
peas *garokh*
spinach *shpinat*
carrots *markof*
tomatoes *pamidory*
potatoes *kartofel*
onions *luk*
rice *rees*
fruit *frukty*
apple *iablaka*
orange *apelsin*
peach *persik*
pear *grusha*
pomegranate *granat*
watermelon *arbuz*
strawberries *klubneeka*

raspberries *maleena*
banana *banan*
grapes *vinograd*
dessert *desiert*
ice cream *marozhenaya*
pastry *pirozhnaya*
cake *pirazhok*
chocolate pudding *shokoladny pudink*

IN CASE YOU GET LUCKY

I love you *ya liublu tebia*
...very much *...silno-silno*

Photo Credits
Photos by **Vladimir Anokhin** except those listed below:
Nik Wheeler: *Cover*, pages 3, 7 *left*, 15, 21, 24, 25, 31, 37, 39, 43, 54, 63, 64–65, 72, 77, 96, 99, 100, 101, 102, 104–5, 106–7, 109, 110–111, 112 *left*, 112 *right*, 113 *left and right*, 115, 118—9, 119, 120, 124, 125, 128, 129, 180, 184, 191, *back cover; top left and middle left*

Recommended Reading

MACKENZIE, DAVID AND CURRAN, MICHAEL W. *A History of Russia and the Soviet Union*. The Dorsey Press, Illinois, 1982.

SOLZHENITSYN, ALEXANDER. *The Gulag Archipelago*. Collins Harvill, New York, 1988.

Folk Art in the Soviet Union. Abrams/Aurora, Leningrad, 1990.

REED, JOHN. *Ten Days that Shook the World*. Penguin, London, 1919.

YELTSIN, BORIS. *Against the Grain*. Johnathan Cape, 1990.

GORBACHEV, MIKHAIL. *Towards a Better World*. Richardson and Steirman, 1987.

Motorist's Guide to the Soviet Union. Progress Publishers, Moscow, 1980.

MCLEAN, FITZROY. *Portrait of the Soviet Union*. Weidenfeld and Nicolson, 1988.

Masterworks of Russian Painting in Soviet Museums. Aurora, Leningrad, 1989.

CRUZ SMITH, MARTIN. *Gorky Park and Polar Star*. Ballantine, New York, 1989.

MAWDSLEY, EVAN AND MARGARET. *Moscow and Leningrad* (in the *Benn Blue Guide* Series). Ernest Benn Ltd., London, 1980.

ANDREWS, WILLIAN G. *The Land and People of the Soviet Union*. HarperCollins, New York, 1991.

HYMAN, CHARLES O. (ED). *The Soviet Union Today*. National Geographic Society, Washington, D.C., 1990.

YEGORYCHEV, VIKTOR. *Opening Day in Moscow*. Novosti Publishers, Moscow, 1989.

Impressionist and Postimpressionist Painting. Aurora, Leningrad and H.L.Levin Associates, New York, 1986.

GAUTIER, THEOPHILE. *Voyage en Russie*. Paris, 1867.

OLSHEVSKY, VADIM. *Paintings in the Tretiakov Gallery*. Novosti Publishers, Moscow, 1979.

RYBAKOV, BORIS. *Treasures of the USSR Diamond Fund*. Izobrazitelnoye Iskusstvo Pubishers, Moscow, 1980.

PIATROVSKY, B.B. (ED). *Egyptian Antiquities in the Hermitage*. Aurora, Leningrad, 1974.

KAPLANOVA S. *VRUBEL*, Aurora, Leningrad, 1975.

Quick Reference A–Z Guide
to Places and Topics of Interest with Listed Accommodation, Restaurants and Useful Telephone Numbers

A accommodation, general *192*
Angara *162, 166*
access *167*
arriving in Russia
by air *181*
by bus *182*
by car *182*
motoring information
Britain *184*
USA *184*
by sea *183*
by train *181*
by charter flights and tour operators *183*
Britain *183*
USA *183*
by special Tours *183*
Britain *184*
USA *183–184*
Intourist Offices abroad *183*
travel documents *184*
what to take *186*
when to go *185–186*
women alone *199*
B **Balakovo** *141*
C charter flights and tour operators *183*
Britain *183*
USA *183*
climate *32*
credit cards *192*
report loss
(203 80 79 (Intourservice) *196*
(254 17 95 (American Express) *196*
crime *197*
cuisine *36*
currencies *192*
currency exchange slip *192*
customs *184–185*
D **Don** *143*
Don Channel *143*
Dubovka *142*
E electricity *197*
embassies and consulates *190*
emergencies *196*
Engels *142*
etiquette *192*
European North
climate *151*
geography *151*
history *151*
F **Far East**
access *176*
attractions
Amur River *172*
climate *171*
geography *171*
history *171*
G geography *32*

H health *190*
health certificate *190*
history *19, 32*
Brezhnev *29*
Coalition Wars *23*
cold war *28*
Crimean War *25*
Gorbachev *29–30, 95*
Khrushchev *28*
Kulikovo Field *20*
Lenin *26, 138*
revolution *26*
Stalin *27, 29*
Vladimir-Suzdal Principate *84*
World War I *25*
World War II *93*
Yeltsin *30*
I **Irkutsk**
access *167*
accommodation
Baikal Hotel *167*
Intourist Hotel (91 353   *167*
attractions
Lake Baikal *166*
Museum of Decembrists
(45 245   *167*
history *166*
restaurants
Hotel Baikal *167*
Intourist Hotel *167*
K **Kamyshin** *142*
Karelia
attractions
Kivach *155*
Kizhi *156*
Martial Waters *155*
Kazan *138*
attractions
Kremlin *138*
Khabarovsk
access *176*
accommodation
Intourist Hotel (34 43 47   *175*
Tsentralnaya Hotel (33 47 59   *175*
attractions
Museum of Art *174*
museum of ethnography *174*
history *174*
restaurants *176*
tourist information
Intourist Hotel (34 43 47   *172*
Khvalynsk *141*
Kiev
access
Borispol International Airport *131*
Kievskoye Highway *131*
River Terminal *131*

accommodation
Bratislava (559 69 20   *129*
Darnitsa Campsite   *129*
Dnipro (229 82 87   *129*
Druzhba (268 34 06   *129*
Leningradskaya-1 (225 71 01   *129*
Leningradskaya-2 (221 70 80   *129*
Leningradskaya-3 (224 42 26   *129*
Lybed (274 00 63   *129*
Mir (268 56.00   *129*
Moskva (228 28 04   *129*
Prolisok Motel (444 00 93   *129*
Rus (220 42 25   *129*
Slavutich (555 79 26   *129*
Ukraina (221 75 84   *129*
attractions
Assumption Cathedral   *126*
Cathedral of St. Sophia   *124*
Church of St. Andrew   *125*
Church of the Intercession   *128*
Desiatinnaya Church   *125*
Kiev Dynamo (football team)   *35, 127*
Golden Gate   *125*
Mikhailovsky Monastery   *125*
Museum of Russian Art   *126*
Pechersk Monastery   *126*
Podol   *128*
St. Vladimir's Cathedral   *126*
history 121
restaurants,
Beer Pubs   *131*
Dubki (440 51 88   *130*
Dynamo (229 40 38   *130*
Krakiv (274 19 08   *131*
Kureni (293 40 62   *131*
Maxim (224 12 72   *130*
Mlyn (517 08 33   *131*
Stolichny (229 81 88   *130*
Zoloti Vorota (212 55 04   *131*
shopping
Central Department Store   *128*
tourist information
Aeroflot (274 51 52   *123*
Ambulance (03   *123*
Boat Terminal Pochtovaya Square
  (416 12 68   *123*
Borispol Airport (295 67 01
  (information)   *123*
Fire (01   *123*
International telephone (071 072
  (074 from hotels)   *124*
passport   *124*
Police (02   *123*
Railways General information
  (223 30 53   *123*
Taxi Bookings in Ukrainian (058   *123*
Kostroma
attractions
Ipatievsky Monastery   *88*
museum of wooden architecture   *88*
Lake Baikal   *161*
mail   *195*
Marx   *142*
money   *192*
Moscow
accommodation
***Cosmos (217 86 80   *77*
***Intourist (203 40 08   *77*

***Metropol (927 60 96   *77*
***Mezhdunarodnaya (253 13 91   *77*
***Moscow Olympic Penta (971 61 01   *77*
***Pullman-Iris (488 80 00   *77*
***Savoy (929 85 00   *77*
***Slavianskaya (941 80 20   *77*
***Sovetskaya (250 72 53   *78*
**Belgrade ((248 67 34   *78*
**Budapest ((924 88 20   *78*
**Leningradskaya (975 30 08   *78*
**Saliut (438 65 65   *78*
**Ukraina (243 30 30   *78*
Molodiozhnaya (210 45 65   *78*
Orlyonok (939 88 44   *78*
Sputnik (938 71 06   *78*
attractions
art galleries, Tretiakov Gallery   *70*
Arbat Street   *64*
Bolshoi Theater   *61*
Cathedral of the Virgin (St.Basil's)   *52*
Central Puppet Theater   *68*
Children's Music Theater   *61*
Church of the Resurrection   *63*
Conservatoire building   *63*
Czar Bell   *57*
Czar Cannon   *57*
Gorky Park   *69*
Grand Palace   *57*
Granovitaya Chamber   *56*
GUM   *53*
Kremlin   *49*
Kremlin museums   *55*
Lenin Museum   *60*
Lenin's Mausoleum   *51*
monasteries
  Andronikov Monastery   *71*
  Donskoi Monastery   *73*
  Novodevichy Convent   *73*
Moscow Spartak (football team)   *35*
Palace of Congresses   *57*
Polytechnical Museum   *58*
Red Square   *49*
theater of animals (281-29-14   *69*
Tomb of the Unknown Soldier   *51*
Tverskaya Street   *62*
Uspensky Cathedral   *55*
car rental
Businesscar (231 82 25   *49*
Europcar (253 13 69   *49*
Innis (927 11 87   *49*
Intourservice (203 00 96   *49*
Mosrent (248 36 07   *49*
Rozec Car (241 78 18   *49*
history 19, 24, 41
Civil War   *46*
Ivan the Terrible   *44*
Mongol invasion   *42*
Napoleon   *45*
Péter the Great   *45*
Stalin   *48*
World War II   *46*
religion   34
restaurants
Aragvi Restaurant (229-37-62   *63*
Arlekino (Italian) (205 70 88   *78*
Delhi (Indian) (255 04 92   *78*
Kropotkinskaya 36 (Russian) (201 75 00   *79*
Peking Hotel (209-24-56   *68*

Praga (Czech) (290 61 71 79
Pullman-Iris (French) (488 80 00 79
Razgulai (Russian) (267 76 13 79
Sakura (Japanese) (253 28 94 79
Sovetsky (Russian) (250 74 49 79
take-out restaurants
 Baku-Livan 79
 McDonald's (200 16 55 79
 Pettina (286 52 17 79
 Pizza Hut (229 20 13 (Tverskaya Street);
  (243 17 27 (Kutuzovsky Prospekt) 79
 The Little Mermaid (Danish Sea Food)
  (248 44 38 79
 Tren-Mos(American) (245 12 16 79
 U Pirosmani (Georgian) (247 19 26 79
 Vienna (German) (971 61 01 79
shopping
 Dom Knigi (House of Books) 68
 Gastronom 62
 Smolensky Gastronom 65
tourist information
 Aeroflot (245 00 02 (central office),
  (155 09 22 (airport) 49
 Intourist office (203 69 62 49
 Vnukovo Intourist (436 29 67 49
transportation
 metro 49
 taxi (927 00 00 49
motoring information 184
 Britain 184
 USA 184
Murmansk
 accommodation
  Severnaya (5 50 40 156
 attractions
  sports 36
 restaurants
  Polarnye zori 156
  Vstrecha 156

N Nakhodka
 access 176
newspapers and magazines 198
Nikolaevsk 174
Novgorod 151–153
 accommodation
  Intourist (7 50 89 153
  motel (7 24 48 153
  Sadko Hotel, (9 51 70 153
  Volkhov Hotel (9 24 98 153
 attractions
  Cathedral of St. Sophia 151
  Kremlin 151
  Party Committee building 152
 history 151
 restaurants
  Detinets Restaurant 153
  hotel restaurants 153
Novocherkassk
 attractions
  Cossack Museum 146
Novosibirsk 163, 166
 access 166
 accommodation
  Novosibirsk Hotel (22 03 13 166
 attractions
  Akademgorodok 166
  museum of ethnography 166
  Museum of Local History (21 42 92 166

Obskoye Sea 166
 restaurants
  Novosibirsk Hotel (Siberian cuisine)
   (22 72 44 166
 tourist information
  Intourist Hotel (91 354 166

P passports 49, 184
Pereslavl-Zalesky 88
 attractions
  Spaso-Preobrazhensky Cathedral 88
Petrozavodsk 155
 accommodation
  Karelia Tourist Complex (5 88 97 156
  Severnaya Hotel (7 63 54 156
 attractions
  Lake Onega 155
 restaurants 156
Privolzhsky 142
Pskov
 accommodation
  Oktiabrskaya (9 94 00 155
  Rizhskaya Hotel (3 32 43 154
 attractions
  Kremlin 154
  museum-preserve 154
  Svyatogorsky Monastery 154
  Vasily-on-the-Hill 154
 environs
  Izborsk 154
  Pechory 154
  restaurants
   Rus 155
 history 153
 restaurants
  Druzhba Hotel
   (in Pushkinskiye Gory) 155
  Oktiabrskaya (9 94 00 or 2 55 93 155
  Rizhskaya Hotel
   (3 32 43 or 9 16 37 154
  Rus (in Pechory) 155
Pugachevskaya 143

R radio and television 197
religions 34
Rostov the Great 88
 attractions
  Ascension Cathedral 88
  Assumption Cathedral 88
  Church of St.John 88
  Odigitry Church 88
Rostov-on-Don 146
Russia
 crime 197
 electricity 197
 etiquette 192–194
 getting around 186
  by air 186
   Aeroflot offices, Moscow
    (245 00 02 187
  by bus 188
  by car 188–189
  by taxi 188
  by thumb 188
  by train 187
   booking (Moscow)
    Intourist information office
     (921 45 13 187
    Intourtrans, 15 Petrovka Street 187
  health precautions 190

holidays and festivals *194*
mail *195*
money *192*
Russian for travelers *200*
staying on (visa) *200*
steam baths *199*
telephone *195*
time *197*
tipping *199*
water *197*
weights and measures *197*
Russian food specialities *79*
Russian for travelers *200*

S | **Samara** *140*
Saratov *142*
Sergiyev Posad *83–84*
access 84
accommodation
  Intourist hotel (225 68 83 , *84*
attractions
  monastery *83*
history 83
Siberia *159–167*
geography 161
history 162
sport *35*
St. Petersburg *91–117*
accommodation
  ***Astoria (219 11 00 *115*
  ***Grand Hotel Europe
    (312 00 72 *115*
  ***Karelia (226 57 01 *116*
  ***Moskva (274 20 51 *116*
  ***Okhta (227 44 38 *115*
  ***Olgino (238 35 51 *116*
  ***Peterburg (542 90 31 *116*
  ***Pribaltiiskaya (356 51 12 *116*
  ***Pulkovskaya (264 51 00 *116*
  **Baltiiskaya (277 77 31 *116*
  **Druzhba (234 18 44 *116*
  **Gavan (358 85 04 *116*
  **Rossiya (296 76 49 *116*
  **Vyborgskaya (246 23 19 *116*
attractions
  Academy of Arts *107*
  Academy of Sciences *107*
  Admiralty *97*
  Alexander Nevsky Monastery *98*
  General Staff *100*
  Hermitage *104*
  House of Books *98*
  Kazan Cathedral *98*
  Kunstkammer *107*
  New Convent *109*
  Peter and Paul Cathedral *96*
  Peter and Paul Fortress *95*
  Smolny *109*
  St.Isaac's *106*
  Winter Palace *99*
  Zoological Museum *107*
car rental
  Sovinteravtoservis (292 12 57 or
    (292 17 45 *95*
environs
  Pavlovsk *113*
  Petrodvorets *112*
  Pushkin *113*
history 21, 93

restaurants
  **Demianova Ukha (Seafood)
    (232 80 90 *117*
  Belye Nochi (319 96 60 *116*
  Chaika (German) (312 21 20 *116*
  Fortezzia (233 94 68 *116*
  Gino Ginelli *116*
  Kavkazsky (Transcaucasian)
    (311 45 26 *116*
  Literaturnoye Kafe (Russian)
    (312 71 37 *116*
  Metropol (European) (310 22 81 *116*
  Na Fontanke (Russian) (311 45 26 *117*
  Neva (Russian) (311 36 78 *116*
  Schwabsky Domik (528 22 11 *116*
  Tbilisi (Georgian) (232 93 91 *117*
  Troika (Russian) (113 53 43 *116*
  Zhemchuzhina (Azerbaidzhani)
    (355 20 63 *117*
tourist information
  emergency fire: (01 *95*
  medical care
    bone fractures (310 45 25 *95*
    dental care (213 55 50 *95*
    dental care (children) (314 25 65 *95*
    eye injuries (272 59 55 *95*
    general (217 02 82; (234 57 72 or
      298 45 96 *95*
  Police (02 *95*
  Telegraph (066 *95*
  Telephone, information: (09;
    International: (07, *95*
  US Consulate (273 21 04 *95*
  Weather (001 *95*
transportation
  Aeroflot 211 79 80 *95*
  Intourist (355 13 30 *95*
  Passenger Port *117*
  Pulkovo Airport
    (293 99 11(domestic flights);
    (291 89 13 (international flights) *95*
  Railways —
    Domestic (162 33 44 *95*
    General information (168 01 11 *95*
    International (274 20 92 *95*
  Sea Terminal (355 19 02 *95*
  Taxi (312 00 22 *95*
steam baths *199*
Suzdal *84–88*
accommodation
  Tourist Complex (2 17 57 *87*
attractions
  Spaso-Yevfimievsky Monastery *86*
environs
  Bogoliubovo *86*
restaurants
  Gostiny Dvor *88*
Syzran *141*

T | telephone *195–196*
  country codes *196*
  Russian city codes *196*
temperature *186*
time *197*
tipping *199*
toilets *198*
tourist information
  Intourist offices in Britain ((1) 538 32 02 *183*

Intourist offices in Canada
  ((514) 849 63 94   *183*
Intourist offices in Russia   *189*
  Irkutsk, 44 Gagarinsky Bulvar. (446 86   *189*
  Ivanovo, 6 Naberezhnaya Ulitsa.
    (785 58   *189*
  Kazan, 9/10 Baumanskaya Ulitsa,
    Suite 212. (32 01 45   *189*
  Khabarovsk, 2 Amursky Bulvar.
    (33 76 34   *190*
  Kislovodsk, Dzerzhinsky Prospekt.
    (534 97   *190*
  Krasnodar, 109 Krasnaya Ulitsa.
    (588 97   *190*
  Kursk, 72 Ulitsa Lenina. (29 98 40   *190*
  Moscow, 16 Teatralny Proyezd.
    (203 69 62   *189*
  Murmansk, 20 Ulitsa Profsoyuzov.
    (543 72   *190*
  Nakhodka, 11 Nakhodkinsky Prospekt.
    (573 44   *190*
  Novgorod, 16 Dmitriyevskaya Ulitsa.
    (742 35   *190*
  Novosibirsk, 3 Ulitsa Lenina. (22 52 81   *190*
  Orel, 37 Ulitsa Maksima Gorkogo.
    (674 63   *190*
  Petrozavodsk, 21 Prospekt Lenina.
    (763 06   *190*
  Pskov, 25 Rizhskoye Shosse. (332 43   *190*
  Rostov-on-Don, 115 Ulitsa Engelsa.
    (65 90 00   *190*
  Smolensk, Motel Feniks. (214 88   *190*
  St. Petersburg, 11 Isaakievskaya
    Ploschad. (214 64 20   *189*
  Stavropol, 2 Ulitsa Bulkina. (391 72   *190*
  Togliatti, 24 Ulitsa Chilina. (22 20 97   *190*
  Tver, 130 Peterburgskoye Shosse.
    (556 92   *190*
  Ulianovsk, 15 Sovietskaya Ulitsa.
    (948 16   *190*
  USA (757 38 84   *183*
  Vladimir, 74 Ulitsa tretiego
    internatsionala. (242 62   *190*
  Volgograd, 14 Ulitsa Mira. (36 45 52   *190*
  Vyborg, 5 Cheleznodorozhnaya Ulitsa.
    (212 58   *190*
tours (specialist tours)   *183*
  Britain   *184*
  USA   *183*
tours operators   *183*
  Britain   *183*
  USA   *183*

Trans-Siberian railway
  booking   *176*
  travel documents   *184*

U
V

Ulianov   *139*
visa   *200*
Vladimir   *87*
  accommodation
    Hotel Vladimir (30 42   *87*
  restaurants
    Russkaya Derevnia (9 71 32   *87*
    Traktir Restaurant (67 53   *87*
    U Zolotykh Vorot 34 55   *87*
Vladivostok   *174*
  access   *176*
  accommodation
    Amursky Caliv (22 55 20   *176*
    Hotel Equator (21 28 64   *176*
    Hotel Vladivistok (22 22 08   *176*
  attractions
    Botanical Garden   *175*
    Golden Horn Harbor   *175*
  restaurants
    Intourist Hotel   *176*
  tourist information
    Intourist representative office
      (25 88 39   *172*
  vocabulary   *201–205*
Volga   *135*
Volga-Don district   *135*
  cruise information
    lock information   *146*
    distances   *146*
Volga-Kama Preserve   *139*
Volgodonsk   *143*
Volgograd (Tsaritsyn)   *143*
  attractions
    Motherland Statue   *143*

W

water   *197*
weights and measures   *197*
what to take   *186*
when to go   *185–186*
White Stone   *83–88*
women alone   *199*

Y

Yaroslavl   *88*
  attractions
    Monastery of the Savior   *88*
    museum of architecture   *88*
  tourist information
    Intourist representative (-12-58   *88*
Yermakovo   *141*

Illustrated Blueprints to Travel Enjoyment

INSIDER'S
GUIDES

The Guides That Lead